3⁰⁰

The Naturalists

The Naturalists

Scientific Travelers in the Golden Age of Natural History

Stephen R. Bown

BARNES
&NOBLE
BOOKS
NEW YORK

Contents

Timeline

1739	**Birth of William Bartram**
1743	Founding of the American Philosophical Society in Philadelphia
1758	Carolus Linnaeus publishes *Systema Naturae*
1756–1763	Seven Years War between France and England. All French territories in North America, along the St. Lawrence, forfeited to England.
1768	The first voyage of James Cook for Tahiti and Australia with the naturalist Joseph Banks
1769	**Birth of Alexander von Humboldt**
1772	Joseph Banks becomes director of Kew Botanical Gardens
1773–1777	William Bartram wanders southeastern North America
1776–1783	American Revolution. British presence in North America is reduced to the lands won from France two decades earlier.
1782	James Watt's invention of the double-acting rotary steam engine
	Montgolfier brothers design the first hot-air balloon
	Birth of Charles Waterton
	Birth of Maximilian of Wied
1787	**Birth of John Richardson**
1789	French Revolution
1791	Publication of Bartram's *Travels*
1792	The slave trade abolished in Denmark
1793	Sir Alexander Mackenzie first crosses North America from east to west
1795	Lemon juice introduced in the British Royal Navy as an antiscorbutic
1796–1814	Napoleonic Wars
1799	**Birth of David Douglas**
1799–1804	Alexander von Humboldt and Aimé Bompland explore South America, Cuba and Mexico
1802	The term "biology" first used by German naturalist Gottfried Treviranus
1803	The Louisiana Purchase—U.S. purchases land west of the Mississippi River and north of the Gulf of Mexico from France; Lewis and Clark expedition to the Pacific coast
1804	Royal Horticultural Society founded in London

1807	Publication of first volume of von Humboldt's *Personal Narrative*
1809	**Birth of John Kirk Townsend**
1812	U.S. declares war against Britain (ends December 24, 1814)
	Academy of Natural Sciences of Philadelphia founded
1812–1813	Charles Waterton's first expedition to Guyana
1815	Final defeat of Napoleon at the Battle of Waterloo
	William Smith produces monumental geological map of England, the beginning of geology as a science
	Steam locomotive developed in England
1814–1817	Waterton's second expedition
1815–1824	Brazil, Chile, Guatemala, Mexico, Venezuela, Equador, Bolivia, Peru, Columbia and Panama achieve independence from Spain
1819	U.S. purchases Florida from Spain
1819–1821	John Richardson's first arctic expedition
1820–1821	Waterton's third expedition
1823	David Douglas's first collecting expedition, to eastern North America
	Death of William Bartram
1824–1825	Waterton's fourth expedition and publication of *Wanderings in South America*
1824–1827	Douglas's second expedition, to the Pacific Northwest and British Columbia
1825	**Birth of Henry Walter Bates**
1825–1827	Richardson's second expedition to the Arctic
1827	Publication of first edition of John James Audubon's *Birds of America*
1829	Publication of the first volume of Richardson's *Fauna Boreali-Americana*
1830	The cell nucleus in plants discovered by Scottish botanist Robert Brown
	Royal Geographic Society founded in London
1830–1834	Douglas's third expedition, to California, the Pacific Northwest, British Columbia and Hawaii
1831	James Clark Ross locates the North Magnetic Pole
1831–1836	The *Beagle* departs England for South America and the Galapagos with Charles Darwin as Naturalist
1832–1834	Maximilian of Wied and Karl Bodmer explore the Missouri River
1834	Spanish Inquisition finally suppressed
	Death of David Douglas
1834–1837	John Kirk Townsend's cross-continental trek
1834	**Birth of John Wesley Powell**
1835–1842	Second Seminole War in Florida
1836	Texas secedes from Mexico

1837	Samuel Morse demonstrates electric telegraph in New York
	Smallpox epidemic devastates American Plains Indians along the Missouri River
1838	Publication of fourth and final edition of John James Audubon's *Birds of America*
1839	Publication of first edition of Maximilian's *Travels*
	Publication of Townsend's *Narrative*
	First electric clock, Carl August
1840	Publication of Townsend's *Ornithology of the United States of North America*
	Louis Agassiz publishes *Etudes sur les Glaciers*
	Last criminals transported from England to New South Wales
1841	Britain claims sovereignty over Hong Kong
1842	Crawford W. Long produces surgical anesthetic from ether
1843	First propeller-driven ship crosses the Atlantic
1844	Paper from wood pulp invented by Fredrich Gottlob Keller
1845	John Franklin leads the *Erebus* and the *Terror* to search for a Northwest Passage
1846	Oregon Boundary Treaty gives the current states of Washington and Oregon to the United States and the current Canadian province of British Columbia to Britain
	U.S. annexes New Mexico
1848	Alfred Russell Wallace and Henry Walter Bates depart for the Amazon
	John Richardson leads expedition to search for the missing John Franklin
	Founding of the Smithsonian Institution
	California gold rush
1851	Population of U.S. 23 million; Germany 34 million; Britain 20.8 million France 33 million
	Death of John Kirk Townsend
1853	Smallpox vaccination compulsory in Britain
1856	Discovery of the original Neanderthal skeleton near Düsseldorf
1859	Charles Darwin publishes *On the Origin of Species by Means of Natural Selection*
	Bates returns to England after 11 years along the Amazon
	Death of Alexander von Humboldt
1861	Start of American Civil War
1862	British zoologist Richard Owen calculates that total known species of birds has increased from 444 to over 8,000 since Linnaeus first published *Systema Naturae* in 1758
1863	Publication of Bates's *The Naturalist on the River Amazons*
1864	Bates appointed Assistant Secretary of the Royal Geographical Society

1865	End of American Civil War
	Abolition of slavery in the United States
	Death of Charles Waterton
	Death of John Richardson
1867	Canada formed
	Alaska purchased from Russia
	Death of Maximilian of Wied
1868	American Museum of Natural History opens in New York
	John Wesley Powell's collecting expedition to Colorado
1869	Powell's expedition down the Colorado River
1871	United States Geographical and Geological Survey of the Rocky Mountain Region, J.W. Powell in charge, continues sporadically for nearly 9 years
1872	Creation of the first national park in the United States, Yellowstone National Park
1875	Publication of Powell's *The Exploration of the Colorado River of the West*
1876	Alexander Graham Bell invents the telephone
1878	Publication of Powell's *Report on the Lands of the Arid Regions of the United States*
1879	Powell becomes director of the U.S. Geological Survey
1880	Thomas Edison and J.W. Swan independently create practical electric lights
1886	Canadian Pacific Railway completed, linking the country from coast to coast
1891	W. J. Judson invents the clothing zipper
1892	Rudolf Diesel patents internal combustion engine
	Death of Henry Walter Bates
1893	Henry Ford builds his first car
1895	Guglielmo Marconi invents radio telegraphy
1896	Hydroelectric generation begins at Niagara Falls
1897	Klondike gold rush
1899–1902	Boer War between Britain and the Boers in South Africa
1902	**Death of John Wesley Powell**
1903	Orville and Wilbur Wright fly first propeller airplane
2000	Founding of the All Species Foundation with the objective of creating a "complete inventory of all species of life on Earth within the next 25 years—a human generation."

Introduction

America offers an ample field for the labours of the naturalist.
On no other part of the globe is he called upon more powerfully by nature
to raise himself to general ideas on the cause of phenomena and their mutual
connection.... The resources which the New World affords for the study of
geology and natural philosophy in general have been long since acknowledged.
Happy the traveller who may cherish the hope that he has availed himself
of the advantages of his position, and that he has added some
new facts to the mass of those already acquired!
—ALEXANDER VON HUMBOLDT, 1803

THE LATE EIGHTEENTH AND EARLY nineteenth centuries in Europe and America saw the dawn of a golden age of science in which society energetically sought to quantify, categorize, and rationally explain the world. The accurate cataloguing of nature was one of the goals of the age, and most plants and animals commonly known today were collected, classified, and named in a great frenzy of scientifically motivated exploration. Until the publication in 1859 of Darwin's *The Origin of Species*, it was believed that there were a finite number of species on the planet and through diligent effort all of nature might be collected and studied.

The scientific collectors were known as naturalists, a term that initially applied to anyone with an interest in the natural world—amateur bug collectors, dedicated professional collectors, and formally educated scientists and thinkers. The science they studied was called natural history, natural science, natural philosophy, or natural knowledge (the terms were used interchangeably). *Merriam-Webster's Dictionary* defines natural history as "a former branch of knowledge embracing the study, description, and classification of natural objects (animals, plants, and minerals) and thus including the modern sciences of zoology, botany, mineralogy, etc. insofar as they existed at that time... [now] restricted to a consideration of these subjects from an amateur or popular rather than a technical and professional point of view." The natural world was broadly defined to include mammals, birds, insects, fish, trees, flowers, and minerals, as well as such things as the winds, ocean currents, and precipitation.

By the 1820s, two distinct groups of naturalists had emerged: field naturalists and closet naturalists. Field naturalists were chiefly amateur scientific travellers and collectors who devoted themselves to collection, descriptive observation, and the literary telling of their adventures in exotic places. Few had the skills or knowledge to properly classify their finds, and those who did publish information on their own specimens often made mistakes that had to be later corrected—an embarrassing scientific gaffe. When an institution such as the Horticultural Society sent out collector David Douglas, or the Academy of Natural Sciences of Philadelphia commissioned John Kirk Townsend, the institution claimed the specimens the naturalists brought back from their expeditions and assumed the responsibility—as well as the prestige—of naming and classifying them. Although the names of new species were often linked to the field naturalist who discovered them, the naming was customarily done by closet naturalists—institutional scientists who, over time, specialized into the fields of botany, ornithology, coleoptery, ichthyology, mammology, ethnology, paleontology, meteorology, and so on. They became taxonomic specialists, particularly as more and more specimens were collected from around the world and the accurate classification of species became increasingly difficult for the amateur field naturalists. The closet naturalists held posts in museums and universities, studying in their laboratories the internal processes of organisms, such as respiration, digestion, gestation and embryonic development, growth, and movement, in order to document the anatomical distinctions between species.

The two groups did not always respect each other's contributions. Philip Gosse, writing in *A Naturalist's Sojourn in Jamaica* in 1851, eloquently expressed the field naturalists' disdain for the study of nature in a laboratory, removed from the context of the living environment.

It is mainly conversant with dry skins, furred or feathered, blackened, shriveled, and hay-stuffed; with objects, some admirably beautiful, some hideously ugly, impaled on pins, and arranged in rows in cork drawers; with uncouth forms, disgusting to sight and smell, bleached and shrunken, suspended by threads and immersed in spirit...in glass bottles. These distorted things are described; their scales, plates, feathers counted; their forms copied, all shriveled and stiffened as they are; their colours, changed and modified by death or partial decay, carefully set down; their limbs, members, and organs measured, and the results recorded in thousandths of an inch; two names are given to every one; the whole is enveloped in a mystic cloud of Graeco-Latino-English phraseology...and this is Natural History!

By the mid-nineteenth century, the closet naturalists looked down upon the field naturalists, no longer viewing them as true scientists; nor would nineteenth-century field naturalists be described as scientists today. Although they studied the same material as modern-day botanists, zoologists, or geologists, they approached the study in a different fashion. Natural history was a blend of science and art—the facts and observable truths of the natural world were mixed with personal narrative and philosophical speculation on the nature of life. It was an aesthetic science, equally concerned with appreciating the beauty of the natural world and using it to comment on human existence, as it was with understanding the vital processes of plants and animals. "Treating it as science," wrote Lynn L. Merrill in *The Romance of Victorian Natural History*, "expecting it to be scientific in the modern sense, does natural history a disservice and neglects its considerable charms."

The field naturalists were as much philosophers as they were scientists. They bridged the gap between art and science by using the concrete collection and classification of new species, the enumeration of the variation of the natural world, as a means of speculating and postulating about life, and celebrating the glory of nature. "Natural history," according to Merrill, "displays some very unscientific qualities that draw it closer to literature: emotion, evocativeness, and connotation.... It can raise fundamental questions about one's place in nature, one's moment in time." The products of the field naturalist's investigations were not anatomical treatises, but literary texts. Books describing their adventures were exceedingly popular and a major source of income, but the books were not scientific, being written as much to entertain as to educate. "Because it depends on facts," Merrill wrote, "natural history writing is allied to science; because it deals with human response and emotion, it is allied to literature."

In keeping with their era, most of the early naturalists were religious. They viewed nature as the manifestation of God, immutable and static yet infinitely varied and pleasing. Studying nature was studying God's creation, hence the more you collected and understood, the closer you came to God. Many of the accounts share a similar tone of awe at the abundance and variety of animals and plants. For them, a walk in the woods was as much a religious or spiritual experience as it was an act of exploration or scientific inquiry.

The golden age of the scientific collectors and travellers lasted from the late eighteenth century until the 1860s. Throughout most of this period, naturalists were still considered to be part of the greater scientific community. Although they focused on travel, adventure, and poetic descriptions of wildlife and landscape, the thousands of new plants and animals they collected were vital to the study of nature and contributed to the nineteenth-century understanding of the natural world. Darwin's theory of evolution through natural selection evolved from the basic principles of natural history—from observing the traits of different species and seeking an explanation for those differences and their change over time.

By the end of the nineteenth century, however, species new to science became much more difficult to discover, and the sheer quantity of information amassed by a century of collecting rendered it impracticable, if not impossible, for one individual to have a comprehensive understanding of all aspects of the natural world. Following its heyday in the early to mid-nineteenth century, natural history was dismissed as an irrelevant exercise in collecting and naming and was superseded by the hard sciences. As respect for natural history as a scientific endeavour diminished, so did its overall popularity, and the demand for new books from scientific travellers also dwindled.

The era of the travelling naturalists was also an era of great change and turmoil in western Europe and America, an era of geographical expansion, exploration, and colonization in which people were constantly bombarded with new information about the larger world. The great scientific explorers were motivated and spurred on by several competing motives that were a complex blend of technology, politics, and industry. Throughout the eighteenth century, ships steadily increased in size and capacity while improved navigational techniques, such as accurate maps and charts and the ability to calculate longitude at sea, made voyages safer and more predictable. By the early nineteenth century, ships routinely carried up to three or four hundred mariners and passengers on voyages lasting months between landings. It was possible to cross the Atlantic with relative ease; indeed, the scope of the globe had been shrunk so that for the first time ever it was possible to travel to distant lands or establish regular trade routes and colonial outposts.

As naval technology improved, western European nations, extending their perennial internecine quarrels across the globe, strove to discover and exploit new and valuable territory. The era of the travelling naturalists was marked by several major global wars. The American Revolution between 1776 and 1783 resulted in the creation of a new country, the United States, out of the original thirteen British colonies along the Atlantic seaboard of North America. The conflict disrupted Atlantic trade and travel and ended William Bartram's wandering in southeastern North America. It had a profound impact on the global balance of power. Apart from Bartram, in the period immediately after the Revolution, most of the travelling naturalists hailed from either England or continental Europe. The new American states were presumably too preoccupied with organizing their country as they expanded westward to send out scientific explorers.

Soon after the American Revolution, Europe experienced the French Revolution and the Napoleonic wars, a series of conflicts that involved Britain, France, and continental European nations from the late eighteenth century until Napoleon's defeat at the Battle of Waterloo in 1815. French and British ships battled around the globe as they sought to disrupt each other's trade and travel. Britain and the United States were also at war between 1812 and 1815. It was not a good time for travelling naturalists—Alexander von Humboldt had difficulty even getting a ship across the Atlantic because of the war.

Britain emerged from the wars as one of the strongest nations on the globe and the strongest naval power, and it was in the relative peace after the wars that the era of the natural history collectors accelerated. Self-funded, curious aristocrats such as British Charles Waterton and German Maximilian of Wied led extensive travel and collecting expeditions into the wilds. In the decades after the Napoleonic wars, however, continental Europe became increasingly insular and conservative, leading to a decline in interest in natural history and the greater world. Maximilian of Wied was one of the last travelling naturalists from continental Europe, while earlier explorers such as von Humboldt lamented the shift away from open scientific inquiry. For Britain, on the other hand, the incentives for the study of nature on foreign continents greatly increased, expanding in conjunction with commercial and colonial aspirations. It was an attempt to understand the bewildering complexity of the new worlds that were being opened through trade and colonization. Professional collectors such as David Douglas, John Richardson, and Henry Walter Bates brought back reams of information and tens of thousands of specimens from areas as diverse as the barren tundra of the Arctic and the torrid morass of Amazonia.

The nineteenth century was also a century of expansion for the United States. After the Louisiana Purchase in 1803—in which France sold to the United States for $15 million all the lands previously ceded to France by Spain, from the Mississippi west to the Rockies and from the Gulf of Mexico north to British North America— American politicians were greatly concerned with exploring their own backyard. In 1803, Thomas Jefferson sent an expedition led by Meriwether Lewis and William Clark to probe the new lands that, despite being populated with numerous independent native peoples, were now considered to be part of the growing republic. Many naturalists eagerly explored the new lands. In the 1830s, for example, John

Kirk Townsend and Thomas Nuttall set off from Philadelphia to determine what animals and plants dwelt in the western domain, a region that had never before been explored by naturalists.

In South America, the early nineteenth century saw decades of war as the Spanish colonial provinces of Mexico, Venezuela, Ecuador, Bolivia, Peru, Columbia, and Panama were embroiled in revolutionary wars that culminated in their independence in 1824. Other South American nations such as Argentina, Uruguay, and Paraguay also achieved independence from Spain around the same time, while Brazil separated from Portugal. In other areas of the globe, such as India, China and Africa, European nations were busy establishing colonial dominion over local societies. The political world after the Napoleonic wars was in a state of constant flux.

Meanwhile, the technologies of the Industrial Revolution, particularly steam power and its adaptations, were transforming the landscape of western Europe and eastern America. The natural world was receding from the lives of everyday people as they moved from farms and small rural towns into cities. No longer were the majority of people outdoors in the fields, but were labouring in factories next to shrieking steam machinery. Grim, dirty hovels were springing up around industrial centres to accommodate the influx of migrants; nature seemed far away. The urban population of Britain increased from about 13 per cent in 1700 to over 50 per cent in 1851; cities and towns were also rapidly expanding in eastern North America. Writers of the time, Henry David Thoreau in the United States, Goethe in Germany, and the Romantic writers in Britain, such as Wordsworth, Shelley, and Coleridge, frequently reflected on the lost rural past or idealized the peaceful tranquility of the natural world. The scientific/travel books of the naturalists themselves were hugely popular, revelling in the beauty and bounty of nature, the excitement of travel, and the sheer simplicity and peace of being away from the polluted centres of population.

Steam locomotives were quickly changing the landscape all over Europe and Britain and the eastern United States, carving up the wilderness for railway lines while drastically reducing the travel time between non-coastal destinations. Forests were being hacked down in great swaths to supply the shipbuilding industry, to fuel the raging furnaces of the factories, and to feed the black bellies of the locomotives that chugged about on ever-increasing lines of track. By the end of the nineteenth century, not only was most of the terrain of the Americas claimed by European-style governments, but unexplored land was scarce. The vast bulk of easily identifiable species of plants and animals had been collected and those that remained undiscovered—there are still new species of insects and plants regularly being discovered even today—were variations on creatures no longer considered exotic after nearly a century of exposure through books, articles, museums, and zoos. When John Wesley Powell ventured down the Colorado River after the American Civil War, he rode west in comfort to the headwaters of the mighty river on the first American cross-continental railway. His was one of the last significant expeditions of the old-style travelling naturalists. There was simply nowhere left for them to go.

While the golden age of the scientific collectors drew to a close in the late nineteenth century, there are still curious scientific travellers who have an interest in understanding or appreciating the natural world. A modern parallel to the travelling naturalists of the golden age might be Wade Davis, explorer-in-residence for the National Geographic Society and author of several books, or the ethnobotanist Richard Schultes, who died in 2001. They are modern-day sightseers and scholars who, in an era of sprawling cities and large-scale trade and travel, are no longer searching to uncover what is new but are, in some cases, pointing out what has been lost to us after two centuries of industrial output and exponential population growth. As wilderness rapidly disappears under the onslaught of urban sprawl, deforestation, mining, and resort development, the numbers and species of animals, birds and insects are declining. Davis, a traveller in some of the remotest regions of the globe, has written about the loss of human languages and cultures, the melding of the diversity of human culture into a global polyglot behemoth, while Schultes was a vocal conservationist known in particular for his work in ethnobotany and ethnopharmacology among the peoples of the Amazon basin. In the Introduction to his book *Where the Gods Reign*, he wrote:

> A number of years ago, I heard a high-ranking South American diplomat describe the Amazon as a "desert of trees that had to be cleared for the benefit of mankind." Yet, investigations by Colombian and foreign botanists have recognised an unbelievably rich flora, and the detailed knowledge of it possessed by its native inhabitants. Advancing acculturation and civilisation everywhere spell the doom of extinction of this knowledge faster even than the extinction of species themselves as a result of forest devastation.

The modern sightseers and scholars are presiding not over an era of growth but an era of decline. In the early twenty-first century the excitement over the discovery of new species of animals and plants has been largely replaced by warnings and concern for the diminishing variety of species in the natural world, the downside of taming the wilderness. It is the tail end of a process begun centuries ago when European nations first developed naval technology capable of sending ships across the great oceans of the world, and a sad conclusion to a movement that began with such energy, curiosity, and optimism.

And yet, the collection and studying of new species has not entirely disappeared. In 2000 a group of scientists from around the world established the All-Species Foundation with the specific objective of creating a "complete inventory of all species of life on Earth within the next 25 years—a human generation." Estimates of the number of undiscovered species on the planet, including microbes, could be as high as 100 million—no one really knows, so despite centuries of work by naturalists, the task remains daunting (although naturalists of the golden age didn't even know of the existence of microbes). Scientists have little information concerning the vast majority of these species, but the members of the foundation believe that a reliable, computer-based catalogue of all of the earth's life "will greatly enhance our capacity to conserve essential biodiversity." The project has been launched at a critical juncture, "given the rate of species loss thanks to humanity operating in ignorance of what's really out there." The All-Species Foundation has revived, with a modern twist, the old dream of the early naturalists.

Much has been written about pre-Darwinian scientific theorizers and thinkers such as Linnaeus, Cuvier, Lamarck, and Mendel, and about Charles Darwin himself, but the scientific travellers and collectors—the field naturalists who provided most of the observations and facts upon which the scientific speculations of the eighteenth and nineteenth centuries were based—have generally been overlooked. They have been dismissed as explorers, overshadowed by grand geographic and military expeditions, and passed over as scientists, in favour of the theorists whose research more closely resembles science as it is studied today.

Sightseers and Scholars is an effort to bring to light the remarkable tales of the field naturalists who scoured the remotest regions of North and South America during the great age of scientific collectors. I decided that the best way to discuss these travellers, adventurers, and storytellers was to tell the tales of their adventures, to show the conditions under which they laboured. I wanted to highlight their unique contribution to the study of the natural world that, although eclipsed by a more thorough study of nature, nevertheless forms an interesting, if dead-end, line of scientific reasoning that went into slow, terminal decline after the publication of *The Origin of Species*.

The characters selected for *Sightseers and Scholars* in no way represent a comprehensive or definitive collection of naturalists but rather a sampling of some of the interesting members of a broad social movement in continental Europe, Britain, Canada, and the United States. It is not an encyclopedic collection of individuals, nor is it an in-depth analysis of the social conditions that gave rise to the great collecting craze. Any book of this nature is personal—the choice of characters is based on my own reading and research. There are dozens, perhaps hundreds, of other naturalists who could have been included here. I cast my net wide and came up with a diverse collection of individuals whom I felt formed a balanced sample from the great age of scientific travellers.

Several criteria influenced my choices. The characters were selected to broadly cover the geography of North and South America, to demonstrate how similar work differed depending on the climate and terrain. Time was also a factor, to show a transition from the wealthy aristocratic amateurs of the eighteenth and early nineteenth centuries to the more formally trained professional collectors of the mid-nineteenth century. And finally, each character had to be a pioneer in some way—the first to thoroughly study, write about, or collect the species from a region, or the first to develop a new approach to the study of nature.

Like all people, the naturalists were products of their own time and culture. There are no women in this collection, for example. It is well documented that women, particularly in Britain, Canada, and the United States, were avid collectors of specimens, made up close to half the members of local natural history clubs, and were voracious readers of the dozens of natural history books published each year. Lynn Barber points out in *The Heyday of Natural History* that "every Victorian young lady, it seemed, could reel off the names of twenty different kinds of ferns or fungus." But women were not the explorers and collectors sent out to distant lands; and consequently they did not write travel accounts of their adventures. During the late eighteenth and mid-nineteenth centuries, women were generally excluded from such activities. They are almost invisible participants in the broad social phenomenon, contributing to its advancement and popularity but never claiming the limelight.

The Royal Geographic Society, the Linnean Society, and the Royal Horticultural Society, for example, admitted no female members, and, as Barber writes, this was "a strong disincentive to research, since it was usually only through their various *Transactions* that findings could be published." American institutions such as the American Philosophical Society and the Academy of Natural Sciences of

Philadelphia did have a small number of women members.[*] Barber also observes that "in natural history as in other fields, there was the usual obstacle that women were not *expected* to achieve anything," and "were encouraged to pursue an interest such as natural history just so long as it was dilettante; once it verged on real intellectual application it became 'fatiguing' and unhealthy." For women, the study of science and nature was restricted to a hobby, although women writers churned out popular natural history books for children and were the—frequently anonymous—illustrators for many works of the period.

The men who did travel were also a product of their time in their reticence to write or comment about their families and personal lives. They wrote almost nothing of their spouses, mistresses, or children—all is concealed behind a veil of social respectability. And so we are left with only sketchy biographical details. An incomplete picture emerges, to be filled in with information from their public letters and books, their commentary on the natural world, and, by inference, from their responses to situations in their narrative.

All in all, the scientific travellers were a remarkably liberal bunch for the times, open-minded and philosophical in their meditations and speculations. As a generalization, despite a propensity to shoot and preserve anything they thought was new or novel and an interest in sport hunting that is perhaps disturbing by modern standards, they were willing, as travellers, to accept and appreciate other people and new and different ways of doing things. They were, for the most part, notably free from the prejudices against native cultures prevalent in European and American society at the time. They were interesting, often eccentric, explorers who ventured as far as they could off the beaten path in order to pursue their quarry—butterflies, beetles, fishes, birds, and plants. Though they were undoubtedly brave, they were not dashing individuals—many of them were retiring and quiet, preferring the solitude of the forest to the social gatherings of high society. Today, many of their scientific

---

[*] Both of these institutions, which still exist today, were the central organizing ones in the United States for the study of the natural world. The American Philosophical Society was founded in 1743 with the objective of pursuing "all Philosophical Experiments that let Light into the Nature of Things, tend to increase the power of Man over Matter, and multiply the Conveniences or Pleasures of Life." The Academy of Natural Sciences of Philadelphia was founded in 1812 "for the encouragement and cultivation of the sciences and the advancement of useful learning." Both institutions organized scientific expeditions or advised travelling naturalists and government officials on matters of scientific interest. They numbered among their members prominent doctors, lawyers, clergy, merchants, and officials; Benjamin Franklin was a member, as was George Washington, Alexander von Humboldt and, later, the young John Kirk Townsend.

contributions are common knowledge—we know that birds migrate, for example, or that bears hibernate, that certain snakes are poisonous, and we can find out almost any plant's name and characteristics merely by consulting a book. But at the time, the travelling naturalists had a profound impact on how the world was understood. They were the forerunners of today's ecologists and biologists, advancing the study of science during its infancy and ultimately contributing the bulk of the information that enabled Charles Darwin to develop the theory of evolution through natural selection.

The hardships and adventures of the scientific travellers are no less fascinating than those of the greatest explorers and are made all the more interesting because of the odd and entertaining books they wrote of their journeys, and their uncommon thoughts and meditations on the natural world and the human place within it during an age of great change and scientific discovery.

PART ONE

Early Naturalists and Scientists

THE QUEST TO MAKE SENSE OF THE bewildering complexity of the natural world is as old as humanity itself. For millennia, survival depended upon having a basic knowledge of edible plants and animals and an understanding of the medicinal properties of various herbs. During the Age of Reason in the eighteenth century, however, the period of the European philosophical movement called the Enlightenment, the study and understanding of the natural world became a passion. As maritime trade expanded and the ships of seafaring nations such as Britain, France, Germany, and the United States circled the globe, mariners returned from their journeys with a multitude of new specimens of animals and plants and natural curiosities that didn't match any of the descriptions found in the ancient texts. The evidence of so many unfamiliar life forms rendered obsolete the old medieval bestiaries and herbals, which had previously classified known animals and plants. Most of these bestiaries intermingled pictures and descriptions of known animals with fantastic creatures such as mermaids, unicorns, and sea monsters that were conveniently said to live in the blank spaces on maps.

Based on the belief that all animals and plants were immutable, set by the creator and reproducing for eternity without change, the seemingly obvious starting point to understanding nature was to collect and classify all the plants, mammals, birds, fish, and insects of the world. An early English naturalist named John Ray (1627–1705), while working on a compendium of plants and animals of the British Isles, realized that a system of classification that would transcend language barriers was needed. The bestiaries and herbals of the time were structured alphabetically, resulting in a different order of information in each translation of a given work. Ray proposed using Latin as the universal language of nomenclature and came up with the term *species* to define organisms that could reproduce with each other. His book *Synopsis of the British Flora* was organized alphabetically in Latin according to species.

The Swedish naturalist Carolus Linnaeus (1707–1778) further developed the classification system by creating two Latin names for each species—what is known as binomial nomenclature—that included the distinctions of genus and species as identifiers for any given specimen. He classified them based on their sexual organs and method of reproduction, a novel approach that provoked indignation among certain prudish members of the intelligentsia. The English botanist Reverend Samuel Goodenough remarked that "a literal translation of the first principles of Linnean botany is enough to shock female modesty." In spite of these reservations, Linnaeus's system was quickly adopted as the standard for communication between botanists. Each of the three "Kingdoms of Nature"—animal, mineral, and vegetable—were subdivided into classes, orders, genera, and, finally, species. The kingdom of animals, for example, included mammals, birds, amphibia, fish, insects, and worms. Linnaeus imagined every living thing to be a part of a great hierarchy from the lowest creatures to the highest—with humans at the apex. In a remarkable tour de force, he named over 7,500 species of plants; by 1759, in the tenth edition of his great work *Systema Naturae*, he had also given official names to nearly 4,500 animals. Linnaeus's classification system is still more or less followed today, with modifications such as the creation of phylum, family, and sub-species to further differentiate creatures.

Taxonomic classification was a useful tool for naturalists seeking to define a universal order. It was now possible to properly place new discoveries within the expanding global schemata—and to be one step closer to the complete cataloguing of nature. The travelling naturalists and scientists of the era who followed immediately after the acceptance of Linnaeus's hierarchy—when science itself was still primitive— had no particular focus when they began scouring remote and uncivilized regions for new natural treasures. Presented with a bewildering yet fascinating and entirely new collection of plants, animals, and landscapes that differed widely from anything they had known in Europe, they began the process of collecting and studying what existed around them. They posed questions, were free with their theories, and were interested in a wide range of scientific pursuits. They were working with a clean slate, and so, with no accurate information about the natural world, speculating on bird migrations, collecting a novel plant, measuring ocean currents, and observing the behaviour of mammals were all of equal interest to them. Profound distinctions between the different approaches to the study of the natural world had not yet emerged, and these early travellers were at the forefront of a tradition that placed great emphasis on recording observations of nature, not just on classifying species. They were all, by necessity, generalists.

Travel was fraught with danger and uncertainty as the earliest naturalists of the eighteenth century wandered through unfamiliar regions without accurate maps. William Bartram, a younger son of America's first naturalist John Bartram, visited lands only beginning to be explored and tamed. The Thirteen Colonies, later the first independent states of the United States of America, consisted of a thin strip of cultivated and "civilized" land along the Atlantic coast. Apart from this narrow band, natives lived much as they always had on the rest of the continent. To the settlers, the wilderness was a wild and dangerous force that needed to be subdued, but to Bartram it was something to be celebrated, evidence of the divine. When Bartram ventured on his journeys, he had no accurate maps, no roads, and, apart from his periodic trips to the coast to send off specimens and to re-supply, no specific destination. He merely wandered, for years, collecting specimens, hundreds of which were new to science. The American Revolution began and ended during the time of his ceaseless ramblings in the wilderness, and he hardly mentions it, apart from a brief period spent in a local militia near St. Augustine preparing for a rumoured British assault. While helping to define the hinterland of the expanding American republic, he wrote a poetic and often whimsical tale of his adventures, interspersed with detailed descriptions of the new plants and animals he encountered.

Writing nearly thirty years after Bartram, the German aristocrat and self-trained scientist Alexander von Humboldt was considerably more pragmatic and practical in his investigations. Between 1799 and 1804, while Napoleon struggled to dominate much of Europe, he roamed the wild interior of northern South America, taking copious notes and shipping vast collections of specimens back to Berlin. Rather than merely marvelling at the abundance of nature in South America, which was admittedly primeval and on a grander scale than anything remaining in western Europe, Humboldt began laying the foundations for solving specific questions concerning the natural world. His interests were broad and far-ranging, yet at the same time quite focused. He wanted to know exactly how a volcano worked, what caused the tides, why one region was arid while another was humid; answers that could not be rationally explained were of little interest to him. However, his account, like the others, combined a travelogue of his experiences in an exotic land with broad-ranging speculations on the natural world and descriptions of new species. A man of Humboldt's temperament would likely have been a scientist rather than a naturalist had he lived fifty years later. But he travelled and wrote at a time when people were still asking the questions that scientists and theorists would try to answer in the coming century.

The early naturalists and scientists of the late eighteenth century and the early nineteenth century had a profound impact on the study of natural history throughout the nineteenth century. Without the wealth of knowledge of the natural world taken for granted today, unsophisticated and unsystematic speculation was the starting point for scientific inquiry.

CHAPTER ONE

William Bartram

Observe these green meadows how they are decorated; they seem enameled with the beds of flowers. The blushing Chironia and Rhexia, the spiral Ophrys with immaculate white flowers, the Limodorum, Arethusa pulcherima, Sarracenia purpurea, Sarracenia galeata, Sarracenia lucunosa, Sarracenia flava. Shall we analyze these beautiful plants, since they seem cheerfully to invite us?—
WILLIAM BARTRAM, *Travels through North and South Carolina, Georgia, East and West Florida, the Cherokee Country, the Extensive Territories of the Muscogulges, or Creek Confederacy, and the Country of the Chactaws*

When he was an old and hunched man, shuffling about the interior of the stone house where he was raised on a verdant farm along the Schuylkill River a few miles out of Philadelphia, William Bartram could look back on a life of turmoil, uncertainty, financial setbacks amid the political upheaval of the American Revolution. He could also reminisce on a life of adventure, danger, and astounding accomplishments in a peculiar and ill-defined calling normally reserved for wealthy and eccentric hobbyists. His career as a naturalist initially showed great promise, but was derailed for many years before he was ultimately vindicated by the 1791 publication of his masterpiece, *Travels through North and South Carolina, Georgia, East and West Florida, the Cherokee Country, the Extensive Territories of the Muscogulges, or Creek Confederacy, and the Country of the Chactaws*. Although his magnum opus was not immediately appreciated upon its publication, it eventually established him as one of the most informed and knowledgeable naturalists of his time.

Bartram's fame in later life drew an endless stream of

William Bartram (1739–1823), America's greatest travelling naturalist.

William Bartram's travels in southeastern North America, 1755–1776.

visitors from Europe and America to confer with him and observe the wonders of his great herbarium—a living museum of the majority of plants native to the eastern United States, specimens accumulated by him and his father during fifty years of roaming the wild and tangled hinterland on the fringes of "civilization," the western boundary of the Thirteen Colonies. William Bartram corresponded regularly with such luminaries as Benjamin Franklin, Benjamin Barton, Thomas Nuttall, and André Michaux about matters of scientific importance. Although he was one of the most widely travelled naturalists at the dawn of the heroic age of scientific exploration, in his later years he seldom ventured farther afield than Philadelphia, claiming that his youthful travels had permanently weakened his constitution.

Born the seventh of eleven siblings on February 9, 1739, William Bartram had a love of the natural world that could easily have come from a childhood spent wandering through acres of exotic plants, groves of peculiar shrubs, and a small forest of trees that his father had begun cultivating a few years before his birth. But his love of adventure in the wilds likely developed in 1854, when, at age fifteen, he accompanied his father on a collecting trip to the Catskill Mountains in New York State. It was here, despite his father's misgivings about the unpredictable prospects of a career that was heavily dependent upon European patrons for livelihood, that his ambition to succeed as a naturalist-artist took root. For most of his life, the adventure and freedom of living simply in the woods would draw him away from his mercantile endeavours and any semblance of a settled existence.

The younger Bartram began sketching birds, trees, flowers, and other vegetation soon after returning from this first trip, imitating the style of Mark Catesby, the famous English ornithologist who had briefly sojourned in the Carolinas twenty years earlier. He spent the winter at school in Philadelphia, and then accompanied his father to the Catskills again in 1755. These expeditions made such a lasting impression on him that he still wrote about them nearly forty years later. "Being youthful and vigorous in the pursuit of botanical and novel objects," he described, recalling his first encounter with a rattlesnake in 1755, "I had gained the summit of a steep rocky precipice, ahead of our guide, when just entering a shady vale, I saw at the root of a small shrub, a singular and beautiful appearance...and was just drawing back my foot to kick it over, when at that instant my father being near, cried out, 'a rattle snake my son,' and jerked me back, which probably saved my life." The torpid serpent, "very beautiful, speckled and clouded," continued its indolent lazing. Although his father "pled for its life" the guide immediately killed it, and Bartram had to be content with its skin and fangs for his collection.*

Although his father referred to him proudly as "my little botanist," and Bartram worked on a commission to collect and draw all species of American turtles he could find for his father's influential English colleague, John Collinson, Bartram's father remained dubious about his son's prospects of earning a living as a naturalist. Collinson, however, was so

Bartram's first big break came in 1768 when a wealthy natural history enthusiast in London commissioned drawings of all of America's "land tortoises."

---

* On another occasion in east Florida a decade later, he again almost trod on a sleeping serpent "about six foot in length and as thick as an ordinary man's leg." Startled, he killed it in a passion and then dragged it back to the fort, "his scaly body sounding over the ground," where it was served up for dinner to the "amazed multitude." For Bartram, though, it was a sad occasion and he couldn't swallow his portion, tender though it was. "He certainly had it in his power to kill me almost instantly," he mused, "and I make no doubt but that he was conscious of it.... I promised myself that I would never again be accessory to the death of a rattle snake, which promise I have invariably kept to."

Franklinia
Gordonia pubescens.

Gordonia pubescens franklinia, later renamed *Franklinia altamaha*, was one of Bartram's greatest finds in 1765. "It is a flowering tree," he reported, "of the first order for beauty and fragrance of blossoms."

impressed with William's work that he showed the drawings to another Quaker naturalist, Dr. John Fothergill, one of England's most noted horticulturists and gardeners. Fothergill, who later became one of William's most important patrons, urged the lad to "observe and draw plants and all varieties of creatures." Still, erring on the side of caution, the elder Bartram apprenticed William to a Philadelphia merchant when he was eighteen so that he could acquire the skills to earn a secure living and be waylaid from the uncertain path of a naturalist and artist. But William, who had grown into a young man with prominent features and a thoughtful countenance, had little interest in practical matters and he continued to devote his time and energy to his drawings. Although he moved to Cape Fear, North Carolina, in 1761 to live with an uncle and establish himself as a trader, his heart was not in it and the business did not prosper.

Four years later, in 1765, the elder Bartram, now sixty-six, was appointed official botanist to His Majesty George III, a position of great prestige but little remuneration. With his first annual stipend he set out on another botanical collecting expedition, this time to Florida, a strange and relatively unexplored land where there were rumoured to be many new and curious specimens of the "vegetable kingdom."* En route, he stopped in Cape Fear to visit William, who persuaded his father to hire

---

* Although Florida was primarily inhabited by the Seminole Indians, it was claimed by England from Spain following the Treaty of Paris in 1763. In 1773, after the American Revolution, it was returned to Spain. Boundary disputes between the United States and Spain, however, continued until 1819 when Spain ceded the territory to the United States. The Seminoles were eventually driven off the land in a series of wars that culminated in the Second Seminole War (1835–1842). When the Bartrams first ventured to Florida, it was nominally English, yet when William published his *Travels* in 1791, it was back in Spanish hands.

him as an assistant, and the two headed off to the swamps and savannahs of Georgia and east Florida together.

The younger Bartram, at twenty-six, fell in love with the South and began an association that would continue for the rest of his life. "How gently flow thy peaceful floods, O Altamaha!" he rhapsodized on seeing the lush growths along the shores of the river in Georgia. "How sublimely rise to view, on thy elevated shores, yon Magnolia groves, from whose tops the surrounding expanse is perfumed, by clouds of incense, blended with the exhaling balm of the Liquid-amber, and odours continually arising from circumambient aromatic groves of Illicium, Myricea, Laurus, and Bignonia." Literary effusion aside, it was not the circumambient groves that would prove to be their greatest discovery during this journey. Along the banks of the Altamaha River, father and son stumbled upon an elegant shrub, or small tree, that they correctly surmised was a new and rare species. William reported, "It is a flowering tree of the first order for beauty and fragrance of blossoms: the tree grows fifteen or twenty feet in height, branching alternately; the leaves are oblong, broadest towards their extremities.... The flowers are very large, expand themselves perfectly, are of a snow white color and ornamented with a crown or tassel of a gold-colored refulgent staminae in their center,... and make a gay appearance. The fruit is a large round, dry, woody apple or pericarp opening at each end."

They named it *Gordonia Pubescens Franklinia* (later renamed *Franklinia altamaha*), the Franklinia tree, after the elder Bartram's good friend Benjamin Franklin.[*]

---

[*] Although the tree was no longer in bloom at the time of their first discovery, William again encountered the tree along the Altamaha River eight years later, in 1773. He spied it the second time enveloped in beautiful creamy flowers and brought seeds back to the garden in Philadelphia and cultivated it. By this simple act, the Bartrams likely preserved it from extinction—it has never been recorded in the wild since 1790. Today, the Franklin tree is a popular American ornamental, with all living specimens descended from the Bartrams' garden.

Annona Grandiflora was one of the many new plants Bartram avidly collected during his travels.

They continued their journey overland to St. Augustine, and then began their most daring foray yet—a canoe excursion up the St. Johns River, surveying the main stream and all major tributaries and lakes, making charts of the waterway's winding course, measuring width, depth, and distances, and providing notes on currents. It was a four-hundred-mile paddle that took many months and likely furnished the younger Bartram with the basic survival skills he needed for his solitary travels and explorations in the following decade. Pitcher plants and Venus flytraps were both fascinating finds on this trip. "How greatly the flowers of the yellow Sarracenia (pitcher plant) represent a silken canopy," he wrote. "The yellow, pendant petals are the curtains, and the hollow leaves are not unlike the cornucopia or Amalthea's horn. What a quantity of water a leaf is capable of containing: about a pint! Taste of it," he implores his reader, "how cool and animating—limpid as the morning dew." William called the Venus flytrap, which is native to South Carolina, "tipitiwichit" and considered it one of his favourites. "Let us advance to the spot in which nature has seated them," he suggests. "Astonishing production! See the incarnate lobes expanding, how gay and sportive they appear! Ready on the spring to entrap incautious, deluded insects, what artifice! . . . carnivorous vegetable!"

The elder Bartram returned to Philadelphia in June 1766, with "a fine collection of strange Florida plants," while William elected to remain in Florida and try raising indigo and rice along the St. Johns River. In this he failed more disastrously than in any other business venture to date, and the following year he boarded a ship for home. He began labouring in obscurity on a farm near Philadelphia. Despite his humble occupation, though, in 1768 he was elected a corresponding member of the American Society held in Philadelphia for Promoting Useful Knowledge (later amalgamated with the American Philosophical Society). Benjamin Franklin and Bartram's father were elected members at the same meeting. In spite of this honour, his prospects as a naturalist remained dim for a few years, and only improved when Peter Collinson secured him a commission from the Duchess of Portland to draw "all Land, River and your Sea Shells, from the very least to the greatest," and another commission from Dr. Fothergill to draw a series of mollusks and turtles.

Around this time Bartram started another mercantile enterprise, but it also faltered after a few years. Facing almost certain bankruptcy, in 1770 he fled Philadelphia for Cape Fear, where he remained for a few years fulfilling his obligations to his English patrons, organizing and drawing specimens. In 1772, he determined to throw off the shackles of commerce and venture to Florida to explore on his own. How he would finance this expedition remained unclear, and on hearing these plans, his father expressed concern over his "wild notion" and summoned him home to help expand the herbarium. William had not been in Philadelphia for very long, however, when he received a letter from Dr. Fothergill offering the financing for an extended expedition through the south, and then west to the Mississippi. "It is a pity that such a genius should sink under distress," Fothergill wrote to William's father.

While the United States hovered on the brink of revolution, the younger Bartram (now thirty-four years old) spent the next five years wandering through much of the wildest and least known terrain in the Carolinas (1773), in Georgia (1773–74) and in eastern Florida (1774), in Cherokee country (all land west of the English-inhabited regions along the coast) by way of Georgia and South Carolina (1775), and in western Florida (1776) before returning in the fall of 1777. He spent much of this time camping in a tent in the woods as a guest of socially

Head of the Great Soft-shelled Tortoise.

Bartram paid considerable attention to capturing the details of specimens including out-of-context close-up sketches.

starved outlying farmers, or staying at Indian trading posts deep inland. Nothing escaped his eye: tree, insect, bird, flower, fish, fruit, mammal, mineral, or mollusk. The great political upheavals that resulted in the creation of the United States of America, and changed forever Bartram's own citizenship, complicating his relationships with his sponsors and seed purchasers, seems to have been far from his mind.

Bartram rode about the hinterland, which to him was surreal in its lushness and variety, loaded with food and "camp equipage." He flitted about for years along murky, ill-trodden, and underused trails through the overgrown foliage and shady groves, skirting the fringes of torrid swamps enshrouded in tendrils of lush cypress, hickory, water hyacinth, great leaf magnolias, and drooping clusters of Spanish moss. He crossed savannas covered in magnificent specimens of black oaks that, he claimed, "to keep within the bounds of truth and reality, in describing the magnitude and grandeur of these trees, would, I fear, fail of credulity." The trunks in one forest averaged eight to eleven feet wide five feet above the ground, and he measured "several that were thirty feet girt." The tulip trees, liquid amber, and beech were equally stately, while in Florida he frequently regaled himself with plump oranges that grew profusely in groves along the glades of the interior. He plucked them from branches above his head, squeezing the juice over his frying fish.

He parleyed his way out of trouble with the Creek and Seminole Indians (who eventually named him "Plant Hunter"), escaped from brigands along unpatrolled byways, and avoided being eaten by carnivores, poisoned by snakes, or sucked beneath the turgid waters of a vast swamp. He was, by his own admission, "continually impelled by a restless spirit of curiosity, in pursuit of new productions of nature." He was astonished at the "avidity" of frogs and fishes in pursuit of their insect prey at dawn and dusk, and he marvelled at the antics of bears when he frightened them by shooting his gun. On one occasion, he came upon a cool stream just below a rapids and he observed a cluster of gravel pyramids strewn about the streambed. The pyramids were inhabited by a congregation of small crayfish who used them as a citadel, "a place of retreat for their young, against the ravages of their enemy the gold-fish," who swarmed the citadels attacking the crayfish. Occasionally, "a small detachment of veteran cray-fish sallied out upon them" and the fish "instantly fled from every side, darting through the transparent waters like streams of lightning." No sooner had the crayfish retreated, however, than the others emerged again to surround the pyramids. "In this manner," he mused, "the war seemed to be continual."*

The crude, rudimentary maps of the terrain he traversed did not deter him, and when he ventured into "Indian country," where the land shown on his maps bore little resemblance to reality, he frequently hired Creek or Seminole guides. Toward the Indians he was unusually generous, at odds with the prevalent attitudes of the times that native peoples were savages and the only way to control them was, in the words of William's own father, to "bang them stoutly." Although on more than one occasion his guide deserted him in the wilderness, he maintained a balanced view of native peoples as human beings deserving of the same respect he accorded to others. "Such is the virtue of these untutored

---

* In his description of the seemingly mundane, he elevated nature writing to an art. "The gold-fish," he recorded, "is about the size of an anchovy, nearly four inches long, of a neat slender form; the head is covered with a salade of an ultramarine blue, the back of a reddish brown, the sides and belly of a flame, or of the colour of a fine red lead; a narrow dusky line runs along each side, from the gills to the tail; the eyes are large, with the iris like burnished gold."

savages: but I am afraid this is a common phrase epithet, having no meaning, or at least improperly applied; for these people are both well tutored and civil; and it is apparent to an impartial observer, who resides but a little time amongst them, that it is from the most delicate sense of honour and reputation of the tribes and families, that their laws and customs receive their force and energy."[*]

William Bartram's characteristic descriptions of the terrain are so specific that it is almost possible to imagine riding along beside him through the English frontier, sharing his wonder. It also provides a window to view the land as it was before the forests were cut down to make way for cultivation, and before civilization crept westward in the following decades. Riding inland from Savannah near the beginning of his trip, he described the changing terrain as follows: "...from the sea coast, fifty miles back, is a level plain, generally of a loose sandy soil, producing spacious high forests.... Nearly one third of this vast plain is what the inhabitants call swamps, which are the sources of numerous small rivers and their branches...twenty or thirty miles upwards from the sea, when they branch and spread abroad like an open hand, interlocking with each other, and forming a chain of swamps across the Carolinas and Georgia, several hundred miles parallel with the sea coast....We now rise a bank of considerable height, which runs nearly parallel to the coast, through Carolina and Georgia...is mostly a forest of the great long-leaved pine, the earth covered with grass, interspersed with an infinite variety of herbaceous plants."

---

[*] On one occasion his imagination got the better of him and he was tempted to liken the noble Seminole to the Greek hero of yore: "What an Elysium it is!" he spouted, "where the wandering Seminole, the naked red warrior, roams at large, and after the vigorous chase retires from the scorching heat of the meridian sun. Here he reclines, and reposes under the odoriferous shades of Zanthoxilon, his verdant couch guarded by the Deity; Liberty, and the Muses, inspiring him with wisdom and valour, whilst the balmy zephyrs fan him to sleep."

The land was shrouded in a canopy of shrubs "of great beauty and singularity"; and the great swamps were "varied with the coppices and hommocks of the various shrubs and trees." Then came the hilly country, covered in pine and extending 150 miles west, "fertile and delightful" and fed by burbling rivulets "either coursing about the fragrant hills, or springing from the rocky precipices...the coolness and purity of which waters invigorate the air of this otherwise hot and sultry climate."

In 1774, Bartram again canoed up the "impetuous current" of the St. Johns River, recreating the journey he had taken with his father nearly a decade before, alone apart from a Seminole guide who deserted somewhere inland because of the horrible conditions and Bartram's tedious preoccupation with the minutiae of the natural world. It was the steamy heat of summer, and he constantly scanned his surroundings for something new, something exotic, something rare; always distracted by a world of magic and marvellous enchantment. "O thou Creator supreme, almighty!" he exclaimed one day. "How infinite and incomprehensible thy works! most perfect, and every way astonishing!"

Bartram observed and was awed by the variety of nature and, in turn, was inspired to write about his discoveries. In his account of his years of travel, his own tales take second place to his observations—whenever he encounters some aspect of nature previously unknown to him, his writing takes on a light of its own, in eloquence and in the sheer delight in the boundless variety of the natural world and its mystical significance, all of which was evidence to Bartram, a deeply religious Quaker, of the influence of the manifestation of God. "This world," he postulated, "as a glorious apartment of the boundless palace of the sovereign Creator, is furnished

A map of the coast of east Florida from Bartram's *Travels* reveals just how little was known of the interior of the country in the late eighteenth century.

with an infinite variety of animated scenes, inexpressibly beautiful and pleasing, equally free to the inspection and enjoyment of all his creatures."

The dreamy Bartram did have one close encounter with providence. While canoeing alone deep in the winding inlets of the inland glades of Florida, "elegantly embellished with flowering plants and shrubs," he was distracted from his musings by a tremendous battle between two "subtle, greedy" alligators.* One enormous beast surged toward the other across the murky lagoon "the waters like a cataract descend[ing] from his open jaws," while "clouds of smoke" issued forth from his dilated nostrils. Apparently, the "boiling surface of the lake mark[ed] their rapid course" and they entwined "in horrid wreaths" before sinking into the gloom. After a frenzied combat the victor emerged, produced "a dreadful roar" and continued its indolent lounging. After the lagoon had returned to tranquility, Bartram leaped into his canoe to skirt across the murky water and catch some fish for supper. Several sneaky reptiles, however, ascertaining his destination, slipped into the water, surrounded his flimsy boat, and attacked on all sides, "several endeavouring to overset the canoe." That he had underestimated their determination, or hunger, was now obvious, yet he was still amazed by the onslaught. Two huge creatures attacked simultaneously, "rushing up with their heads and part of their bodies above the water, roaring terribly and belching floods of water over [him]." Their vicious jaws snapped so close to his head that he was stunned, and, he fearfully recounted, "I expected every moment to be dragged out of the boat and instantly devoured." Fortunately, he managed to beat them off with a club and then paddle quickly to safety. Later, when he was scaling fish by the shore, he looked up to see a sly creature

---

* Alligators and crocodiles are both native to the swampy morass of the southeastern United States. Bartram used the terms interchangeably, and so it is impossible to know specifically which creature he actually encountered.

emerging from the lagoon and swiping its tail. Bartram leaped back, and it only "brushed off several fish." The "incredible boldness of the animal," he recorded with great understatement, "disturbed me greatly."

He later learned why there was such a "prodigious assemblage of crocodiles at this place." As the sun set, the river "appeared to be one solid bank of fish, of various kinds, pushing through this narrow pass" into a nearby lake. The reptiles, apparently, were clambering over each other and quarrelling to be near the fish. "It would have been easy to have walked across on their heads," he suggested, "had the animals been harmless." It was this scene that astonished and frightened him. The "horrid noise of their closing jaws, their plunging amidst the broken banks of fish, and rising with their prey some feet upright above the water, the floods of water and blood rushing out of their mouths, and the clouds of vapours issuing from their wide nostrils, were truly frightful." It was with great apprehension that he bedded down on his little islet that night, with scenes of the feeding frenzy before his eyes. He records having seen an alligator with three large fish in its mouth at the same time "squeeze them betwixt his jaws, while the tails of the great trout flapped about his eyes and lips, ere he had swallowed them." Although he was "occasionally awakened by the whooping of owls, screaming of bitterns, or the wood-rats running amongst the leaves," the tremendous appetite of the devouring alligators had apparently been sated.

On another, more peaceful, occasion Bartram witnessed a large spider barring his path through the woods. After recovering from his initial shock, he observed that the spider was engaged "on predatory attempts against the insect tribes," and he quietly drew near to watch the proceedings. The spider, he noted, had its eyes set on a large fat "bomble" bee that "was visiting the flowers, and piercing their nectariferous tubes." The spider drew closer, with the stealth, or so it seemed to Bartram, of a Seminole approaching a deer. With

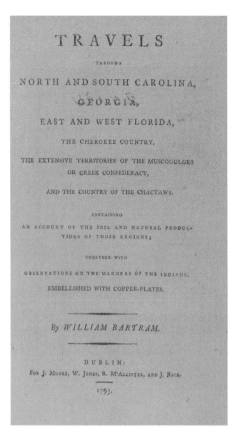

Title page of an Irish edition of Bartram's *Travels.*

short leaps, timed at the precise moment that the bee was busy inside a flower, the spider slunk forward, and then "instantly sprang upon him." The bee with the spider on its back immediately flew into the air, but was jerked back at the end of a tether, a strand of silky web that bound them to the earth. "The rapidity of the bee's wings, endeavouring to extricate himself, made them both together appear as a moving vapor," he reported, "until the bee became fatigued by whirling around . . . quite exhausted by his struggles, and the repeated wounds of the butcher, became motionless, and quickly expired in the arms of the devouring spider." The victorious spider shinnied up the strand and removed itself to feast upon its prey, but perhaps, speculated Bartram, "before night became himself, the delicious evening repast of a bird or lizard."

Birds also fascinated him. He noted that they became quieter at night, and expressed his observation as only Bartram could: "At the cool eve's approach, the sweet enchanting melody of the feathered songsters gradually ceases, and they betake themselves to their leafy coverts for security and repose." He spent considerable time observing migration patterns and debunking early theories on where birds went in the winter. Some theories suggested that they went to the moon, others that they found caves and hollow trees and hibernated; and, Bartram noted with incredulity, "even at this day very celebrated men have asserted that swallows, at the approach of winter, voluntarily plunge into lakes and rivers, descend to the bottom, and there creep into the mud and slime, where they continue overwhelmed by ice in a torpid state until the returning summer warms them again into life. . . . This notion, though the latest, seems the most difficult to reconcile with reason and common sense." Although he admitted to being "entirely ignorant of how far southward they continue their route," he was completely convinced that almost all birds, "beautiful and entertaining beings," did migrate somewhere for different seasons. Bartram included a catalogue of 215 species of birds as an addendum to his published *Travels*. Although nearly half proved to be incorrect, the renowned ornithologist Elliott Coues remarked nearly a century later that Bartram had formed "the starting point for a distinctively American school of ornithology."

On several occasions during his five-year odyssey Bartram suffered from fevers and other mysterious ailments. Only occasionally did he return to Savannah or St. Augustine to mail off correspondence and send specimens to Dr. Fothergill in England, or just to relax. On one such occasion at Fort Frederica near the coast of Georgia, he stared east into the "majestic scene," heard "the solemn sound of the beating surf strik[ing] our ears; the dashing of yon liquid mountains, like mighty giants, in vain assail the skies; they are beaten back, and fall prostrate upon the shores of the trembling island." He reached Baton Rouge in late October 1775, but constant travelling in harsh climates and conditions had worn him down and he began thinking of returning to Philadelphia. In 1776, he joined a group of American volunteers in Florida to defend against a rumoured British invasion from St. Augustine (an invasion that fortunately never materialized). For the most part, though, the Revolution had little impact on him because he was so far removed from the settled regions along the coast.

When William Bartram finally decided to end his ceaseless rambles, in late 1776, his body was weakened by the ravages of fevers and years of difficult living. He turned north and arrived in Philadelphia in January 1777, at the height of the Revolutionary War, to find his father suffering from frailty and old age. The elder Bartram died soon thereafter, in September, apparently from anxiety over the fate of his botanical garden in the wake of advancing British troops. The

Ixia Calestina

Many of Bartram's plant drawings, such as the *Ixia calestina*, capture a surreal, sleepy-looking quality that matched his effusive ornate descriptions.

war never reached the garden, however, and William elected to remain there while he finished organizing his specimens and writing his travelogue. On July 4, 1783, the war ended and he was no longer a British citizen, but a citizen of the United States of America.

Bartram's explorations resulted in dozens of paintings and sketches, descriptions and collections of new species of plants, and reports on Indian culture, soil conditions, topography, birds, mammals, reptiles, amphibians, and fishes. It was a truly broad compilation of information, the first collection and description of the flora and fauna of the wild lands to the west of the new American states. He kept a meticulous journal during his travels, which was eventually forwarded to Dr. Fothergill. William then spent the next decade slowly compiling the text for *Travels*. Unfortunately, an eye ailment that he contracted in Florida made him extremely sensitive to light; direct sun caused tears to flow down his cheeks, and he scrawled away on his manuscript, sometimes in so much pain that he kept his eyes shut, a condition that explains the long delay in publishing his book.

His sketches and paintings reveal the dual components of his character—the artist and the scientist; they are alternately dreamy and improbable or precise and painstakingly accurate. Some look like something out of *Alice in Wonderland*, a surreal melange of disparate ecosystems, distorted in scale and association yet executed with remarkable attention to detail on individual species: snails creep along loamy detritus; droopy fronds of sleepy-looking plants sway on delicate curving stems; elliptical pads splay out over placid pond water; ill-shaped serpents swallow squirming frogs next to pelicans peering down into the hazy depths; playful alligators writhe in the swamp, gobbling fish and snorting water through their nostrils, "bellowing in the spring season." Others, such as his depictions of specific plants, however, are unerring in their exactitude, showing minute details such as insects clustered along a stem, the subtle speckles along a turtle's shell, or the spidery tendrils of an immature root bulb. In some cases, his drawings and accompanying description were so precise that they were used as the defining information about a species in preference even to a dried specimen.

In America, there was considerable criticism of *Travels* and its evident poetic inspiration, which had an influence on the Romantic poets Shelley, Coleridge, and Wordsworth, among others. Many could not believe some of his accounts, such as his tale of the alligators, which seemed too overblown to be credible; others were disturbed by his sympathetic depiction of the natives; some criticized his elegant, flowery language as being unscientific, or, in one review, "very incorrect and disgustingly pompous." Although it appeared in eight or nine editions in six different countries in Europe, including Britain, Germany, Holland, and France in the first decade alone, only a small printing originally went ahead in the United States. It is difficult to speculate what effect, if any, the somewhat muted reception to his life's work had on Bartram, but his writing after 1791 was limited to a few scientific publications and plant descriptions, some of which he forwarded to his friend Benjamin Smith Barton, a professor of botany at the University of the State of Pennsylvania, who published them, sometimes without proper credit, in his own texts on botany.

Although knowledge of how organisms functioned was largely non-existent, Bartram was at the forefront of a scientific tradition that would see the understanding of the world

Hydrangea Quercifolia

In some cases, Bartram's drawings and accompanying description were so precise that they were used as the defining information about a species in preference even to a dried specimen. In his drawing of the *Hydrangea quercifolia*, for example, he showed a view of the tree as well as close-ups of the leaf and flower.

greatly expanded. His ideas about the interrelationships between species and the environment, the concept of an ecosystem, were groundbreaking, if only speculative. And his idle thoughts about "the continual circulation of animal juices" in living creatures is both simplistic and uncannily accurate, considering the lack of any means of empirically measuring such things. His dismissal of the preposterous theories of seasonal bird disappearances was an early example of the quest for scientific explanations of natural phenomena that would become increasingly important in America and Europe throughout the nineteenth century. Bartram had no way to test his hypotheses, but in the coming years other scientists would ask similar questions and continue to strive for a greater understanding of the complexity of the natural world.

Despite his concern that his exertions had broken his health, Bartram lived to the grand old age of eighty-five, tending the garden and playing host to visiting statesmen, scientists, authors, and artists who flocked to see both him and America's first botanical garden—a garden that still exists as Historic Bartram Gardens along the Schuylkill River. Around the turn of the century, he was invited by Thomas Jefferson, who had purchased and presumably appreciated his book in 1791, to be the naturalist on a military and scientific expedition to the Far West (what would become known as the Lewis and Clark expedition). But because of his age, he didn't feel up to the task of a cross-continental trek through more uncharted wilderness.

William Bartram, who had never married, spent his final years living on the farm along the Schuylkill with his brother and family. After their father's death in 1777, the garden and farm had passed to William's brother John. In the end death was kind. William collapsed early one morning in July 1823; he had just finished scrawling the description of the natural history of a plant, and was enjoying a "morning survey" of his glorious garden.

While Bartram belonged to a religious tradition of Quakers who believed that God could be understood by studying nature, almost thirty years after his retirement from field excursions another scientist was setting out on a grand five-year expedition to South America with a different perspective. Rather than providing descriptions of nature as a means of defining "creation," the German aristocrat Alexander von Humboldt extended the speculative queries of William Bartram to include even more aspects of the natural world—from winds, tides, and geological formations to the relationship between elevation and plant species to the functioning of the internal organs of animals. Like Bartram's, the breadth of his curiosity was astonishing.

CHAPTER TWO

Alexander von Humboldt

Nature is an inexhaustible source of investigation, and in proportion as the domain of science is extended, she presents herself to those who know how to interrogate her, under forms which they have never yet examined.

—ALEXANDER VON HUMBOLDT, *Personal Narrative of Travels to the Equinoctial Regions of America During the Years 1799–1804*

Alexander von Humboldt (1769–1859), the most influential scientific traveller of the nineteenth century.

"From my earliest youth I felt an ardent desire to travel to distant regions, seldom visited by Europeans," wrote Friedrich Heinrich Alexander, Baron von Humboldt, of his early desire to explore the natural world. Humboldt and his companion, the reserved French botanist Aimé Bonpland, spent nearly five years roaming the hinterlands of South America in the early nineteenth century, traversing the savannahs, clambering to the top of the highest peaks, navigating swamps and rivers and visiting the principal cities and rudimentary outposts of the Spanish colonies. Humboldt was drawn on by a seemingly insatiable curiosity and desire to observe the marvellous diversity of the animal and vegetable life of the "torrid zone." On his return to Paris in 1808, he published his monumental opus, *Personal Narrative of Travels to the Equinoctial Regions of America During the Years 1799–1804*, a staggering twenty-three-volume report and travelogue describing his and Bonpland's five-year journey and adventures. It was the first written account to provide detailed descriptions of the flora and fauna of the continent, the first scientific treatise on the region, and was most noteworthy for pointing out relationships between seemingly incongruous phenomena and proposing links between different aspects of the natural world.

The questions Humboldt posed had never been asked before and would consume natural historians for the better part of the next century. The theories he formulated during his years studying nature in South America became accepted knowledge and formed the foundation for the study of physical geography and meteorology. Contemporary science was unable to account for much of what he observed. Although he was not the first scientist to study aspects of South America, his account incited such interest that in the following decades the scientific study of Spanish America became a passion for countless other scientific explorers such as Charles Waterton, Maximilian of Wied, Alfred Wallace, Henry Walter Bates, and Charles Darwin. It was because of the sheer breadth and scope of Humboldt's questioning and powers of observation that Darwin later called him "the greatest scientific explorer who ever lived."

Humboldt was born on September 14, 1769, the eldest son of a wealthy and influential family whose estate sprawled along the outskirts of Berlin. His parents had slated him for a career in the civil service and he spent a disillusioned year studying economics at the University of Frankfurt before transferring first to the University of Gottingen to study physics, chemistry, geology, mineralogy, and languages, and then to the School of Mines in Freiberg to study mining technology. He completed his formal education in 1792 and took his intellectual and critical approach to the world with him when he received an appointment as mining inspector with the Prussian government. He experimented with and studied

Alexander von Humboldt's exploration of the equinoctial regions of South America, 1799–1804.

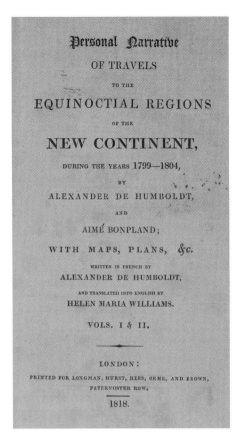

Personal Narrative

OF TRAVELS

TO THE

EQUINOCTIAL REGIONS

OF THE

NEW CONTINENT,

DURING THE YEARS 1799—1804,

BY

ALEXANDER DE HUMBOLDT,

AND

AIMÉ BONPLAND;

WITH MAPS, PLANS, &c.

WRITTEN IN FRENCH BY
ALEXANDER DE HUMBOLDT,

AND TRANSLATED INTO ENGLISH BY
HELEN MARIA WILLIAMS.

VOLS. I & II.

LONDON:

PRINTED FOR LONGMAN, HURST, REES, ORME, AND BROWN,
PATERNOSTER ROW,

1818.

Title page of an early edition of Humboldt's *Personal Narrative to the Equinoctial Regions of the New Continent,* a groundbreaking work that influenced scientific thinking for decades.

electricity, gases in the mines and air quality, and terrestrial magnetism—early attempts to modernize the primitive mining techniques then in practice. Humboldt remained in the civil service only while his parents lived, and promptly resigned in 1796 after they passed away, leaving him a large inheritance. "No longer deluded by the agitation of a wandering life," he wrote, "I was anxious to contemplate nature in all her variety of wild and stupendous scenery; and the hope of collecting some facts useful to the advancement of science, incessantly impelled my wishes toward the luxuriant regions of the torrid zone."

He embarked upon a strict regimen of self-study of barometric pressure, humidity, temperature, and navigation so as to be indispensable to any scientific expedition. His first opportunity, a private English expedition to Egypt in 1798, was thwarted when Napoleon's armies invaded the North African country, and his second opportunity, with a French scientific expedition to Mexico, California, New Guinea, and Madagascar, was also cancelled when France withdrew the funding to concentrate on the war. Increasingly frustrated after years of delay, he invited the young French botanist Aimé Bonpland, who had also been assigned to the French expedition, to join him on a private excursion to Africa. This venture, too, was derailed when they were unable to secure transportation.

The two wandered to Spain in 1799 in the hope of finding passage on a ship, but the Napoleonic wars in Europe had significantly disrupted trade and travel. During the winter, however, they received an astonishing offer from the Minister of State, Mariano Luis de Urquijo, to secure diplomatic privileges for a scientific excursion to Spanish America (at their own expense). They would be allowed to take any scientific instruments they chose and to pursue their scientific interests, which included measuring the height of mountains, recording astronomical readings, comparing soil composition, and, as Humboldt related, to "execute all operations which I should judge useful for the progress of the sciences.... Never had so extensive a permission been granted to any traveler, and never had any foreigner been honoured with more confidence on the part of the Spanish government." It was a surprising gesture, and Humboldt was happy to pay his own and Bonpland's expenses for the rare opportunity to explore the mysterious lands of Spanish America.

After months of preparation their ship hoisted sails and headed west from Spain on June 5, 1799. "From the time we entered the torrid zone," he wrote, "we were never wearied with admiring, every night, the beauty of the southern sky which, as we advanced toward the south, opened new constellations to our view." Once the voyage was truly underway, and he was farther from Europe than America, Humboldt's exuberance was tainted by a wistful melancholy. He might not ever see his homeland again and the endless days sailing west provided ample opportunity to reflect on his decision. "Separated from the objects of our dearest affections," he wrote in his journal, "entering on a new state of existence, we are forced to fall back on our own thoughts, and we feel within ourselves a dreariness we have never known before."

Melancholy did not entirely dampen his curiosity, however, and his journal contains numerous speculations on the cause and temperature of ocean currents, the climate, the winds, and navigation techniques. He was amazed when, after days of not seeing a single living creature or plant, the ship "entered a zone where the whole sea was covered in a prodigious quantity of medusas [jellyfish]." Although the ship's sails were baggy and it was becalmed in doldrums, the medusas continued on their way, a great swath of writhing tentacles and glistening gelatinous bags slowly propelling themselves south. When even the stragglers had finally vanished from sight, Humboldt was overcome with questions: "Do these animals come from the bottom of the sea?" he wondered, "which is perhaps in these latitudes some thousand fathoms deep? Or do they make distant voyages in shoals?"

He captured some and tested them for a response to "galvanic electricity" but his experiments produced no conclusive insight. "If we place a very irritable medusa on a pewter plate," he observed, "and strike against the plate with any sort of metal, the slight vibrations of the plate are sufficient to make this animal emit light." Why, he could not say. How, he found equally baffling. Another experiment consisted of rubbing the medusa with wood, and this also caused the medusa to produce light. "In what manner ought we to consider the effect of the friction, or that of the shock?" he wondered. "This is a question of difficult solution." Such experiments and speculations produced three pages of journal entries in his book, and it whetted his appetite for scientific discoveries in the New World.

The remainder of the voyage was uneventful, apart from Humboldt's disagreement with the captain over the plotting of longitude; the captain's methods were too primitive and error-prone, he felt. He secretly kept his own measurements and calculations and was quietly pleased that his predictions were consistently more accurate than the captain's. On July 16, 1799, he sighted land. "At break of day, we beheld a verdant coast, of picturesque aspect. The mountains of New Andalusia [present-day Venezuela], half veiled by mists, bounded the horizon to the south. The city of Cumaná and its castle appeared between groups of cocoa-trees."

Although Cumaná was not their preferred port of landing, the sinister appearance of disease, possibly typhus, among some of the crew provoked a prudent change of plan. They hastily disembarked and wandered along the orderly cobblestone streets of the town to introduce themselves and present their passports to the governor Don Vincente Emparan, who proved to be an open and friendly man "much interested in everything that related to natural philosophy." In preparation for a prolonged stay, they leased a large, comfortable house, well suited to astronomical observations, as a base for their planned forays into the hinterland. They also hired a Guayaqueria Indian guide named Carlos del Pino. He was tall, bronze-skinned, "of excellent disposition, sagacious in his observations, and he had been led by intelligent curiosity to notice the productions of the sea as well as the plants of the country." It was an auspicious beginning.

During the next two months the naturalists and their guide explored the environs of Cumaná and wrote about every activity they avidly pursued, including measuring the tides, the temperature (in the caves compared with shady groves and under the beating sun), the elevation of the mountain peaks, and the humidity. They visited the salt mines, observed and measured a solar eclipse, and examined the remains of an earthquake from two years earlier, speculating on its cause. They followed paths down lush valleys to tobacco plantations, scrambled up mountains, and descended into deep gorges. They were guided into the great Cavern of the Guacharo where they killed several guacharo birds, unknown to European naturalists, for their specimen collection. Bonpland paid special attention to parasitic plants and the diversity of vegetation in different temperature and elevation zones and collected his first new plant, a smallish shrub he named *Avicennia tomentoso*. During their forays into the frontier, and on later excursions, they were the guests of missionary friars stationed in small settlements along the rivers of the interior. Humboldt was very pleased by their hospitality, especially since he was a Protestant.

Humboldt and Bonpland were awed by the incredible diversity of nature in South America, which was on a grand scale compared with Europe. "A dazzling light spread through the air," he wrote, "along the whitish hills strewed

TRAVELS AND RESEARCHES

OF

BARON HUMBOLDT.

OLIVER & BOYD, EDINBURGH.

This woodcut shows the luxuriant forest through which Humboldt and Bonpland travelled. "We almost accustomed ourselves to regard men as not being essential to the order of nature. The earth is loaded with plants, and nothing impedes their free development.... The crocodiles and the boas are the masters of the river; the jaguar, the peccary, the tapir, and the monkeys traverse the forest without fear and without danger; there they dwell as in an ancient inheritance. This aspect of animated nature, in which man is nothing, has something in it strange and sad."

with cylindric cactuses, and over a sea ever calm, the shores of which were peopled with alactras (a brown pelican, of the size of a swan), egrets, and flamingoes. The splendor of the day, the vivid colouring of the vegetable world, the forms of the plants, the varied plumage of the birds, everything was stamped with the grand character of nature in the equinoctial regions." They were also introduced to the sturdy mules of the region when climbing the rugged hills, and were very impressed with their quality and forbearance, comparing them favourably to those in Switzerland and the Pyrenees. "In proportion as a country is wild," Humboldt proclaimed, "the instinct of domestic animals improves in address and sagacity."

He and Bonpland took special interest in anything that seemed odd or peculiar in the local people, paying special attention to physiological phenomenon. They were particularly intrigued by tales of a man who "suckled a child with his own milk." According to local tales, when the mother was ill the man reputedly took his child to bed and "put it to his bosom and soon the irritation of the nipple caused his breasts to swell with milk." Apparently he suckled his child two or three times a day for five months, and although "he drew on himself the attention of his neighbours, he never thought, as he would have done in Europe, of deriving any advantage from the curiosity he excited." In order to verify the story Humboldt sent for the man and his son to visit him in Cumaná, and there "M. Bonpland examined with attention the father's breasts, and found them wrinkled like those of a woman who has given suck. He observed that the left breast in particular was much enlarged." Humboldt devoted five pages to descriptions of all other accounts of similar occurrences with men and animals in ancient times in Europe. "The greater part of these phenomena having been noticed in times very remote," he wrote, "it is not uninteresting to physiology that we can confirm them in our own days." Another aspect of physiology that intrigued him was the relativity of heat and cold. After only a few weeks in the equatorial heart of South America he felt cold when the temperature dropped to 21 degrees centigrade. Such a narrow and fickle band of temperature for humans to define heat and cold, he thought, "was worthy of the attention of physiologists."

Natural Bridges of Icononzo.

After thoroughly exploring the region surrounding Cumaná, Humboldt and Bonpland cast their eyes on a more remote and potentially dangerous destination than any they had yet undertaken—a journey up the Orinoco River into the heart of the continent, a region that had never been visited by modern naturalists. Not only would they have the opportunity to cross the Llanos, the great plains of Venezuela, but they might also lift the shroud of mystery surrounding the Casiquiare River, the rumoured link between the Amazon and the Orinoco watersheds. If it existed, the Casiquiare would be an unusual phenomenon where the waters of a single stream supply two great river systems, and Humboldt wanted to either verify or disprove its existence. Bonpland was also inspired by tales of strange new species of plants and animals said to dwell in those remote parts.

In November 1799 they booked passage on a small ship and sailed from Cumaná to La Guaira and then rode overland to Caracas, where they remained, preparing for the journey,

The wild scenery of equatorial South America amazed and inspired Humboldt's curiosity. The mode of life of the local peoples and their relationship to the land— how they survived amid such wildness—was one of his many interests.

The unusual lakes, forests and mountains of South America were a great inspiration to Humboldt.

View of the Lake of Guatavita.

until February 1800.* "We had to choose the instruments that could be most easily transported in narrow boats and to furnish ourselves with guides for an inland journey of ten months, across a country that is without communication with the coasts." Rather than heading directly up river, however, the peripatetic pair set off on a circuitous route west from Caracas to inspect Lake Valencia after they heard rumours of an unexplained decline in the lake's water level in recent years. The local residents were convinced that a large subterranean cavern or grotto must be sucking the water away, since there

---

*While in Caracas, a pleasant city that had a "perpetual spring," Humboldt and Bonpland had to explore the surrounding terrain. One excursion led them to the dual peaks of the Silla de Caracas, which Humboldt, as soon as he learned it had not been properly surveyed or measured, insisted on climbing. It was a difficult ascent despite the guides and host of servants carrying the provisions. Unfortunately, the quartermaster miscalculated the food required and one evening near the summit Humboldt was shocked when he observed the meagre fare set out for the meal. "Our repast did not last long," he noted sardonically. "Olives, which might have afforded a satisfactory meal to a poet, devoted to study, and leading a sedentary life, appeared an aliment by no means sufficiently substantial for travellers climbing mountains." The view from the summit, however, was spectacular.

was no visible outlet. After studying the lake, however, Humboldt proposed a more prosaic and oddly modern conservation-oriented solution to the mystery—climate change brought about by deforestation. "The changes, which the destruction of the forests, the clearing of plains, and the cultivation of indigo have produced within half a century in the quality of water flowing in, on the one hand, and, on the other, the evaporation of the soil and the dryness of the atmosphere present causes sufficiently powerful to explain the progressive diminution of the lake of Valencia. . . . By felling the trees that cover the tops and sides of the mountains, men in every climate prepare at once two calamities for future generations; the want of fuel and a scarcity of water. . . . When forests are destroyed, as they are everywhere in America by the European planters, with an imprudent precipitancy, the springs are entirely dried up, or become less abundant. The beds of rivers, remaining dry during a part of the year, are converted into torrents whenever great rains fall on the heights. As the sward and moss disappear with the brushwood from the sides of the mountains, the waters falling in rain are no longer impeded in their course; and instead of slowly augmenting the level of the rivers by progressive filtrations, they furrow during heavy showers, the sides of the hills, bearing down the loosened soil, and forming sudden and destructive inundations. Hence it results, that the clearing of the forests, the want of permanent springs, and the existence of torrents are three phenomena closely connected together."

After studying the region around Lake Valencia, the two naturalists continued on their journey to the Orinoco, heading toward the Llanos in March. En route they visited the plantation of Barbula to investigate another curiosity they had heard about—the *palo de vaca*, or cow tree, which produced a stream of apparently nutritious milk-like substance when the bark was slit. It was, they reported after tasting the glutinous fluid early one morning, "tolerably thick, destitute of all acrimony, and of an agreeable and balmy smell." Humboldt sent samples of the milk to colleagues in Europe for analysis and devoted over four pages of his narrative to discussing its beneficent properties and its similarity to animal milk. He also noted that the tree grew only in the Cordillera of the coast within a narrow band near Lake Maracaibo. "Nothing appears isolated," he observed, "the chemical principles that were believed to be peculiar to animals are found in plants; a common chain links together all organic nature." The interconnectedness of the natural world, something William Bartram had mused about decades earlier, evolved into one of Humboldt's greatest philosophical beliefs during his four-year jaunt. He increasingly observed and pondered how one aspect of the natural world had an influence on others; how climate or temperature or elevation affected plant growth, which in turn influenced water levels, temperature, and so forth.

From Barbula, the duo and their entourage rode west onto the arid, flat Llanos near Mesa de Paja. The baked, cracked earth of the plains stretching as far as he could see fascinated Humboldt in its opposition to the luxuriant growth of the coast. "The chief characteristic of the savannas or steppes of South America," he wrote, "is the absolute want of hills and inequalities, the perfect level of every part of the soil.... This resemblance to the surface of the sea strikes the imagination most powerfully, where the plains are altogether destitute of palm trees; and where the mountains of the shore and of the Orinoco are so distant that they cannot be seen." Two days of riding through the windless dusty plains brought them to a lonely ranch, "a solitary house in the steppes, surrounded by a few small huts, covered with reeds and skins." The herds of cattle, oxen, and horses wandered freely and the men laboured under the burning sun. "All around us the plains seemed to ascend to the sky, and the vast and profound solitude appeared like an ocean covered with sea-weed.... There is something awful, as well as sad and gloomy, in the uniform aspect of these steppes."

The next day they set off for Calabozo, a bustling cattle

centre, before full light to avoid the "devouring heat of the tropical sun." Here they met Carlos del Pozo, a local man who had read the writings of Benjamin Franklin and other scientists and had constructed an electricity machine. He agreed to help Humboldt and Bonpland capture some elusive and dangerous electric eels to jointly further the study of electricity. Despite Humboldt's offer to pay handsomely for each captured specimen, and despite their astonishing assertion that chewing tobacco rendered you immune to the electrical shock, the locals were reticent to get too close to the eels lurking in a nearby pond. After discussing the matter amongst themselves they brought in a herd of about thirty horses and mules and drove them into the water, where they soon excited the eels from their lethargy. "The extraordinary noise caused by the horses' hoofs," Humboldt wrote, "makes the fish issue from the mud and excites them to combat. These yellowish and livid eels, resembling large aquatic serpents, swim on the surface of the water and crowd under the bellies of the horses and mules." With sticks and furious yelling, the horses were prevented from leaving the pool, and in the frantic frenzy the eels discharged repeatedly.

"The eel, being five feet long, and pressing itself against the belly of the horses, makes a discharge along the whole extent of its electric organ," Humboldt related. Several of the panicked beasts, after receiving shocks "from all sides in organs the most essential to life, and, stunned by the force and frequency of the shocks, disappear under the water. Others, panting, with mane erect and haggard eyes expressing anguish, raise and endeavour to flee from the storm by which they are overtaken." Within five minutes two horses had drowned and the others were wild with pain and shock before the energy of the furious eels began to lag. Unable to discharge their electrifying shock, the eels "approach timidly the edge of the marsh, where they are taken." Five large eels were captured by this less than humane method and the naturalists spent the next few days delightedly experimenting. Although they discovered nothing new or conclusive, they were introduced to the pain the horses must have endured. "If by chance you receive a stroke before the fish is wounded or wearied by a long pursuit," Humboldt recorded, "the pain and numbness are so violent that it is impossible to describe the nature of the feeling they excite."

They pressed on across the windblown plains until the end of March when they neared the Apure River. Arriving at the mission community of San Fernando de Apure, they hired a *lancha*, paddled by four Indians with a thatched cabin in the rear, to transport them down the Apure to the Orinoco. Onto the small boat were packed enough provisions for a month, along with luxuries such as sherry, oranges, and tamarind donated by the head missionary. Fish, manatees, and turtles provided a welcome respite from rations as they slowly floated west through a land wild and strange in its beauty. The naturalists were astonished with the grand spectacle of life along the river. One night, Humboldt wrote, it "was calm and serene, and there was a beautiful moonlight. The crocodiles were stretched along the shore. They placed themselves in such a manner as to be able to see the fire. We thought we observed that its splendour attracted them, as it attracts fishes, crayfish, and other inhabitants of the water.... When the jaguars approached the skirt of the forest, our dog, which till then had never ceased barking, began to howl and seek for shelter beneath our hammocks. Sometimes, after a long silence, the cry of the tiger came from the tops of the trees; and in this case it was followed by the sharp and long whistling of the monkeys, which appeared to flee from the danger that threatened them."

The forest was not a quiet place. A few hours after dark the nocturnal chorus of its varied denizens reached a climax, with the moans of apes, the roaring of jaguars and cougars, the howling of the peccary and the sloth, and the cries of the curasso, the parraka, "and other gallinaceous birds." Their evening serenade was so loud they often lay awake late into the night while the braying continued, pondering a hundred sounds they could not identify. "It was impossible to close our eyes," Humboldt related.

Despite the great profusion of life, much of it surprising and new (particularly prominent during the unquiet evenings as a chorus of cacophonic squawks, slithers, rustles, and sporadic roars), the absence of other humans along their route was vaguely disquieting to the naturalists. Humboldt wrote, "In that interior part of the New Continent, we almost accustomed ourselves to regard men as not being essential to the order of nature. The earth is loaded with plants, and nothing impedes their free development.... The crocodiles and the boas are the masters of the river; the jaguar, the peccary, the tapir, and the monkeys traverse the forest without fear and without danger; there they dwell as in an ancient inheritance. This aspect of animated nature, in which man is nothing, has something in it strange and sad.... Here in a fertile country adorned with eternal verdure, we seek in vain the traces of the power of man; we seem to be transported into a world different from that which gave us birth."

After a week of paddling, on April 5, the group cruised past the junction where the Apure flowed into "a country of a totally different aspect." After a few rough spots the river broadened and "an immense plain of water stretched before us like a lake as far as we could see. White top waves rose to the height of several feet from the conflict of the breeze and the current. The air resounded no longer with the piercing cries of the herons, the flamingoes, the spoonbills, crossing in long files from one shore to another." The forest loomed huge on the horizon, shimmering and steaming in the heat of the sun, but seldom approached the shore of the vast placid river. A wide swath of sandy beaches "constantly parched by the heat of the sun, desert and bare as the shores of the sea" blended the shore of the river and the edge of the forest. They had reached the Orinoco, "one of the most majestic rivers of the New World."

After hauling their supplies and boat over several unnavigable sections, they launched into the mighty river and headed upstream until rapids forced them to transfer to a much smaller and uncomfortable canoe, paddled by Indians whose songs were "sad and monotonous." At points they longed to find a spring for fresh water. The river, particularly close to the shore, was so turgid, brackish, and silty, it had to be strained through cloth before they could drink it. "The waters of the Orinoco are alike loaded with earthy particles," Humboldt lamented, "they are even fetid, where dead bodies of alligators are found in the creeks lying on banks of sand or half-buried in the mud." Somehow they avoided sickness.

During the next few months the party continued along the river systems of the interior, navigating the Orinoco upstream to the Atabapo, which they followed inland, and portaged over to the Pinichin, which led them downstream into the Negro. They floated down the Negro until May 10, 1800, when they arrived at the anticipated Rio Casiquiare, the mythical waterway that joins the Negro with the Orinoco. Humboldt was astonished at the sight of the mythical waterway. It was not as he suspected, a small unnavigable creek, but rather was "as broad as the Rhine." Proving the reality of the Casiquiare was perhaps the most cherished accomplishment of Humboldt's journey. "After all we had endured," he wrote, "I may be permitted, perhaps, to speak to the satisfaction we felt having reached the tributary streams of the Amazon, having passed the isthmus that separates the two great systems of rivers, and being sure of having fulfilled the most important object of our voyage, determining astronomically the course of that arm of the Orinoco, which falls into the Rio Negro and of which the existence has been alternately proved and denied during half a century."

The otherworldly scenery in the heart of the continent was nowhere more spectacular than along the Casiquiare. Although they seldom ventured far inland from the river shore, they beheld a land "loaded with plants, among which rise the palms crowned with leafy plumes; the banks are reflected in the waters; and the verdure of the reflected image seems to have the same vivid hue as the object itself directly seen." Bonpland collected samples of the many varieties of lichens that were "cleaving the rock," was amazed by the "little portions of sand nourishing succulent plants," and "layers of black mould deposited in the hollows." He dried his specimens and crammed them into the limited space on the boats, provoking a bemused indulgence on behalf of the Indian guides, who helped him devise a method for preventing the humid climate from ruining the valuable collection.

However, Humboldt was more concerned with taking notes of portages, rapids, and travel conditions along the route. The missions that lined the rivers provided a respite from the endless days of camping along the shores, although even there they fell prey to flies and mosquitoes. Bonpland's hands and face became particularly swollen because he continuously exposed them while collecting and working on his plant specimens. "We had suffered severely from the sting of insects," Humboldt remembered stoically, "but we had withstood the insalubrity of the climate." And despite the sweltering heat, relief from a cool bath was denied them. Fear of the "caribe fish" (so named "because no other fish has such a thirst for blood") lurking in the murky pools was enough to frighten the hottest and dirtiest traveller into a state of resignation. To test the accounts of its viciousness, the two naturalists tossed hunks of raw, bleeding meat into the river and eagerly peered into the depths to spy the result. "In a few minutes a perfect cloud of caribes had come to dispute their prey." Although they were small, only three to four inches long, they tore the flesh to shreds in minutes, each fish devouring a mouthful before retreating with its morsel. They captured several and dissected them on shore. Humboldt devoted several pages to their physical characteristics, feeding patterns, digestive capabilities, and comparing the physiology of the different varieties of the fish, such as the commonly known piranha. He was equally fascinated by crocodiles, manatees, howler monkeys, and turtles, and wrote detailed descriptions of their habits, preferred foods, skeletal structure, and so on. He noted how the caimans and crocodiles lay dormant in the mud during the dry season and woke only when the rains came. By digging in the earth, he uncovered several torpid reptiles that scuttled away quickly in search of a stream or pond.

Humboldt's powers of observation were remarkable. He was intrigued by the antics of howler monkeys, recording the timing and pitch of their wailing, those occasions when it ceased altogether, and when it rose it volume and intensity in a group chorus. The incessant "mournful" wailing was so loud and constant that his guides informed him that "to cure asthma, it is sufficient to drink out of the bony drum of the hyoidal bone." Although he doubted it was true, Humboldt recorded that, according to the natives, the howler's extraordinary strong voice "must necessarily impart to the water poured into it the virtue of curing affections of the lungs. Such is the science of the vulgar, which sometimes resembles that of the ancients." In spite of his disdain, he was nevertheless fascinated to learn how the natives soaked dead boas in pools to "obtain, by means of putrefaction, the tendinous parts of the dorsal muscles, of which excellent guitar-strings are made at Calabozo, preferable to those furnished by the intestines of the... monkeys."

Another example of the ingenuity of the inland natives that intrigued Humboldt was the use of curare. Humboldt and Bonpland, not surprisingly, were particularly interested in recording the physiological effects of the poison on animals and the ingredients that composed it, and they sought out the companionship of an elderly shaman, the "poison master," to verify their suppositions. "He has," observed Humboldt, "that self sufficient air and tone of pedantry of which the pharmacopolists of Europe were formerly accused.

'I know,' said he, 'that the whites have the secret of making soap, and manufacturing that black powder which has the defect of making a noise when used in killing animals. The curare, which we prepare from father to son, is superior to anything you can make down yonder (beyond sea). It is the juice of an herb which kills silently, without any one knowing whence the stroke comes.'" From the poison master they were able to accurately identify most of the plants used in the preparation of the paste and the majority of the process. Five dense pages are devoted to their observations and speculations about the poison and its similarity to poisons produced along the Amazon. Humboldt was compelled to conclude, however, that "an interesting chemical and physiological investigation remains to be accomplished in Europe on the poisons of the New World. . . . Our botanical knowledge of the plants employed in making poison can be but very slowly acquired." When the British naturalist Charles Waterton explored the jungles of Guyana thirty years later, the secret of curare was still unsolved, and he conducted his own experiments to determine its physiological effects.

By June, Humboldt and Bonpland had retraced their journey by floating back down the Orinoco, arriving at the city of Angostura where they remained a month taking stock of their specimens and recuperating from a debilitating bout of typhus and dysentery that laid Bonpland out for several weeks. "After the life we had led in the wood," he wrote, perhaps with great understatement, "our dress was not in the very best order. . . ." Bonpland had, however, acquired "a rich harvest of plants," and Humboldt had acquired the experience and foundation for much of his later philosophizing and speculation on the "interconnectedness of nature." It was with great difficulty that they loaded their specimen bundles and numerous cages of live animals aboard a ship destined for Cumaná, where they waited a few months for passage to Havana, Cuba. The voyage was slow and difficult, yet Humboldt compared it favourably to his canoe trip in

Venezuela. "The inconveniences endured at sea in small vessels are trivial in comparison with those that are suffered under a burning sky, surrounded by swarms of mosquitoes, and lying stretched in a canoe, without the possibility of taking the least bodily exercise."

During his stay in Havana, Humboldt studied the land with his usual intensity, wandering through the botanical gardens, reading government reports, and examining all aspects of island life and culture. To Humboldt, Cuba was as fascinating as the wilds of Venezuela's heartland, but more for his interests in culture, economy, climate, and industry.* Because of the wars in Europe and the notorious pirates of the Caribbean, Humboldt and Bonpland took special precautions shipping their priceless collections and notes back to Europe. From Havana, they boxed and shipped forty-two crates containing over six thousand equinoctial plants, seeds, shells, insects, mammal skeletons, and skins and "what had hitherto never been brought to Europe, geological specimens." Humboldt also forwarded to Europe three copies of hundreds of pages of extensive field notes that would form the foundation of his celebrated account.

The two naturalists planned to continue on to Mexico and then to the Philippines, but a timely note in a European newspaper alerted Humboldt that the French scientific expedition he and Bonpland had originally sought to join was to leave

---

* One aspect of Cuban society, however, irritated the otherwise uncritical German scientist—slavery. "Slavery," he later wrote, "is no doubt the greatest of all evils that afflict humanity.... In vain have writers of ability, seeking to veil barbarous institutions by ingenious turns of language, invented the terms 'Negro peasants of the West Indies,' 'black vassalage,' and 'patriarchal protection.' That is profaning the noble qualities of the mind and the imagination, for the purpose of exculpating by illusory comparisons, or captious sophisms excess which afflict humanity, and which prepare the way for violent convulsions.... The state of slavery cannot be altogether peaceably ameliorated, except by the simultaneous action of the free men."

after all, and was heading to Peru. Humboldt wrote the captain and informed him that both he and Bonpland would alter their itinerary and meet the expedition in Lima the next year.

In March 1801, the two set sail again for South America to continue their studies and explorations. After a tedious month sailing in a small ship to Cartagena, they decided that they were more suited to overland travel and set off to Lima by way of Quito, never suspecting that they would spend eighteen months on this journey. They, of course, chose the more difficult route because it seemed more interesting. "The mountain of Quindiu," reported Humboldt, "is considered as the most laborious passage presented by the Cordillera of the Andes. It is a thick forest, entirely uninhabited. . . . It contains no cabin, no means of subsistence; at every time of year, the travelers take enough provisions for a month, because often the melting of the snows and the sudden flooding of the mountain streams isolates them, so they cannot descend. . . ." It proved to be a narrow deep-worn track along the windswept ridges of the high Andes, winding through alpine valleys and over treacherous passes; mud-slickened stones covered the path and droopy fronds of huge plants shadowed away the sun. It rained frequently. When the path was blocked, by a column of slowly meandering oxen, for example, the two naturalists and their own entourage of oxen and mules (loaded with their collections, instruments, and supplies) climbed "up the wall of earth which borders the crevice and kept [themselves] suspended by hanging on to the roots that have penetrated into the soil." Many a time they slipped in the mud, lacerating skin and tearing clothing. After a few months their shoes were worn away on the jagged rocks and they were forced to travel barefoot.

They reached the ancient city of Quito, Ecuador, in January 1802, after a gruelling journey, recuperating for only a few months before pushing on. Despite hearing news that the French scientific voyage had again changed plans and was not destined for South America at all, they still wanted to

While in Peru, Humboldt and Bonpland climbed as high as they could up Chimborazo and enjoyed the amazing panorama.

A View of the Mountains of Chimborazo and Carguairazo, in South America.

visit Lima and en route travelled in luxury over the Inca road, which Humboldt found comparable to the ancient Roman roads of Italy. The broad, level thoroughfare was quite a change from picking their difficult way over boulder-strewn highland paths at the head of a dozen beasts of burden. While in Peru, the two scientists climbed the highest mountain peaks (Pichincha and Chimborazo), peered over the ledge of active volcanoes, and finally descended into the fertile lowlands of the Pacific coast. "We now," wrote Humboldt with evident pleasure, "for the first time, commanded a view of the Pacific. We saw it distinctly, reflecting along the line of the coast an immense mass of light, and rising in immeasurable expanse until bounded by the clearly-defined horizon." Although Bonpland continued his gathering of new plants and preserving them for later study, Humboldt devoted less time to studying flora and fauna and was mostly preoccupied with observing rock formations, measuring the elevation of mountains, recording climate, and correcting slight inconsistencies in the region's charts.

The climate in most of western South America was not conducive to preserving specimens, and the difficulty of travel, apart from the Inca road, made hauling them about a trying experience. "Sad experience taught us but too late," Humboldt lamented, "that from the sultry humidity of the climate, and the frequent falls of the beasts of burden, we could not preserve the skins of animals hastily prepared, nor the fishes and reptiles placed in phials filled with alcohol." The weighty mineral samples Humboldt eagerly gathered from the Andes were a particular problem. "The conveyance of these objects," he wrote, "and the minute care they required, occasioned us such embarrassments as would scarcely be conceived, even by those who have traversed the most uncultivated parts of Europe. . . . Often, in order to add to our collections of new mineral substances, we found ourselves obliged to throw away others."

Despite the difficulty of travelling with a pack train of mules and oxen, Humboldt and Bonpland managed to traverse much of western South America, and it was here, next to the coast, that Humboldt had one of the most memorable insights of his entire journey. While visiting a cluster of unusually well preserved

Azteck hieroglyphical A. in the Vatican Library.

Inca ruins along the coast, Humboldt was struck by the high level of humidity and cloudy skies that seemed in contrast to the dryness of the land. A brief visit to the island of Mazorca, which was covered in hundreds of feet of guano (nitrogen-rich bird dung used as a fertilizer), suggested to him that it hadn't rained there for centuries despite the humidity. After measuring the ocean temperatures, he speculated that the unusual phenomenon of a humid desert was caused by a particularly cool ocean current that chilled the air above it. When the coastal air blew over the land it became warm, increasing its capacity to absorb moisture, which it sucked from the land. The clouds floated east and dumped rain at the base of the mountains. As a result of his astute observations, the cold

Although Humboldt found Mexico too settled compared with the Amazon basin, he was impressed by the ruins of its ancient civilizations, particularly the stylized writings of the Aztecs.

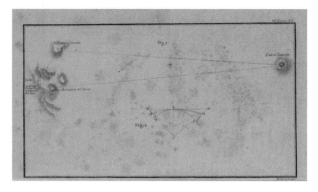

This drawing from Humboldt's *Narrative* shows his early calculation of an isotherm, a groundbreaking observation that certain plants thrived at the same elevations in different regions.

ocean current off the Peruvian coast used to be called the Humboldt current; it is now known as the Peru Current.

Near the end of 1802, the two naturalists boarded a ship in Lima and sailed to Mexico, where they remained for a year, travelling and organizing their specimens. Mexico was much more settled, and offered less in the way of exotic new species not known to science. In January 1804, they set off for a brief visit to Philadelphia and Washington, to visit President Jefferson, and, finally, weary of the constant travel and, perhaps, yearning for home, they returned to France in August 1804, a few weeks before Napoleon was proclaimed Emperor. It had been a remarkable and epic journey through much of South and Central America. They were the first naturalists to venture into much of this terrain, and the observations they made of the strange creatures that dwelt there gave European scientists their first reliable picture of the region.

Humboldt made his way to Berlin, but returned to Paris in 1808 when Napoleon seized Prussia, stifling intellectual freedom. For twelve years he and Bonpland and other scientists worked to prepare for publication much of the information gleaned from their years in Spanish America.* Humboldt, sometimes collaborating with other naturalists, continued writing, raising more questions about the natural world, introducing new concepts and ideas, and providing

---

* Bonpland helped Humboldt with the publication of works on botany and zoology, and then accepted a professorship in natural history in Buenos Aires in 1816. In 1821, he was captured by the Paraguayan dictator Jose Gaspar Rodriguez de Francia and spent the next decade under house arrest, able to pursue his botanical studies, but not to leave the country. He was finally released in 1831, and decided to remain in South America for the rest of his life.

more information about the geography, commerce, and social customs of Spanish America. Humboldt marked on his maps the many temperature readings he had taken and drew a line connecting them—the relative spacing of the lines, called isotherms, showed relative temperature gradients, and these still appear on certain maps today. In botany, he studied not only the specific characteristics of the plants he and Bonpland collected, but also their distribution relevant to climate and elevation, attempting to show how certain plants flourished in certain temperature gradients or isotherms.

Volcano of Jorullo.

This drawing from Humboldt's *Narrative* shows a desert landscape with mountains in the distance. The etching shows the remarkable detail that the artist went to great lengths to achieve.

Humboldt was just as interested in studying the intervals between earthquake tremors, the relationship between climate and elevation, or the strength of electricity in an eel as he was in dissecting the larynx of a howler monkey or determining the ingredients in a deadly poison. His narrative, as the only source of accurate information about South America, had a profound effect on the scientific community in Europe at a time when they were energetically striving to develop an understanding of an increasingly interconnected world brought about by expanding travel and literature.

In Paris, Humboldt was lionized as the great light of his age. Scientific societies sought his membership and honoured him, geographical features were named after him, and governments granted him pensions. He was offered many lucrative academic and corporate positions in both Mexico and Germany, but declined them in order to pursue his theorizing without obligation. Much of his fortune was spent in publishing his own books and pursuing his scientific experiments. In 1827, against his wishes, he was compelled to return to Berlin at the behest of the Prussian government that

Researches, Concerning the Institutions and Monuments of the Ancient Inhabitants of America was one of the many works produced by Humboldt in the decades after his return from the Americas.

was paying him a modest stipend, upon which he now depended.

Humboldt argued for the unfettered study of science and the humanities in an attempt to stop the increasing insularity and conservatism in Europe following the Napoleonic wars. He watched European liberalism deteriorate and was frustrated with the restrictions on and censorship of the press. Yet as the years passed, he grew increasingly financially dependent upon a government he could no longer support. He died at the age of eighty-nine on May 5, 1859 (the same year Charles Darwin published *The Origin of Species*), bequeathing his few meagre possessions to his servant, who for years had weathered his periods of financial insecurity.

Alexander von Humboldt elevated the study of natural science from idle speculation and unsubstantiated theorizing to a higher level with greater emphasis on rigorous testing, empirical measuring, and defendable conclusions. He asked a plethora of questions in an attempt to grasp the totality of the natural world and its functioning and interrelationships. His conclusions were not always accurate; however, his greatest contribution to the development of natural science was not his conclusions but his questions. In 1845, at the age of seventy-six, he published the first volume of *Kosmos*, an immensely popular and groundbreaking five-volume work in which he tried to encompass his entire personal philosophy in one series, seeking to show the unity and interdependence of nature and to reconcile the vague ideals of the eighteenth century with the more exacting scientific requirements of the nineteenth.

His influence on European science was so great that by

the time of his death, many of his theories were considered standard subjects of study, or were so widely accepted that his contributions went unrecognized or unacknowledged by a new generation of naturalists. The starting point for innovative study began where his theories left off. Although he was once the most preeminent naturalist in western Europe, his brilliant theorizing and observations were considered passé by the time of his death. It was probably either his greatest source of pride or his greatest disappointment.

PART TWO

Inquisitive Aristocrats

IN THE EARLY NINETEENTH CENTURY the study of natural history was primarily the preserve of the wealthy or aristocratic. With little government support for expeditions to distant lands, and with public interest in natural history just starting to expand beyond the educated elite, only wealthy individuals could organize extensive field excursions in pursuit of scientific specimens. For these dedicated and inquisitive amateurs, as for the eighteenth-century naturalists, scientific exploration involved travelling to exotic lands where the greatest number of new species could be found and where the natural world was as different as possible from their own home. They set out to observe odd and interesting animals, speculate on natural phenomena, and collect specimens for later study.

The inquisitive aristocrats of the early nineteenth century fall somewhere between the early scientists, with their omnivorous interests, and the professional scientists and field naturalists of the later nineteenth century. Although they were dedicated to the study of the natural world, the aristocrats' approach was more akin to that of the eighteenth-century scientists than it was to the specialized collectors who were beginning to emerge. They were not scientists in the true sense, but self-educated generalists at the beginning of an age of specialization, unscientific in their studies and conclusions. When Charles Waterton first began wandering through the jungles of Guyana in 1812, the term "naturalist" encompassed anyone studying the natural world, from the most whimsical amateur to the most rigorous professional anatomist, but by the 1830s the term applied mostly to unsystematic travellers, collectors, and writers whose subject was the natural world.

Because they could afford to, the inquisitive aristocrats remained generalists, equally intrigued by all aspects of nature, widely versed in recent scientific writings, and still believing that a single dedicated individual could keep abreast of all the new developments within the scientific community. They travelled and wrote of their exploits because they wanted to, not out of financial necessity, and, as a result, their books reflect their own interests rather than those of a patron or sponsor. They never set out to prove anything conclusive, just to observe and comment on nature in regions where no other naturalists had previously ventured.

The aristocratic wanderers lacked the financial compulsion to devote every minute of their working lives to searching for new specimens, just as they lacked the formal training of the closet naturalists. The number of new species they amassed was not anywhere near the volume gathered by the professional collectors, and their theories on animal behaviour or climate variation, for example, remained somewhat erratic, failing to earn the respect of the emerging specialists. It is impossible to know specifically what creatures Waterton encountered in the rain forest because he did not bother to learn how to classify species according to the Linnean system. His detailed descriptions of bird calls and behaviours were of limited value because later ornithologists had no way of identifying to which species he was referring.

Waterton had no specific scientific training, nor did he have a scientific temperament. Independently wealthy, he was concerned primarily with exotic travel, describing the behaviour and activities of creatures that he knew were misunderstood, and writing a florid and outlandish account of his journey. In the coming decades, there would be little room for amateurs like Waterton, whose contribution to science was purely descriptive and anecdotal. But in the 1820s, much of what he had to say, particularly relating to how and where creatures lived, what they ate, and so on, provided fresh and insightful information on the natural world. Even so, many in the scientific community criticized his anecdotal and sensational style, though his book sold phenomenally well to the general public. Waterton wandered and wrote on the cusp of the age when the distinction between closet naturalists and field naturalists was still blurred, when a self-funded, self-directed amateur could explore a region and still hope to contribute to science.

Prince Maximilian of Wied travelled and collected in Brazil in the 1820s, at the beginning of the natural history craze sweeping Europe and North America, and produced a glossy well-illustrated book of his journeys. His final expedition took him up the Missouri River in the 1830s. He was not a professional specimen collector and he had no need for the income that could be generated from selling duplicate specimens. Without the monetary compulsion to collect, the prince turned his interest in natural history toward ethnology—an as yet to be defined field where an amateur with a professional attitude and thorough technique could still make a valuable contribution. His extensive notes on the Indians of the Missouri River, and his companion's detailed paintings, far outstripped anything he could have done as a collector of specimens.

By the 1830s, self-motivated generalists like Waterton and Maximilian were able to make only small contributions to the scientific development of natural history. They were surpassed by professional closet naturalists in the universities and museums, and by professional collectors in the field.

Charles Waterton

*England has long ceased to be the land for
adventures. Indeed, when good King Arthur reappears to claim his
crown he will find things strangely altered here.*
—CHARLES WATERTON,
Wanderings in South America

An 1821 painting of the forty-two-year-old Charles Waterton shows him in ruffled shirt and necktie, with a high forehead, straight nose, and an erect posture. He has a quizzical and pensive expression and shares the scene with a small stuffed bird perched on the index finger of his right hand. In the foreground, the mounted head of a cross-eyed cat rests upon a large unidentifiable tome on an elegant table. It is an unconventional portrait of an unconventional man.

Waterton stood about five foot eleven and always had his hair neatly cut short (except, presumably, when he fumbled about the uncharted wilds of South America, barefoot and ill-clad). When he was in England, his public appearance was of respectability, wholly at odds with his private behaviour and thoughts. He strolled shoeless about his own gardens, clambered into the uppermost branches of ancient oaks to observe nesting birds, and he always slept on the bare floor with only a wooden block as a pillow. Despite his renowned generosity and soft heart, Waterton was not an easygoing man. He quarrelled with other naturalists over seemingly small differences of opinion. William Swainson once wrote

Charles Waterton
(1782–1865).

that "the man is mad—stark, staring mad," after reading a letter from Waterton criticizing John James Audubon for some minor disagreement involving the olfactory faculties of vultures or buzzards.

When Waterton felt he was correct he would launch into a vicious personal diatribe against his opponents in various natural history magazines such as *Loudon's*, the *Edinburgh Review*, and in his own collection, *Essays on Natural History*, published in various editions beginning in 1838. Eventually editors stopped printing his letters and essays, and he resorted to publishing his own pamphlets and personally distributing them. Judging by his own writings and the accounts of the editors of his collected essays (who wrote after his death), he was as interested in attacking his perceived enemies—anyone who disagreed with him on any issue of natural history—as he was with discussing the details of observations of natural history. It seems that as he aged, his judgment deteriorated and his personal attacks escalated.

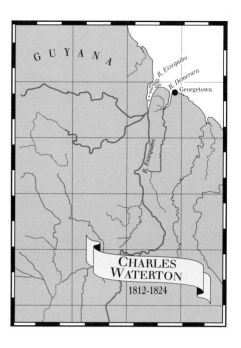

Charles Waterton's wanderings in Guyana, 1812–1824.

Because his pronouncements often proved incorrect, Waterton was not universally respected in the scientific community, and he only reluctantly admitted his own fallibility. He was prone to overstatement when making his case and bristled if he was referred to as an eccentric, which he surely was. But he also made significant contributions to the knowledge of many birds and mammals of South America, and challenged long-cherished myths concerning the behaviour of these creatures. As a field naturalist, he took pride in deflating the erroneous presumptions of closet naturalists about the behaviour of animals. A summation of his career in the 1840 edition of *Lardner's Cyclopaedia* referred to him as a traveller, and "an unscientific, but very observing naturalist, whose American travels contain many excellent observations

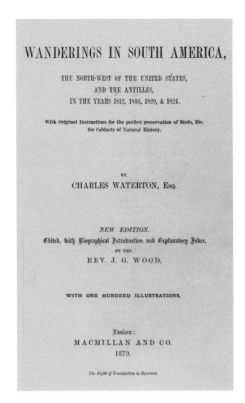

WANDERINGS IN SOUTH AMERICA,

THE NORTH-WEST OF THE UNITED STATES,
AND THE ANTILLES,
IN THE YEARS 1812, 1816, 1820, & 1824.

With Original Instructions for the perfect preservation of Birds, Etc.
for Cabinets of Natural History.

BY
CHARLES WATERTON, Esq.

NEW EDITION.
Edited, with Biographical Introduction and Explanatory Index,
BY THE
REV. J. G. WOOD,

WITH ONE HUNDRED ILLUSTRATIONS.

London:
MACMILLAN AND CO.
1879.

The Right of Translation is Reserved.

Title page of one of the many editions of Waterton's popular and entertaining *Wanderings in South America.*

on the animals of Guyana and Demerara." Waterton remained a devout Catholic throughout his eighty-three years and was strongly opposed to Charles Darwin's theory of evolution through natural selection when it appeared in 1859. Creation, he felt, was to be studied, not criticized, and he brooked no dissenting opinion on this issue.

Precise details of Waterton's private life are scarce. All the information on his early years come from his own autobiographical introduction to later editions of his book *Wanderings in South America*, and virtually all that regarding his later life comes from a biography written after his death by his friend and personal physician, Dr. Richard Hobson of Leeds.

Born into a Catholic aristocratic family at Walton Hall, near Wakefield, Yorkshire, in 1782, squire Waterton never shook his boyhood predilection for practical jokes, climbing trees, and generally getting into trouble, despite a proper upbringing and education. And it was perhaps out of consternation that his parents sent him at age eighteen to reside with two uncles in the town of Malaga in Spain. The journey apparently had the opposite of the desired effect, instilling in him a desire for further adventure and an awareness of his strong constitution. While he was there an epidemic of the "Black vomit" killed both his uncles and thousands of others, and after surviving his own bout with the dreaded disease (which he doesn't specifically identify), he fled back to England in spite of the quarantine. "I was seized with vomiting and fever during the night," he recorded. "I had the most dreadful spasms and it was supposed that I could not last out till noon the next day. However, strength of constitution got me through it." The memory of countless vultures feasting upon the corrupting flesh of the fallen, who numbered in the thousands and couldn't be buried fast enough, stayed with him all his life. He wrote about it in his autobiography nearly forty years later.

Waterton did not remain long recuperating in England and was soon off to Demerara in autumn of 1804, to attend to his father's sugar plantations, which were likely situated near Georgetown, then still named Stabroek and under Dutch control. During the seventeenth century, the Dutch, English, and French began settling around the mouth of the Essequibo River, soon dominating the native Warrau people. The region remained under Dutch control until 1815, when Britain assumed political control over Berbice, Demerara, and Essequibo (later united as British Guyana in 1831). Sugar plantations were extremely profitable during the days of slavery, and although Waterton gives no precise figures on the size or value of the family estates, they must have been extensive because when his parents died he inherited the family's English holdings, while his siblings retained the Guyana plantations. He never mentions returning to them on any of his other journeys to Guyana after his initial journey in 1812. Slavery was abolished in 1834, thirty years after his first trip to the region.

Waterton relates very little information regarding the years he spent as a plantation manager, including his opinions on slavery, but it was at this time that his interest in natural history truly took root. During his tenure on the plantation he frequently took short journeys into the tropical forest to observe exotic animals. It was here also that he solidified his "abstemious" attitude—he observed that the greatest deaths from tropical diseases arose in those men who daily consumed large draughts of rum punch, and he vowed never to fall prey to that particular fate. He returned to England in 1806 (following the death of his father) to assume his inheritance of the family estate, but within the year he sailed across the Atlantic again to continue

LAKE, LOOKING WESTWARD.

On his first journey in 1812 Waterton was primarily interested in the bewildering scenery of Guyana—the monstrous trees and peculiar plants.

COUCOURITE.

Coucourite Palm was one of the many species of tree that impressed Waterton on his journeys.

managing the plantation on behalf of his siblings. In 1812 he resigned, presumably making arrangements for the plantation's sale or management, and went off into the unexplored jungle for adventure and to study natural history. Over the next twelve years, he made four extensive forays into the jungle to satisfy his seemingly inexhaustible curiosity and to debunk many myths concerning the peculiar and little-known animals that dwelt under the shadowy canopy of the great forests.

On his first journey, the overwhelming size and diversity of the vegetation held him in awe. He strolled through sequestered glades, passing foaming cataracts and stands of towering trees sprouting from the damp forest floor, shielded from moon and sun by an impenetrable canopy of green. He passed over open savannah, skirted swamps, and canoed down sluggish serpentine rivers. The perfumes of the trees and flowers were spicy and heady after a rain, and great drooping leaves large enough to envelop him completely dripped sweet water from their uncoiling fronds. He revelled in the humid, muggy evening air, when choruses of frogs blended with the swish of bat wings and the incessant hum of a thousand varieties of insects. He rejoiced when the sun occasionally peeked through the thick foliage. "Welcome as a lost friend," he rhapsodized, "the solar beam makes the frame rejoice, and with it a thousand enlivening thoughts rush at once on the soul, and disperse, as a vapour, every sad and sorrowful idea which the deep gloom had helped to collect there."

Many of the monstrous trees, such as the mora, the ducalbaly, or the green heart, had trunks like giant multifingered hands thrust into the earth and were covered with clusters of shady parasite plants dangling tendrils to the ground. A swaying latticework of vines climbed to the canopy and swooped away into the gloom. All was punctuated by the echoing bark of monkeys and baboons, the staccato squawks and fruity calls of the birds, and the subtle rustling of an unseen host of bizarre insects. It was not at all like the green glens and pleasant Yorkshire hills of his youth. "The finest park that England boasts," he claimed in awe, "falls far short of this delightful scene."

Rather than engaging in specific scientific objectives on his first South American sojourn, Waterton was content to wander and wonder at the grandeur of nature, speculating on the interrelationships between species and poking at the myths surrounding certain creatures he observed first-hand. He frequently travelled alone, occasionally with native guides, and was always well armed. He shot dozens of animals and birds as specimens to be stuffed and displayed when he returned to England. He became very philosophical on this journey, perhaps from loneliness. "Those [trees] whose heads have been bared by time," he speculated, "or blasted by the thunder-storm, strike the eye, as a mournful sound does the ear in music; and seem to beckon to the sentimental traveller to stop a moment or two, and see that the forests which surround him, like men and kingdoms, have their periods of misfortune and decay." And, either to discourage others from duplicating his travels or to magnify his own accomplishments, he wrote, "It would be a tedious journey for him who wished to travel through these wilds, to set out from Stabroek on foot. The sun would exhaust him in his attempts to wade through the swamps, and the Mosquitoes at night would deprive him of every hour of sleep."

Although Waterton is vague about his daily whereabouts and route—presumably he used the Essequibo River as an artery to the interior—one of his specific objectives on his year-long journey was to venture deep inland until he met

EGRET.

One of the many birds that fascinated Waterton was the white-plumed egret. He sketched a specimen one evening near "a sort of a small grotto on the edge of a pond" where it had "sunk to sleep."

Waterton prided himself on his skills as a taxidermist, but was saddened when the brilliant colors he observed in nature faded after death. The Cock of the Rock (*Rupicola aurantia*) "on account of its plumage is in great request with bird stuffers." Unfortunately, the colour, a brilliant orange, faded away when exposed to sunlight.

with the natives who produced curare poison.* No sooner did he have the recipe for the poison (a "gloomy and mysterious" procedure in which a medicine man ground fiery round ants, secret roots, and rare flowers into a dusky powder and filtered it like coffee through a fine net) than he began testing it on various animals, apologizing, of course, to his readers for harming animals in his haphazard experiments. "The wourali-poison destroys life's action so gently, that the victim appears to be in no pain whatever," he wrote to mollify squeamish readers, "and probably, were the truth known, it feels none, saving the momentary smart at the time the arrow enters."

He tested the poison on a wide array of creatures including various birds, a sloth, a fox, an ox, and a dog, and in all cases the result was the same—a slow, sleepy death. The dog, for example, "in three or four minutes began to be affected, smelt at every little thing on the ground around him, and looked wistfully at the wounded part. Soon after this he staggered, laid himself down, and never rose more. He barked once, though not as if in pain. His voice was low and weak; and in a second attempt it quite failed him. He now put his head betwixt his for-legs, and raising it slowly again he fell over on his side...his heart...continued faintly beating several minutes after every other part of his body seemed dead."†

* Curare, which Waterton called waurali, was a commonly used paste that was applied to the tips of blow-darts. It was so powerful that the smallest amount would kill the largest creature within minutes. Occasionally, a hunter would nick himself while preparing a weapon and would soon perish. Waterton devoted considerable time to searching for an antidote, without success.

† Fascinated by the deadly poison, Waterton even tested it on a she-ass when he returned to England, and kept the animal alive through artificial respiration for two hours until the poison had worn off, proving, in a rudimentary fashion, that its effect was primarily upon the respiratory system. For about a year after the experimental surgery, however, "she looked lean and sickly...but began to mend in the spring after, and by midsummer became quite fat and frisky."

Waterton returned to England in 1813 debilitated by sickness. A "tertian ague" (probably malaria) he acquired deep in the hinterland after wading through a torrid marsh during a tremendous downpour continued to periodically lay him low for the next three years. But no sooner had his health ("this long-looked for, ever welcome stranger") rebounded than he set off again for his old haunts in the wilds of South America. England, it seems, was only where he recuperated in anticipation of his next adventure.

His second journey, from March 1816 to April 1817, was more for travel than exploration. He visited many of the coastal towns and cities from Guyana south into Brazil and then wandered through the wilds, but never so far afield as he had on his first journey. He informed his readers of his method of travel: "A hat, a shirt, and a light pair of trousers, will be all the raiment you require," he wrote. "Custom will soon teach you to tread lightly and barefoot on the little inequalities of the ground, and show you how to pass on, unwounded, amid the mantling briers." Even Waterton lacerated his foot on a sharpened branch or stone on more than one occasion, or was feasted on by the Chegoe, a small flea-like creature that burrowed under the toenail and laid its eggs in a flesh-nest. Undeterred, he maintained his barefoot policy even after returning to England.

During this second foray, Waterton concentrated on observing birds and made some interesting discoveries regarding the behaviour, mating preferences, flight patterns, preferred foods, and calls of various avian species. He was one of the first naturalists to observe and describe large numbers of South American birds in their natural habitat. He proudly claimed to have "a pretty just knowledge formed of their haunts and economy." He wrote of hummingbirds (native to the Americas), purple-breasted cotingas, multi-hued campaneras, parrots, the greenish houtous, the striped and ludicrously large-billed toucans, bocloras, cassiques (or mockingbirds), yawaraciris, bitterns, egrets, blue herons, waracabas, and other rare and exotic birds not found in Europe. Although some of the species Waterton encountered and described were undoubtedly new to science, he lacked the training to properly identify them, and because he provided no specific taxonomic information, it is impossible to know definitively what birds he was discussing, except in the most obvious instances.

He described the infamous goatsucker and defended it against critics who accused it of sucking milk from shepherds' flocks under cover of darkness. "When the sun has set in the western woods," he wrote, "…it is then that the Goatsucker comes out of the forest, where it has sat all day long in slumbering ease, unmindful of the gay and busy scenes around it." Contrary to the common notions, Waterton asserted the innocence of the "harmless, unoffending" bird. "How foul a stain has inattention to facts put upon thy character!" he lamented, arguing that rather than subsisting on milk, goatsuckers feasted upon the pestiferous flies that plagued the herds. The docile beasts placidly allowed the birds to leap at their underbellies, devouring any unwanted flies. "Were you to dissect him," he recorded (and he probably did in the interest of science), "you would find no milk there. It is full of the flies that have been annoying the herd."

Waterton attempted to dispel misleading myths about other species as well, such as the woodpecker, which foresters blamed for destroying trees. From his observations, he claimed the birds were only eating the insects already lodged in a failing tree. Also of particular interest to him was the "King of the Vultures." It is a "fact beyond all dispute," he related, "that when the scent of carrion has drawn together hundreds of the common vultures, they all retire from the carcass as soon as the King of the Vultures makes his appearance. When his majesty has satisfied the cravings of his royal stomach with the choicest bits from the most stinking and corrupted parts, he generally retires to a neighbouring tree, and then the common vultures return to gobble down his leavings." He described the king as "very handsome, and seems to be the only bird which claims regal honours from the surrounding tribe." The two hundred or so species he studied and collected were, he wrote, "only as a handful from a well-stored granary," and the hundreds if not thousands of others were "all worthy of the attention of a naturalist, all worthy of a place in the cabinet of the curious."

When he sailed for home in 1817, Waterton may have anticipated an end to his wanderings, but it was not to be so. After a few restless years, during which he toured the Continent,* prepared his journal, and developed new techniques for taxidermy, he was again dreaming of Guyana. "Guyana whispered in my ear," he proclaimed, "and seemed to invite me once more to wander through her distant forests." By 1820 he was again sailing up the river Demerara to Georgetown. He went to visit an old friend, a planter he had known from his days managing his family's sugar plantations, in a region on the fringe of European settlement and soon discovered that not all had remained the same while he was away. The house appeared abandoned and decaying and his friend was nowhere to be seen. It was a melancholy day that inspired him to pen a poem:

> 'Tis now the vampire's bleak abode,
> 'Tis now the apartment of the toad;
> 'Tis here the painful Chegoe feeds,
> 'Tis here the dire Labarri breeds,
> Conceal'd in ruins, moss, and weeds.

---

*When he was in Italy, he marched barefoot into Rome like a pilgrim and had his feet cut to shreds on the uneven cobblestone road. He then proceeded to clamber to the tallest pinnacle of St. Peter's and place his glove over the steeple, perhaps just to prove he could do it. Only when Church authorities expressed alarm at his impious behaviour did he shuffle again to the top and remove his offending glove.

But the dilapidated mansion was well situated for forays into the jungle. He decided to use it as a storage depot for his specimens and a base for his excursions. After hiring some workers to mend the crumbling portions, he prepared to roam the hinterland. He reminded his readers, in case they had forgotten, that his preferred method of travel was shoe-less—shoes would have "irritated his feet, and retarded [him] in the chase of wild beasts." His other bit of advice to prospective naturalists and explorers was a bit more dubious. Never leave behind, he casually suggested, a good supply of "laudanum, calomel, and jalap, and the lancet" for cures against fever and other illness brought on by "exposure to the noon-day sun, to the dews of night, to the pelting shower and unwholesome food."

Waterton's peculiar form of self-medication involved frequent bloodletting (performed on himself when under the dreary influence of a fever) accompanied by heroic doses of calomel and jalap, sometimes up to ten times the standard dose.* On one occasion when he had a "severe" fever, he lay in a stupor for more than a day, sapped of all energy, plagued by throbbing temples and pain in his lower back. He took ten grains of calomel and a pinch of jalap and large draughts of warm tea. By the next evening his pulse had risen to one hundred and thirty, and the "headache [was] almost insup-portable, especially on looking to the right or left." His solution was to bleed himself. He "opened a vein, and a large orifice, to allow the blood to rush out rapidly; I closed it after losing sixteen ounces." Not surprisingly, his pulse was temporarily reduced. But by evening it had resumed its incessant pounding, and the following morning he took "five more grains of calomel and ten of jalap" before subsiding into

---

* Calomel is a tasteless white powder, a compound of mercury that was used at one time as a purgative and an insecticide; jalap is a purgative drug derived from the tubers of a Mexican plant; laudanum is a tincture of opium that used to be prescribed as a painkiller and sedative. Bloodletting was a common medical treatment during Waterton's time.

another delirious sweating stupor. Fortunately, he revived after another day, convinced that the bloodletting, calomel, and jalap had saved his life. He must have had an iron constitution, for his "physic" in all likelihood prolonged the illness and might have killed a weaker man.

Waterton's interest was in the observation and study of natural history, and not in mapping and geography. During this third foray, his actual destinations and travel route are as vague as ever, and, if he had any notion of where he wandered, he makes little effort to mention it. (Knowledge of the interior of many South American countries including Guyana was vague at best, so it is possible Waterton himself had no accurate idea of where he had travelled.) Several mammals hitherto little understood in Europe were the focus of his third journey: the sloth, the ant-bear (anteater), and the vampire bat.

Regarding the sloth, he was particularly vigilant in correcting the assumptions of European closet naturalists. "Those that have written on this singular animal," he wrote, "have remarked that he is in a perpetual state of pain, that he is proverbially slow in his movements, that he is a prisoner of space, and that as soon as he has consumed all the leaves of the tree upon which he has mounted, he rolls himself up in the form of a ball, and then falls to the ground." This is all false, he argued. After studying the animal in its native habitat for a considerable time, Waterton came to very different conclusions. "These errors," he believed, "have naturally arisen by examining the sloth in those places where nature never intended that he should be exhibited." He pointed out that he never saw a sloth in the wild anywhere but in the upper branches of large trees, not scuttling about the ground like a rodent. Previous scientists, he claimed, lacked his devotion and willingness to undergo the deprivation and hardship necessary to obtain accurate information. The sloth "is a scarce and solitary animal....He inhabits remote and gloomy forests, where snakes take up their abode, and where

Waterton took special pleasure debunking the erroneous notion that sloths were a deformed and ill-adapted species, pointing out that in his own travels he observed the sloth only high in the canopy of the forest and not crawling painfully on the ground.

LITTLE ANT-BEAR.

The ant-bear, or anteater.

cruelly stinging ants and scorpions, and swamps, and innumerable thorny shrubs and bushes, obstruct the steps of civilized man." (Whether he considered himself civilized is a matter for debate, but this was the theory he put forward to explain the ignorance of modern science.) He noted that sloths have no soles to their feet, have long claws that impeded ground movement, and have awkward, short hind legs and long forelegs—all these characteristics were certainly impediments for ground travel, but not for arboreal excursions. When he put a captured sloth on the ground, it would slowly and painfully drag itself to the nearest tree. Waterton postulated that the sloth was admirably suited to life in the trees, seldom left the forest canopy, and was not, according the prevailing belief, a mutated abomination, a celestial defect, an unhappy progeny of cruel nature. "It enjoys life as much as any other creature," he claimed. "The sloth is as much at a loss to proceed on his journey upon a smooth and level floor, as a man would be who had to walk a mile in stilts upon a line of feather beds."

Waterton also went to great pains to dispel the illusions surrounding the anteater, particularly the largest variety that was "a stout and powerful" animal six feet long from snout to tail. (Characteristically, he gives no specific scientific information regarding, for example, reproduction, lifespan, or taxonomic classification). But he did record that the creatures dwelt in the deepest recesses of the forest, near low, swampy ground "where the troely-tree grows." Waterton observed one particular aspect of the ant-bear's physiology that was new to science: "as yet unnoticed in the pages of natural history...two very large glands situated below the root of the tongue." The glands emitted a glutinous liquid that slid down the appendage and helped suck up ants. He concluded that they were, like many other creatures he encountered, "harmless and inoffensive."

Waterton was also fascinated by the vampire bat—the "nocturnal surgeon." With his own bloodletting propensities, he was particularly drawn to these bats, which inhabited abandoned houses and shadowy groves where they hung upside down, like ill-shaped fruits, from the swaying branches of trees deep in the jungle. He met many people who complained that the vampire bats (which came in two species, the smaller one that feasted chiefly on birds and the larger one that pursued mammals and humans) bled their domesticated animals and were the cause of great sickness. On one occasion he was resting at a planter's house with a gentleman who was the victim of a nocturnal visit by a vampire bat. Hearing the man cursing under his breath, Waterton asked, "What's the matter, sir?" The man was surly and replied impatiently, "What's the matter? The vampires have been sucking me to death." He then showed Waterton his toe, still oozing blood from where it had been tapped. Waterton attempted levity by suggesting that a European surgeon "would not have been so generous as to have blooded him without making a charge." The man was not amused. Waterton desperately wanted to be sucked by a vampire bat, and for months slept with his toe protruding from his hammock "to tempt this winged surgeon." But it was not to be; only his companions were blessed with a free bloodletting.

Returning to England in 1821, Waterton spent three restless years before again crossing the Atlantic to his beloved Guyana in 1824. His purpose on his fourth and final journey was to continue his observations of species he had previously documented rather than observing new ones. After his return, he set out to write an account of his adventures.

When his book, *Wanderings in South America*, one of the first books by a travelling amateur naturalist, was unleashed into the sleepy, respectable world of British closet naturalists in 1825, it made quite a splash and provoked the usual pedantic murmurings that occur when an unusually fresh book becomes popular. The language was too flowery; the scenarios too whimsical; the stories too outrageous; the conclusions too outlandish; the observations too unscientific. Waterton may have anticipated such criticism when he wrote the preface to the first edition: "I offer this book of Wanderings with a hesitating hand. It has little merit, and must make its way through the world as well as it can.... Perhaps it is destined to add one more to the number of slain, in the field of modern criticism." But, he defiantly added as an afterthought, "If critics are displeased with it in its present form, I beg to observe that it is not totally devoid of interest, and that it contains something useful."

The book was a great success, with editions in print as recently as 1909, nearly forty years after his death. And, although many of Waterton's observations on the behaviour of animals, such as the sloth or ant-bear, seem trite or obvious by modern standards, when he wrote of them in 1825 there was little information available about these species and it was impossible to distinguish between fact and fantasy. Most of the information about these creatures was based on the study of museum specimens, and, in many cases, assumptions of the behaviour of an animal were extrapolated or based on a rudimentary comparison with European animals. For example, sloths were often stuffed and displayed as if they were travelling across the ground in an uncomfortable and painful-looking position, while anteaters were shown to walk like other large mammals, with their large claws painfully curled under their feet. Large snakes were often displayed without the real head (because most specimens were obtained after a serpent was killed, usually by beheading) and a wooden head was substituted "with teeth which are large enough to suit a tiger's jaw; and this tends to mislead the spectator, and give him erroneous ideas."

Although Waterton contributed greatly to the knowledge of certain creatures of his jungle, he did not bother to identify minute details or variations within species. He never recorded the Latin names of any creature he encountered and never bothered to identify new species or sub-species, focusing instead on observing the behaviour of certain well-known but little-understood animals. Many of his astute observations of animals in their natural habitat were couched in such fanciful language that it minimized the impact of his findings. He represents a classic example of the rift that was then developing between field and closet naturalists. The two groups were beginning to diverge—one concerned exclusively with observations in the wild; the other with dissecting and studying specimens independent of their living environment. While in Waterton's time both groups called themselves naturalists, the closet naturalists eventually branched into the more professional pursuit of science, calling themselves biologists later in the century. They rightly pointed out the irrelevance of detailed, careful descriptions of species or painstakingly accurate descriptions of a bird's call notes if it was impossible to know what exact species of bird it was. The field naturalists, for their part, correctly pointed out the absurdity of understanding the internal working of an animal without having an idea of how it lived.

Waterton also had a very unscientific penchant for adventure and spectacle. He was a sensationalist, and some of his stories seemed so outlandish that they detracted from the credibility of his observations, although they caused his book to sell very well. On one occasion he claimed to have captured a huge eighteen-foot boa-constrictor with his bare hands, punching it unconscious when it leaped at him. Afterwards, he dragged it back through the woods to his camp and kept it in a bag under his hammock throughout the night so that he could dissect it in the morning. "Had Medusa been my wife," he wrote, "there could not have been more continued and disagreeable hissing in the bedchamber that night."

On another occasion his claims included the manhandling of a large cayman (alligator or crocodile). He had been searching unsuccessfully for a huge specimen for weeks (the sneaky beasts consistently devoured the fish that was placed

CAYMAN.

Waterton used the terms alligator, crocodile and cayman interchangeably, so one never knows exactly which creature he is referring to in his writings.

over a shark hook each night and slipped away at dawn). Finally, in frustration, he hired a few local Indians to help capture one. One of them tossed away the shark hook and quickly made his own trap, a flexible wooden contraption with barbed tips designed to expand and hook in the cayman's mouth. The next morning they awoke to find "a cayman ten feet and a half long fast to the end of the rope." It was snarling and snapping its powerful jaws, thrashing about the lagoon in a frightful manner.

Waterton resolved on a bold plan to capture it (he didn't want to shoot it for fear of damaging its skin). Grabbing a long mast from the canoe, he swaddled it in sailcloth and prepared to ram it down the beast's mouth if it charged too quickly. His small troupe of helpers began hauling in the beast from the murky depths where it now lay hidden under the water. As soon as the cayman was within a few yards of him, he saw that it "was in a state of fear and perturbation." He then "sprang up, and jumped on his [the cayman's] back, turning half round as I vaulted, so that I gained my seat with my face in the right position." With his legs straddling the gut of the cayman, he held on tightly as it furiously bucked and lashed its tail, meanwhile yelling at his cohorts to drag the plunging reptile farther ashore. (Should any readers express curiosity as to how he kept his seat, Waterton offered this reasoning: "I hunted some years with Lord Darlington's fox-hounds.") As soon as the cayman was exhausted, he lashed its mouth closed and tied up its forefeet behind its neck. They threw it trussed up into their canoe and removed themselves to their camp where Waterton "cut [its] throat; and after breakfast was over, commenced the dissection."

Not only did Waterton relish telling tales such as the one in which he was riding the cayman, but he would go out of his way to eat strange animals and describe the taste of the flesh, no doubt to shock his prudish readers. The larvae of blue wasps, for example, which apparently secretly hung their nests from hidden leafs and would "sally forth to punish you severely" if you disturbed them, could be roasted and were considered a delicacy by the natives. "I tried them once," he casually remarked, "by way of dessert after dinner, but my stomach was offended at their intrusion." He also feasted upon many other tropical delights such as "boiled ant-bear and red-monkey," which he proclaimed were "unknown even at Beauvilliers. in Paris or at a London city feast."

SALEMPENTA.

Waterton took great pleasure in shocking readers by describing the peculiar and exotic animals he ate while wandering in Guyana. The Salempenta (*Teius teguexin*) was one such beast that reputedly tasted like a "delicate young" chicken. "New comers," he observed, "are at first averse to eating a lizard of any description, but they very soon find out their mistake, and would even prefer an iguana or Salempenta cutlet to a chicken."

Waterton was as interested in anything curious or different, in odd or exotic experiences, and in hunting expeditions as he was in the study of natural history. Rigorous study was not his forte; he refused to temper his writings to make them more formal and stuffy and infused them with his own particular brand of humour. It was easier for some to put him down as a mere eccentric than to try to decipher his sense of humour. Sometimes he intentionally distorted the appearance of his stuffed specimens to fool observers (in one instance, for example, he manipulated the head of a monkey to resemble a bearded gentleman and printed an image of it titled "The Nondescript" in the frontispiece of his book!)

Considering Waterton's other peculiar traits, most of his stories are probably true. Certainly few people prowled the jungles riding caymans or punching boa constrictors, but few slept on the floor with a wooden block for a pillow, wrote proudly that in their late sixties they frequently climbed large oaks to better observe the crows, or lived in a veritable museum full of stuffed exotic beasts from South America, including a ten-and-a-half-foot alligator in his parlour.

After his fourth expedition in 1824, and the publication of *Wanderings* in 1825, Waterton never again returned to South America. He focused his attention on writing many essays on

NOCTIFER.

In addition to the fantastical Nondescript, a monkey manipulated to resemble a bearded man that he printed in one of his books, Waterton used his skills as a taxidermist to create many other "blended" creatures for his cabinets. One of these was the Noctifer or Spirit of the Night, a combination of bittern and eagle owl.

natural history that drew on his earlier experiences. Perhaps he felt too old, approaching fifty, for the rigours and hardships of jungle travel. In 1829, at age forty-seven, he had married the seventeen-year-old daughter of one of his friends. The following year, however, Anne (Edmonstone) died giving birth to their only child, Edmund. It was after her death that his eccentricity escalated. Dr. Hobson relates tales from the 1850s of Waterton hiding under a hall table when visitors arrived, and then crawling out barking like a dog and attempting to bite them. At dinner parties he would demonstrate his ability to scratch his head with his large toe. In his later years he was a very peculiar individual.

Waterton spent his final years, apart from a few forays to the Continent, on his ancestral estate, Walton Hall in Yorkshire. He created a vast, sprawling garden complete with wooded hills and a lake, surrounded the beautiful park with a nine-foot stone wall and instructed his gamekeeper never to harm the birds. All this extravagance, he claimed, was "paid for with the wine I didn't drink after dinner." For many years he settled into a pattern of rising at 4:00 a.m., drinking his tea in the evening, retiring early, and waking at midnight for prayer in his private chapel. Those who knew him at this time reported that he was a kind and gentle man, generous (yet anonymous) with his charitable donations. On his habitual evening stroll about the estate, he always took care to bring bread to feed a goose that waited patiently by a small bridge. If he forgot he would murmur, "How shall we ever get passed [*sic*] that goose?" and wait at a distance until it departed so he wouldn't have to disappoint it. He died in his home in 1865 after slipping on a log and falling heavily on his hip. In his final hours, his concern was that others would not be inconvenienced by his passing.

At a relatively early age, Waterton had pondered and come to an understanding of one of the universal truths of the natural world—the impermanent and capricious nature of life, strong as iron yet fragile as a delicate flower in spring. "Put thy foot on that large trunk thou seest to the left," he exhorted his readers on one of his equinoctial tramps early in his life. "It seems entire amid the surrounding fragments. Mere outward appearance, delusive phantom of what it once was! Tread on it, and like the fuss-ball, it will break into dust. Sad and silent mementos to the giddy traveller as he wanders on! Prostrate remnants of vegetable nature, how incontestably ye prove what we must all at last come to, and how plain your mouldering ruins show that the firmest texture avails us naught when Heaven wills that we should cease to be!"

Waterton was as much a storyteller as he was a naturalist, and his muse was the natural world; his contribution to science was as much in raising awareness of the importance of the natural world as something worthy of study, and in celebrating its diversity and beauty, as it was in presenting a coherent explanation for natural phenomena. And, like the early scientists who had come before him, he knew the natural world was not as simple as it at first appeared.

In the years after Waterton returned to England and published *Wanderings in South America*, another aristocratic wanderer, German prince Maximilian of Wied had returned from an expedition to Brazil and was planning another to the remote regions of the American West. There, to his own surprise, the prince's interest in animals and little-known plants would be supplanted by an intense interest in the people he encountered.

CHAPTER FOUR

Prince Maximilian of Wied

*By way of settlement, we may preserve here in America
neither the aborigines nor the wild beasts, because the beginning of settlement
is always the destruction of everything.*
—PRINCE MAXIMILIAN OF WIED,
Travels in the Interior of North America

Prince Maximilian of Weid (1782–1867) shown here third from left along the Missouri River in 1833 when he was fifty-one years old.

From its source high in the Rocky Mountains of Montana, the Missouri River rushes from the ragged hills and rolls on east across the plains for several hundred miles, a broad and dirty serpentine band, before curving south and joining the Mississippi near St. Louis. It is 2,565 miles long, the longest river in the United States, and it drains the waters of ten states and part of two Canadian provinces. Although a series of dams have mostly tamed its wild waters, in the 1830s it was a capricious and treacherous torrent, coloured murky brown from eroding prairie silt. In the spring the river rapidly surged in size, flooding and shifting around ever-moving deadly sandbars hidden under the turbid surface. Great trees, uprooted in violent storms and sucked from the crumbling banks, loomed like macabre skeletons, their heavy half-submerged branches clawing the sky and swaying with the strong current. Herds of deer, elk, buffalo, and antelope came to the shore to drink in the evenings, while beavers, muskrats, bears, and a host of birds swam in the broad waters.

It was the great artery of travel and commerce, from St. Louis in the United States west into the "free Indian territory" where the American Fur Company was pushing its enterprise. In the early 1830s, several rudimentary fur outposts lined the shores of "Old Muddy" as far west as Fort Mackenzie in the shadow of the Rocky Mountains. Each year the company pulled from the Upper Missouri as many as 40,000 buffalo hides, and over 100,000 furs and skins of other creatures such as beaver, muskrat, mink, lynx, weasel and fox. In 1832, the first steam-powered boat pushed west as far as Council Bluffs, just past St. Louis, in an attempt to increase commerce along the great river and improve travel. A year later, a trio of European travellers purchased passage on an American Fur Company steam paddlewheeler. They were on a scientific expedition to the western fringe of the United States.

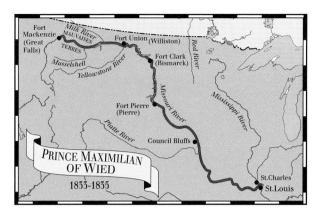

Prince Maximilian's journey up the Missouri River, 1833–1835.

The leader of the small band was a stocky fifty-one-year-old German prince named Alexander Philipp Maximilian of Wied-Neuwied. Serious eyes and a slight frown disguised an open, unpretentious manner and frank curiosity in all things novel in the natural world. In addition to the prince's manservant, a skilled hunter and taxidermist named David Dreidoppel, there was a tall, dashing young Swiss artist named Karl Bodmer hired by Maximilian to visually document the expedition. Before hiring the young man for the expedition, the prince took great pains to nip in the bud any notions Bodmer may have had about living in luxury on a royal tour—"I must also note that Mr. Bothmer [*sic*]," he wrote, "should not, on the basis of my social station, make any conclusions about my standard of living since I always live very simply. No wine cellar or other victuals will be brought along. When I travel I always guide myself by the customs of the country. On the ship we will have good food and wine; in America this will often be lacking." The guaranteed salary, however, was more than enough to entice the fledgling artist to cross the ocean on a dangerous expedition to the frontier of a wild continent. Over the course of their journey, Maximilian and the young Bodmer developed a genuine friendship and mutual respect.[*]

The trio had boarded a small ship in the Dutch port of Rotterdam in the spring of 1832 and arrived in Boston on July 4 at the height of an Independence Day celebration. Despite the tedious, continuous strains of "Yankee Doodle," the prince was pleased to report that the "motley assemblage" conducted themselves with sobriety and produced "no impropriety of conduct or unseemly noise." However, he had no interest whatsoever in touring the cities of the eastern seaboard—apart from Philadelphia, which had emerged as the American centre for science and art. Unfortunately, Maximilian's enjoyment of that city was tainted by an outbreak of cholera, and, for some time, he failed to make contact with the city's circle of prominent American naturalists affiliated with the American Philosophical Society or the Academy of Natural Sciences of Philadelphia. Eager to get on with his collecting, he quickly headed west across Pennsylvania to less "civilized" parts of the country.

The three men spent their first winter at New Harmony, Indiana, where Maximilian had intended only a brief visit with two eminent American naturalists, Thomas Say and Charles-Alexandre Lesueur. After he suffered "serious indisposition, nearly resembling cholera," however, his two-week stopover stretched into a five-month residence. Despite his illness, the sojourn was a pleasant one for the German

---

[*] Despite the nearly thirty years that had passed since Lewis and Clark had travelled up the Missouri (and beyond), no other scientist-naturalists had ventured to the farthest reaches of the river.

Great herds of bison routinely came to the river's edge to drink. These huge beasts were the primary source of food for the native peoples and the fur traders. They were driven to near extinction by the end of the 19th century.

Bodmer's painting of the mouth of the Fox River depicts the scenery along the Missouri River as it was before roads, dams and cultivation.

Like many other early travelers, Maximilian enjoyed the "sport" of hunting grizzly bears, which at that time were quite common on the great plains.

Maximilian and Bodmer (right) meeting a band of Minnetaris outside a fur-trading fort along the Missouri River

Maximilian recorded that from the center of this shrine of human and bison bones, the Mandan Indians beseeched their gods.

Bodmer painted many of the native peoples' shrines and cairns along the Missouri River. This eerie mound of stones and bones was titled *Magic Pile of the Assiniboine Indians*.

From Fort McKenzie, Maximilian could see the Rocky Mountains in the distance. Threats from the Peigan and the dire warnings of the Indians and the traders, however, persuaded him to abandon his plans of continuing west to winter in the mountains.

Near Fort McKenzie, Maximilian and Bodmer witnessed a vicious battle between the Peigan Indians and the Assiniboine. The Peigan and Blackfeet Indians were the dominant military peoples in the foothills of the Rocky Mountains. They used threats and violence to keep the fur traders from encroaching upon their territory.

Overlooking Fort Clark, the American Fur Company outpost where
Maximilian and Bodmer spent the winter of 1832–1833.

Mandan Indians near Fort Clark. Maximilian and Bodmer had the good
fortune to spend the winter of 1832-1833 among the Mandan, recording all
they could of the social customs and mode of life of these peoples.

Maximilian's and Bodmer's contribution to the understanding of Plains Indian culture on the cusp of radical change brought on by the fur trade (and later by a series of epidemics) far outstripped their nominal contributions to natural science. Bodmer captured for posterity events such as the Bison Dance of the Mandan Indians, which might otherwise have been lost.

Niagara Falls, although inspiring enough for Bodmer to paint, were a disappointment to Maximilian, who was much more interested in the wild lands of the west and the numerous native peoples he encountered along the Missouri River.

naturalist. While Bodmer set off on a solo trip south to New Orleans, Maximilian spent the winter reading from Say and Lesueur's voluminous library on natural history and strolling in the woods with his congenial naturalist friends. He added quite a few new specimens to his growing American botanical and zoological collection and filled his journal with observations on the flora and fauna. When he set off for St. Louis in the spring, he probably knew more about the American West and its native inhabitants than most Americans.

Maximilian had been dreaming of a journey to the wilder portions of North America for a number of years. As with many of the early naturalists, details about his personal and family life are sketchy. Born the eighth of ten children in a castle on the Rhine in 1782, he apparently developed an early passion for natural history, pursuing his studies at the University of Göttingen under Professor Johann Friedrich Blumenbach, the reputed father of (the discipline of) physical anthropology. His career in science, however, was derailed by the Napoleonic wars. He fought at the Battle of Jena, was captured by the French, and was later released during a prisoner exchange. After his release he was promoted to major-general in the Allied army and led troops on an advance against Paris in 1814. When the war ended, the prince organized a two-year scientific expedition to Brazil, probably inspired by his friend and mentor, Alexander von Humboldt, whom he met in Paris. It was one of the first non-Portuguese scientific expeditions to the region.

In Brazil, Maximilian was a diligent observer and collector, devoting himself to his studies and amassing a vast number of botanical, zoological, and ethnographic specimens. He was particularly intrigued by the native peoples and their customs, an interest he would bring with him to North America. Many nights he sat around campfires in the gloomy and humid jungle, observing the Indians and partaking in exotic feasts of roasted monkey. When he returned to Germany he devoted the better part of the next decade to preparing his observations for publication. The result was a two-volume report with an atlas portfolio, imitative of the works of von Humboldt in its scope and breadth of questioning and study. The book was translated from German into Dutch, English, French, and Spanish, and secured Maximilian's reputation as a naturalist and explorer. Even before he had finished his Brazilian studies, the prince was already dreaming of a new adventure. "Thoughts of another journey are now going through my head...," he wrote to a colleague, "and I am thinking strongly of northern America. Which region of this interesting land? I think the interior regions of the Missouri would be highly interesting because of its tribes?... Doesn't North America also have much of interest for Botany?" In preparation for the journey he spent years reading everything he could find on the natural history of the interior of North America, including Lewis and Clark's account of their trip to the Pacific, Major Stephen H. Long's records of a trip to the great plains, and Thomas Nuttall's account of his early Western wanderings.

Nothing he had read, however, had prepared him for St. Louis. The three travellers had reached the thriving, chaotic yet strangely cosmopolitan centre of the American fur trade in March 1833. It was a rowdy and rapidly growing frontier town of seven thousand. In contrast to many of the towns they had passed through on their westward journey, St. Louis boasted a central district lined with fine shops, in addition to the busy docks clogged with barges and steamboats that plied north along the Missouri and south down the Mississippi. From St. Louis, Maximilian had several options—he could take the Santa Fe trail to New Mexico, head directly west across the prairie to the Rocky Mountains, or follow the Missouri north into Indian territory.

A chance meeting with another westward-bound European wanderer, Captain William Drummond Stewart, nearly settled his travel plans. Stewart, a Scottish baronet and also a veteran of the Napoleonic wars, urged the prince to head west with him for a year of sport and adventure in the Rocky Mountains. "It would have been agreeable for me to travel in his company," Maximilian noted. But he decided against it on the advice of more experienced frontiersmen who suggested he follow the Missouri and stay as a guest at the American Fur Company outposts en route. His scientific objectives did not mesh with the intention of the amiable Scottish baronet—it would probably have been difficult to make accurate scientific collections while worrying about hostile Indians, shooting buffalo, or tracking down mountain men at the rendezvous, the annual gathering of trappers in the Rocky Mountains. The American Fur Company steamboat could also easily accommodate all his specimens and scientific equipment, including reference books, jars of preserving fluid, plant presses, and frames for drying animals and bird skins. This route would also be much safer and offer a greater chance of meeting various Indians in friendly circumstances at the trading posts.

Maximilian quickly began organizing the journey. Although he planned to live off the land as much as possible, certain provisions were indispensable—"coffee, sugar, brandy, candles, fine gunpowder, shot of every kind, colours, paper," as well as trade goods for the Indians such as "calico, knives, brass bells, burning glasses, cinnabar, red ribbon." He also deposited $300 with the company as credit against purchases upstream in the coming year. Although he was advised of what to expect, reality far exceeded the prince's wildest hopes.

In April 1833, the American Fur Company steamer sallied forth up the Missouri bound for the Far West. The dock was thronged with cheering company hands and the deck was crowded with about a hundred rowdy free trappers, deckhands and *engagés* bellowing as the engine belched smoke and the boat surged into the broad waters heading upstream.* The ship's cannons boomed and were followed by a volley of small shot from the heavily inebriated *engagés*. Although the sunset on the first night was "blood red . . . stupendously beautiful," the weather soon turned grim, and the river became a treacherous obstacle course of sandbars and vicious snags that could easily rip the bottom of a heavily laden steamboat. They were lashed by a series of storms, with winds whipping whitecaps on the water, tearing away chunks of the bank and filling the river with debris. The ship laboured against the current and wind, swerving to dodge the obstacles. Sometimes the *engagés* were sent ashore to haul the ship along with ropes as they trudged through the spring muck, clambering over fallen trees and rocks along the shore. The trip soon turned into a treacherous slog of unremitting toil for the *engagés* and deckhands.

"At the mouth of the Little Nemahaw River the Missouri was very shallow," recorded Maximilian. "Our vessel having received several violent shocks by striking, and a storm, accompanied by heavy rain, arising, we ran aground, about noon, on a sand bank, and were obliged to put out a boat to take soundings, but the wind, which blew with increasing violence from the open prairie on the south-west, drove us further into the sand bank. Every moment it became more furious; our vessel lay almost on her side. . . ." Fortunately the ship was righted by the labours of the *engagés*, but other dangers plagued the travellers. One early morning wake-up call was particularly shocking to the otherwise nonchalant prince. "Early in the morning," he remembered, "a large branch of a tree, lying in the water, forced its way into the cabin, carried away part of the door case, and then broke off, and was left on the floor. . . . One might have been crushed in bed," he noted in alarm.

The ship, named the *Yellow Stone*, frequently pulled to

* *Engagés* or voyageurs, according to Maximilian, were "the lowest class of the Fur Company. Most of them are French Canadians, or descendants of the French settlers on the Mississippi and Missouri."

shore for firewood to stoke the primitive, clanking boilers. The voyage was slow going, allowing Maximilian and Dreidoppel to venture ashore and range across the wooded prairie hills shooting animals and scooping up novel plants. "The underwood of the forest consisted chiefly of *Laurus Benzoin* and *Cercis Canadensis*," he observed, recognizing various species of wild grasses. "The ground was covered with *Equisetum hymenale*, from one and a half to two feet high." On another day the lucky prince was returning to the *Yellow Stone* when "the pilot called out that there was a rattlesnake very near to me.... I looked...[and] stunned it with some slight blows [and] put it into a vessel in which there were already a live heterodon and a black snake, where it soon recovered. The three agreed very well together, but were afterwards put into a cask of brandy." The collecting was not perfect, however. Maximilian was annoyed that "the noise and smoke of our steamer frightened all living creatures; geese and ducks flew off in all directions."

While the boat continued to thrash its way laboriously upstream, the prince made notes on the many varieties of birds and examined three large catfish that were hauled from the river. But on May 3, near the present-day city of Omaha, Maximilian discovered his true interest in the American West—the native peoples. He was treated to an Omaha ceremonial dance under the prairie moon. "The splendid sky was illumined by the full moon," he remembered, "silence reigned around, interrupted only by the noise of the frogs, and the incessant cry of the whip-poor-will...." About twenty Omaha Indians, one with a "savage and martial appearance," danced and jumped to the incessant pounding rhythm of drums. "Chanting 'Hi! hi! hi!' or 'Hey! hey! hey!,' they leaped apposite each other, with great exertion, for about an hour....This dance was very interesting to me, especially in connection with the beautiful evening scene on the Missouri. The bright light of the moon illumined the extensive and silent wilderness; before us, the grotesque band of Indians, uttering their wild cry, together with the loud call of the night raven, vividly recalled to my mind scenes which I had witnessed in Brazil." Bodmer was as enthralled as the prince, furiously sketching the scene with special attention to the minute details that are a trademark of his paintings.

By mid-May the party was chugging north through the territory of the Poncas and the Dakotas. Storms and river debris continued to hinder their progress—occasionally, when the ship lurched onto a sandbar, the entire company dashed to the opposite side to rock the ship off the shoal. Soon Maximilian observed his first antelope and his first bison, and was pleased that the farther from St. Louis they voyaged, the more Indians he encountered. All aspects of native culture interested Maximilian, and he kept meticulous notes on the cultural practices of the various peoples he encountered, describing them in detail and comparing everything from burial and mourning practices and ceremonial dress to culinary etiquette and spiritual beliefs. With company agents as interpreters, Maximilian was able to communicate and ask the Indians he encountered a wide variety of questions. He took an even greater interest in recording everything about them than he did for his natural history specimens. Near Fort Lookout, Maximilian was introduced to a band of Sioux and, while Bodmer painted the chief in full ceremonial garb, the prince learned as much as he could of their culture and wrote it in his journal. Regarding their burial practices, for example, he recorded that "among the peculiar customs of the Sioux, is their treatment of the dead. Those who die at home are sewed up in blankets and skins, in their complete dress, painted and laid with their arms and other effects on a high stage, supported by four poles, until they decomposed.... Those who have been killed in battle are immediately interred on the spot.... Very often, however, they lay their dead in trees; and we saw, in the neighbourhood of this place, an oak, in which there were three bodies wrapped in skins." His journal describes in detail the different customs of the Missouri people, always in his sober, serious tone. He was a meticulous observer of facts, prone to understatement and deadpan delivery of information.

The group reached Fort Pierre, one of the largest fur trading outposts along the river, by early June. Situated just before the Missouri begins its great arc to the west, the post was a sprawling primitive palisade with a commanding view of the plain and river. As was the custom, the guns blazed away in salute, and the ship answered with a ragged, prolonged burst of small shot. The stopover lasted barely long enough for Maximilian and his entourage to transfer themselves to a new steamship, the *Assiniboine*, that quickly lurched into the current of the river. They were floating through the wild prairie now, "prairies, with their hills, steep clay banks, and stripes of forest." And later, "the country, on the south bank, appeared to us to have some resemblance with many parts on the banks of the Rhine; but, on the right bank, there soon appeared those singular hills, resembling fortifications." As they continued north and the presence of wildlife became more prominent along the river shore, Maximilian was appalled that "members of the party who stayed aboard blazed away at anything that moved on shore for the sheer sport of it. Wolves, swans, and beavers fell victim to their fire."

At Fort Clark, near present-day Bismarck, North Dakota, Maximilian recorded his encounter with a band of Crow Indians who were visiting. "The haughty Crows," he wrote, "rode on beautiful panther skins, with red cloth under them, and, as they never wear spurs had a whip or elk's horn in their hand. These mounted warriors, with their diversely painted faces, feathers in their long hair, bow and arrows slung across their backs, and with a musket or spear in their hands . . . were a novel and highly interesting scene." The Crow women were no less novel, and he described—somehow without a shred of humour—how they helped him drive off the multitude of pestering stray dogs with a series of well-placed stones. Bodmer painted constantly, trying to meet the prince's exacting requirements. Much to Maximilian and Bodmer's dismay the ship waited only a single day at each fort before pushing on—the season was short for delivering and collecting goods, and the company had little interest in the prince's work.

As the ship slowly and loudly plowed west, Maximilian noted the changes in the terrain and climate of the Upper Missouri from temperate and reasonably green to dry and barren—"though," he admitted, "various plants, interesting to the botanist, are everywhere to be found." His collecting seemed like such odd behaviour to many of his fellow travellers that it sometimes caused a minor commotion. On several occasions two amiable Indians, "very quiet, obliging men" who also travelled aboard the steamer, tried to help him gather. They "never returned from an excursion on shore," he wrote, "without bringing me some handfulls of plants, often, it is true, only common grass, because they had observed that we always brought plants home with us."

After passing through a series of hills "rising one above the other; some covered with verdure, some of a yellowish colour, mostly without life and variety," they arrived on June 24 at Fort Union, a sprawling palisade enclosure with a large American flag flying in the wind. They were now about 1,800 miles upriver from St. Louis. Fort Union was one of the principal fur trading outposts and the final depot for steamboat navigation on the Missouri. They remained here as guests for nearly two weeks, awaiting the arrival of a keelboat to continue their journey to Fort McKenzie.* The fort was a busy

---

* Keelboats were stoutly built barges with long deep keels to help keep direction in the strong current of the Missouri. They had a mast for a primitive sail and a large rudder. The *Flora*, on which Maximilian travelled, was sixty feet long with a beam of sixteen feet. In addition to a vast amount of cargo for Fort McKenzie, it housed fifty-one people. Quarters were cramped, but no one dared sleep on the shore for fear of attack by Indians or bears.

place situated on a low, flat prairie capable of housing thousands of Indian tents. Cactus covered the ground, a painful irritant to unwary wanderers. While they waited, countless bands of Assiniboines and Crees arrived at the fort, while others left for the buffalo hunt. They had ample time to collect specimens of new plants and birds, but Maximilian was particularly grateful for the opportunity to learn as much as he could about the Assiniboine and Cree ways of life. Bodmer continually sketched and painted all he could of Indian life and drew portraits of warriors, women, and children.

On July 6, 1833, the *Flora* pushed out into the current and slowly made its way west. Although the prince was grateful for the peace and quiet, without steam power travel was even more difficult and unpleasant for the *engagés*. The heavy boat either had to be poled with iron-shod poles, rowed with unwieldy, long sweep oars, or dragged at the end of a rope; only occasionally did a slight breeze fill the baggy sail. Once they were past Fort Union, Maximilian saw a terrain unlike any he had seen before, eerie and barren in its solitude. "The prairie was dry and yellow," he recalled, "the least motion, even a wolf crossing it, raised the dust." They could see huge herds of buffalo on the horizon leaving a billowing tan cloud behind them as they thundered through the grass.

"During our voyage today," he wrote on July 18, "I could not help making comparisons with my journeys on the Brazilian rivers. There, where nature is so infinitely rich and grand, I heard, from the lofty, thick, primeval forests on the banks of the rivers, the varied voices of the parrots, the macaws, and many other birds, as well as of the monkeys, and other creatures; while here, the silence of the bare, dead, lonely wilderness is but seldom interrupted by the howling of the wolves, the bellowing of the buffaloes, or the screaming of the crows. The vast prairie scarcely offers a living creature." Maximilian, however, did observe and shoot a blue-gray "butcher bird," a bald eagle, "a couple of sparrow hawks, a kind of lark, and [some] wild geese," as well as catching "a great many butterflies, which were hovering about the flowers in the burning rays of the sun." He was most astonished with the bewildering array of grasshoppers, "many of them of beautiful colours," as he rambled through the wild prairie along the riverbank. As far as he could see, "there were the bleached bones of the buffaloes and elks, and their immense horns." On the downside to this marvellously novel scene were "a great many ant hills, and mosquitoes, and several other kinds of troublesome stinging insects."

The hunting of large animals alleviated the tedium of river travel for the prince and Dreidoppel, as well as for the traders. Whenever they saw a beast, the ship slowed, and hunters rowed ashore in a smaller boat and crept downwind preparing for the kill. It was not always for subsistence, however, that these creatures were shot. One day they saw "an immense buffalo bull, which approached us slowly, not suspecting any danger." The prince and several others hid in a ravine and, when the "majestic" animal strutted past, they let fire. "The magnificent creature lay stretched out about forty paces above the ravine." The barge had slowly poled upriver in the meantime, so they hurried back to the boat, leaving the carcass for the crows.

Bears were another favourite target for sport shooting, and they pursued and killed any they saw. On one occasion they spied a large bear on a sandbank and, as they drew near, they noted that it was feasting on a dead buffalo cow that was half-buried in the mud. Several hunters, including Dreidoppel, launched a small boat and paddled quickly to shore and positioned themselves downwind. "The ravenous bear," Maximilian reported, "sometimes raised his colossal head, looked around him, and then greedily returned to his repast" as the hunters crept closer. They fired several shots in quick succession and "the bear rolled over, uttered fearful cries, tumbled about ten steps forward, scratched the wounded places furiously with his paws, and turned several times completely over." A hunter then ran up and blasted his rifle into its head. Soon the "huge beast lay stretched out: it was fastened by ropes to the boat, and conveyed in triumph to the ship, where it was measured, and a drawing made of it."

While Bodmer painted the incident, a rueful Maximilian lamented that he had missed the chance to shoot a bear. "I much regretted that I had not taken part in the sport," he wrote, "but I had not believed that it was possible, in such an open, unprotected spot, to get so near the bear. . . . It would have been easy to shoot many of these animals, by posting ourselves near the dead buffalo cow . . . but our time was too short and precious." The boat continued on its way through the diminishing wilderness.

A few days after that incident they saw another bear swimming in the river and immediately discharged fifteen rifles at it, but it miraculously escaped into the aspen forest, "though probably wounded," Maximilian noted. That afternoon they shot a "she bear with two cubs." Two days later, on July 21, they killed another bear, but, as the boat was getting crowded with all of the prince's specimens, "we contented ourselves with carrying off as trophies only his head and fore paws."* Fed up with the crowding, each night the *engagés* "accidentally" swept his specimens, "the skins, skulls of animals, and the like," off the deck of the ship where he had carefully placed them to bleach in the sun. "We had made a numerous and interesting collection of natural history," he recorded, "many articles of which we were obliged, for want of room, to leave on deck. . . . In this manner I lost many highly interesting specimens; and on our keel-boat, with the most

* Hauling a sixty-foot keelboat up the river was a tiring and tedious job. Maximilian tallied the animals downed for food and sport by the fifty-two men on the 650-mile voyage from Fort Union to Fort McKenzie: "Buffaloes—54; Elks—18; Blacktailed deer—13; Common deer—26; Antelopes—2; Bighorns—2; Bears—9; Wolves—1; Skunk—1; Porcupines—1; Hares—2; Eagles (bald)—6; Horned owls (big)—5; Prairie hens—3; Wild geese—10; Prairie dogs—10; Rabbits—1."

favourable opportunities, it was hardly possible to make a collection of natural history, if I except the herbarium, which we kept in the cabin, under our eyes...."

By late July they had entered the land known as *the mauvaises terres*, the badlands, an eerie congregation of weirdly eroded mountaintops and spooky organic clay formations— stark, moulded hills, ill-shapen and weathered. "In general," Maximilian observed with his critical eye, "the bare gray masses of the eminences on the bank were so singularly formed that it was impossible not to wish that an able geologist might make a minute investigation of the chain. Their tops, like towers, pillars, etc. were contrasted with the clear blue sky, and the sun caused them to cast deep shadows." During the following ten days, near the Musselshell River in present-day central Montana, the terrain became increasingly mountainous and desolate. "The mountains here presented a rude wilderness," he wrote, "looking in part like a picture of destruction.... The Mauvaises Terres seems to be unique in its kind, and this impression is strengthened when you look up and down the river. Only the croaking of the raven was heard in this desolate waste, which even the Indians avoid." Bodmer was kept busy filling his sketchbooks with views of the peculiar scenery while Maximilian captured a prairie dog for his zoological collection, as well as a rattlesnake. He somehow prevented the snake from being pitched into the muddy river while it lay splayed open, drying on the deck.

After passing the badlands, however, they saw in the distance "beautiful, medium sized mountains and, at their foot, fresh green forests, a gratifying aspect since we had seen nothing but naked whitish mountains for so long." They were entering the territory of the powerful and warlike Blackfeet Indians. August 5 was an exciting day. At the foot of some large "eminences," the plain that rolled down to the river's edge was covered with the leather tents of a large congregation of Atsina (allies of the Blackfeet). The largest tent was flying an American flag. "The whole prairie was covered in

Indians, in various groups, and with numerous dogs; horses of every colour were grazing round, and horsemen galloped backwards and forwards." Eight chiefs were brought on board the small keelboat for greetings and gifts. They were soon followed by a swarm of others swimming across the channel or paddling small buffalo-hide boats loaded with dried meat, leather, and animal skins for trading. "Our keelboat was suddenly entered on every side and crowded with them," Maximilian recalled. The "tall and slender men" soon covered the deck and ran throughout the cabins demanding brandy, powder, and shot. "Our situation was everything but agreeable," the prince wrote with increasing alarm, "for these same Indians had entirely demolished a fort, on the frontiers of Canada, two years before, killed a clerk and eighteen other persons....If it was their intention to treat us in a hostile manner, there was no way to escape." Although no hostilities or disputes arose, Maximilian was relieved when a favourable wind blew the *Flora* farther from shore.

Four days later the keelboat rounded a wide bend in the river and beheld "the foremost chain of the Rocky Mountains, looking like a distant blue range." Fort McKenzie, the westernmost outpost of the American Fur Company, the first trading outpost in the Blackfeet territory, was situated at the base of some brown grassy hills, with the river flowing in front of it. The fort was only a year old, having been hastily slapped together in 1832 in an effort to expand the trade—generally against the will of their primary customers, the Blackfeet, who, at best, viewed it with ambivalence, but were sometimes hostile to the implicit invasion.

When the keelboat approached Fort McKenzie on August 9, a large encampment of perhaps two thousand Blackfeet was waiting around the primitive palisade prepared for trade. Maximilian noted that "a most interesting scene presented itself." A number of orderly Blackfeet warriors were lined up while the principal chiefs strode forward. The ship was greeted by a thundering explosion of cannons and "the fire of musketry among the mass of the Indian warriors was uninterrupted, and their war cry sounded over to us, while our vessel, in spite of the rain, kept up a brisk fire." After a greeting ceremony with the important dignitaries, Maximilian entered the fort and was grateful for a private, though small, dark and drafty room.

Maximilian's curiosity was raised to the highest pitch by the opportunity to meet the reclusive and often hostile Blackfeet Indians, and he devoted most of the following month to interviewing all the important chiefs and learning as much as he could of their customs, including the trading formalities between the two sides, the elaborate rituals, mutual gift-giving, and pipe smoking. While Bodmer painted vignettes of camp life and portraits of the principal leaders, Maximilian was busy recording his own observations on their clothing and ornaments, style of tents, domestic animals, food and medicine, marriage customs, battle behaviour, and domestic duties. Of the women he wrote they "have to perform all the heavy work. They pitch the tents, chop sod, and lay it around the hem of the tents at the base. They cook, cut, gather and carry home the firewood, tan the hides, and care for the pieces of clothing. In short, they are rather busy."

The bartering and bacchanals continued for days after the arrival of the keelboat and renewed itself whenever a new band of Blackfeet arrived. One day Maximilian noticed two small tame bears romping about at the end of a tether between several tents. Although he wanted the bears for his collection, he was not pleased with having to trade whisky to obtain them, and he alluded to the devastating effect liquor was having on Indian society. "The Indians," he recorded, "...gave everything to get their favourite drink. Many came singing and dancing and offered their wives and daughters in exchange for whiskey. Others brought horses, beavers, and other skins, and we saw indescribable scenes. The young as well as the old got something to drink, and even the very small children here and there could neither stand nor walk."

On the morning of August 28, the Blackfeet were surprised by several hundred Assiniboine warriors. The gates of the fort were quickly shut and bolted, and, from relative safety, Maximilian witnessed a short but brutal conflict, with muskets blazing, warriors screaming, and horses galloping wildly through the encampment. Many of the Blackfeet, bleary from drinking all night, were slain before the attackers were finally driven off. Dead and scalped bodies lay strewn around the collapsed and burned tents, while the moaning of the severely wounded, including children, rose like a dirge from the smouldering plain. In the midst of the battle, to the shock of those around him, Maximilian had to be restrained from rushing out the gates into the fray. The "Indian who had been slain near the fort especially interested me," he recorded, "because I wished to obtain his skull. The scalp had already been taken off, and several Blackfeet were engaged in venting their rage on the dead body." Before he could get closer, however, it was mutilated beyond recognition.

During Maximilian and Bodmer's stay, there were frequent and violent conflicts between the members of the various Indian bands who arrived to trade. Many died during the drunken brawling and many threats were made against the men of the fort. It was this frighteningly cavalier attitude to death and the dire warnings of the Indians and the traders that prompted Maximilian to abandon his long-cherished notion of pushing on west to the Rocky Mountains. "A great number of the most dangerous Indians surrounded us on all sides, and had in particular occupied the country towards the Falls of the Missouri, which was precisely the direction we should have to take." Supplies were also running low at the fort, and Maximilian decided to return downstream for the winter, to the relative safety of Fort Clark, among the friendly Mandans and Minnetarees.

On September 14 they loaded a small oar-powered Mackinaw boat until it was heaped with natural history collections, including a large cage with the two small bears, and set off. The specimens consumed most of the space and it was a very cramped journey for Maximilian, Bodmer, Dreidoppel, a helmsman, and three *engagés* hired to get them safely south. They had to venture to shore each evening to sleep, a practice considered extremely dangerous and almost always avoided because of the possibility of being attacked in their sleep. The bears moaned and growled constantly, irritating them, and soon dark clouds rolled overhead and dumped rain into the uncovered boat, soaking them and drenching their supplies. "In the morning we were in a lamentable plight," Maximilian recorded. "We were all of us, more or less, wet and benumbed, as the boat had no deck, and we found, to our great dismay, that this new vessel was very leaky." As soon as the sun peeked through the clouds the next day, the group pulled ashore and painstakingly unpacked all the crates, chests, and trunks and laid the specimens out to dry. "How grieved were we to find all our clothes, books, collections, some mathematical instruments, in a word, all our effects, entirely wet and soaked." As they shivered around a smouldering fire in the chilly autumn evening, winds frequently gusted across the prairies blowing the drying specimens into disarray. Maximilian was greatly distressed. "My extensive herbarium had to be laid, on account of the wind, under the shelter of the eminences of a small lateral ravine, which took me the whole day, and yet all the plants became black and mouldy."

The pleasant weather returned as they headed farther south, and they soon found themselves amidst the quiet splendour of wilderness on the cusp of the seasons. Their small and quiet boat allowed them to see herds of bison and elk milling about the shore, drinking, ignoring them as they passed. At night buffaloes bellowed, elks whistled, wolves howled, and owls cried, and great flocks of geese honked as they flew overhead on their way to warmer climates. It was a naturalist's paradise to be lulled to sleep by "the nocturnal chorus of the wilderness." On September 22, Maximilian was inspired to write: "during the whole day we saw many buffaloes and elks, and a skunk on the bank, which escaped us, and a small flock of the whooping crane, one of the finest birds of North America, which was on its flight to warmer regions. The moon shone with extraordinary splendour when we lay [sic] to for the night, while the howling of the wolves and the whistle of the elks were all around." Bodmer devoted time to producing studies of many of the animals they encountered along the river—during the two-week voyage they saw not a single other human. They had floated safely to Fort Union by the end of September, and remained there a month before pushing on south to their ultimate winter destination. By mid-October the first snow covered the land, and many of the leaves had yellowed and dropped to the earth.

While waiting for a more river-worthy boat to be built at Fort Union, Maximilian laid his entire collection out to dry in his room at the fort and went bison hunting. He also secretly obtained an Indian skull for his collection by sneaking it off a burial scaffold on the windy plains. On October 30, they loaded supplies into a somewhat larger boat and pushed off for the final stretch downriver to Fort Clark. The days were short and the temperature not much above freezing, even at midday. Apart from some difficulty hunting enough food to keep the captive bears happy, and one instance where the frisky beasts almost ran to freedom, it was a quick and uneventful journey.

Fort Clark, much to the prince's consternation, proved to be small and cramped, and the three travellers were assigned a hastily constructed, squat little hut in which to spend the winter. "The large crevices in the wood which formed the walls, were plastered up with clay, but the frost soon cracked it, so that the bleak wind penetrated on all sides." It had two drafty rooms, one of which became a workroom for the carpenter. Since no wood had been stored during the summer, each morning a group of men tramped off several miles to the closest stands of poplar and returned with a load of green frozen logs that cracked and hissed in the primitive stone hearth, sending up billowing clouds of noxious smoke. It was an unusually harsh and brutal winter, made worse by the overcrowding in the fort and the primitive conditions. "On the 3rd [of January 1834] the mercury sank into the ball and was frozen.... At night the cold was so intense, that we could not venture to put our hands from our bodies, lest they should be frozen.... Our boots and shoes were frozen so hard in the morning, that we could scarcely put them on; ink, colours, and pencils were perfectly useless" until warmed by the sputtering fire. Still, Bodmer continued his frenetic sketching and painting and Maximilian, when he could, scrawled in his journal.

The naturalist and the painter spent every spare moment visiting the Mandans and Minnetarees or entertaining them in the cramped fort. Maximilian frequently tramped across the frozen prairie to the nearby towns, received visiting chiefs in his single room, and recorded everything he could regarding their winter ceremonies and celebrations. He observed them at work and at play, in celebration and in mourning, working and joking. Bodmer sketched all he could, convincing numerous Indians to pose for endless hours while he laboured on their portraits. One painting of great significance to American ethnology was of the interior of a Mandan lodge, executed with the guidance and suggestions of a local chief and showing in detail almost everything of Mandan material culture. Because the paintings were executed with specific and exact attention to ethnographic detail, they are invaluable as a source of information on native culture and custom before the onslaught of European and American settlers altered forever the delicate balance of prairie life that had flourished for centuries. Maximilian and Bodmer's contribution to the understanding of Plains Indian culture on the cusp of radical change brought on by the fur trade (and later by a series of epidemics) far outstripped their nominal contributions to natural science.

As the winter dragged on, conditions at the fort grew worse; the temperature remained uncharacteristically cold, the wind continued to seep through the gaps in the walls, and the food supply was reduced to starvation rations. Wild game such as bison, elk, and deer, normally a large part of the winter diet, were not readily available. Perhaps the harsh weather had driven them to other areas. Maximilian noted that the hunters brought in about twelve bison, and not much else, the entire winter, to feed a complement of dozens. In the fall he had documented that "the stores of the fort were at this time well filled; there were goods to the value of 15,000 dollars, and, in the loft, from 600 to 800 bushels of maize, which a great number of Norway rats assiduously laboured to reduce." By late winter they were living on a daily weak gruel made from rotting rat-infested corn and, in early March, Maximilian recorded, "our diet consisted almost exclusively of maize boiled in water, which greatly weakened our digestion." In early April the inhabitants of the fort were so hungry and weakened that they feasted upon a partially decomposed corpse of a drowned elk released from the ice in the thaw.

Soon the prince was showing the first signs of the dreaded scurvy. When his leg swelled with blood and the strength was sapped from him, he retreated to his lumpy bed, too ill to rise, and remained there for weeks. "During the tedium of my confinement to bed," he recorded in mid-March, "I was enlivened by the frequent visits of the Indians, and I never neglected to continue my journal, which, from fever and constant weakness, was often very fatiguing." Though many feared he might perish before spring, his indomitable spirit kept him hanging on. He rallied when some Indian children collected wild onion bulbs that were turned into a lumpy broth-like paste. With doses of this primitive but effective antiscorbutic, the coming warmth, and the increasing quantities of fresh meat brought in by the hunters, he was soon recovered enough to get around.*

In mid-April, with spring in full bloom and the snow quickly retreating, Maximilian was ready to leave. The Mackinaw boat was loaded with as many specimens as it could safely carry, and they pushed off into the river, arriving at St. Louis six weeks later. In St. Louis, the trio remained only long enough to construct larger crates for the valuable specimens and larger cages for Maximilian's bears, which had conveniently hibernated through the dreadful winter. They pushed on to New Harmony and finally returned east along the more northern route Maximilian had originally planned, now free from the cholera epidemic. Along the route through Cincinnati, Cleveland, and Buffalo, the prince continued his study of zoology and botany and collection of specimens, while Bodmer painted novel scenes such as Niagara Falls. But this tame land was not inspiring to either of them after their Missouri adventure. They boarded a steamer and chugged down from Albany to New York where they, and the two bewildered bears, sailed to Europe on July 16, two years after arriving in Boston.

Unfortunately, many of the specimens that were to follow Maximilian downriver later in the season were lost when a steamboat caught fire and sank in mid-river. Even with the

---

* It was his hosts at the fort that sickened Maximilian the most during his adventure along the Missouri. Confined in the tiny fort all winter, their lack of cleanliness provoked an uncharacteristic rebuke from the reticent prince—recorded only in his personal journal and edited out for publication. "We are tired of life in this dirty fort to the highest degree," he wrote. "Our daily routine is conducted in such a filthy manner that it nauseates one . . . we now have a filthy attendant and cook named Boileau who wears a fur cap, sits down among us and handles the cups and plates with his disgusting fists after cleaning his nose according to the manner of our peasants. . . . The little boy has a gap in his trousers, both in the front and the back, so that he may relieve himself quickly and without formality on the floor of the room, which happened frequently during meals. . . . In short, our sojourn here was a hard test."

loss of these specimens, Maximilian had in Europe one of the largest and most significant collections from the American West at that time. He had amassed a tremendous quantity of the ethnographic, zoological, botanical, physiological, artistic, and historic material that is now located in museums in the United States and Europe. But it was Bodmer's art and the prince's detailed journal and observations that proved to be the most valuable legacy of their two years on the American frontier.

Apart from his two-volume account of his travels (translated into English and French a few years after its initial publication in German in 1839), he wrote nearly twenty articles devoted to American wildlife in German scientific journals. From his original watercolours, Bodmer produced eighty-one aquatint engravings that were issued separately in the two years following the publication of the book. Unfortunately, the cost of production and the time Bodmer took to complete the engravings hurt sales and the project was not profitable. Like other lavishly illustrated natural history books of the time, such as Audubon's *Birds of America*, the cost of purchasing a first edition exceeded the yearly salary of a skilled labourer.

Although not much of Maximilian's personality is revealed in his descriptive yet carefully neutral text, a little of the man can be gleaned from reading between the lines. His unpretentious curiosity gave him a remarkable ability to breach cultural barriers, to get people talking. He was equally at home discussing the finer points of a plant's natural history with a respected naturalist as he was negotiating with rough and rugged frontiersmen or discussing Blackfoot cosmology with a renowned elder. Maximilian made few enemies and his retiring and pleasant disposition likely opened many doors for him and Bodmer. (Many of the native dignitaries Bodmer painted agreed to the hours of posing only at Maximilian's request). He was also an uncommonly generous employer, looking after the interests of Dreidoppel and Bodmer far beyond his obligations.

The prince was no doubt a complex and intellectual man, intensely interested in the social customs and life patterns of many of the world's peoples in addition to the study of natural history so popular during his time. The reason he was drawn to America in the first place—the abundance of unknown plants and animals and the untamed wildness of the western regions—kept him interested in it all his life, reading, studying, and writing about it for years, although he never returned. Maximilian, who remained a bachelor, spent his final years strolling about his castle and the tame and manicured forests of his estate. Little is known of his personal life. He maintained a lively interest in the scientific developments in natural history, including the work of Charles Darwin, whose *Origin of Species*, published in 1859, radically and permanently altered the intellectual foundations of the study of natural science upon which naturalists of Maximilian's era based their conclusions.

Maximilian and Bodmer maintained a relationship until the prince died in 1867 at the age of eighty-four. Two years before his death they collaborated on an illustrated compendium of North American reptiles and amphibians. Bodmer was then living in Barbizon, France, where he was a successful illustrator and a noted landscape painter. After Maximilian died, Bodmer never again painted an American subject. He died in Paris in 1893. The work from his journey to the American West was definitely the apex of his creative achievement.

Three years after Maximilian returned to Europe, but before his book was published, a smallpox epidemic swept up the Missouri aboard an American Fur Company steamboat. The effect on Plains Indian culture was devastating. The Mandans and the Minnetarees, followed by the Assiniboines, Arikaras, Sioux, and, finally, the Blackfeet, were ravaged by the disease. It wiped out approximately a quarter of the tribal populations, permanently altering the landscape and ending the flourishing of their culture. Many of the people Maximilian had befriended on his journey, and who are depicted in Bodmer's paintings, perished in agony. The Mandans, with whom Maximilian and Bodmer spent more than five months in their final winter, suffered the most and were thought to be extinct by the end of 1837.

The epidemic was the forefront of a wave of change that would see the land transformed— disease decimated the native populations, wildlife was wantonly slaughtered by increasing numbers of traders and travellers, and incoming settlers tore up the turf for farms. Soon roads crossed the prairie and towns grew along the rivers. The great bison herds were so diminished that they could no longer support the peoples who depended upon them for sustenance.

Maximilian and Bodmer made their journey during a narrow band of time when the trading forts provided a contact point between the two cultures and a safe means of travel into the wild land. They saw the American frontier in its full glory, at the zenith of its unique culture with an unaltered natural landscape, and their writing and art form a significant part of the record of that time and place. It was a land, Maximilian remembered wistfully years later, where "a solemn silence prevailed...where Nature, in all her savage grandeur, reigned supreme."

By the 1830s when Maximilian made his journey, the world of the natural historians was already changing. The casual observations and philosophical speculation of aristocratic amateurs like Waterton and Maximilian were becoming obsolete and irrelevant. Scientific study and speculation increasingly became the role of formally trained institutional professionals. The inquisitive aristocrats with their entertaining travel accounts and an ear for a good story have a more direct lineage to the professional collectors who followed them, than to the closet naturalists with their rigorous

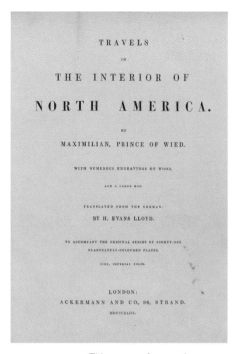

TRAVELS

IN

THE INTERIOR OF

NORTH AMERICA.

BY

MAXIMILIAN, PRINCE OF WIED.

WITH NUMEROUS ENGRAVINGS ON WOOD,

AND A LARGE MAP.

TRANSLATED FROM THE GERMAN,

BY H. EVANS LLOYD.

TO ACCOMPANY THE ORIGINAL SERIES OF EIGHTY-ONE
ELABORATELY-COLOURED PLATES.

SIZE, IMPERIAL FOLIO.

LONDON:
ACKERMANN AND CO., 96, STRAND.
MDCCCXLIII.

Title page of an early English edition of Maximilian's *Travels in the Interior of North America*, the book that accompanied Bodmer's eighty-one colour plates.

scientific proof and their elaborate system of classification. But the professional collectors didn't have the luxury to peruse the natural world according to their interest. They were much more focused on the task of collecting specimens of anything new or unidentified. They would not have spent the time talking to the native peoples and recording their customs as Maximilian did—they could not have afforded to.

PART THREE

Professional Collectors of the Golden Age

BY THE 1830S, A BROADER RANGE OF people in all levels of society began to enjoy and study natural history, which rose in importance and popularity as the century progressed. Particularly in Britain and, to a lesser extent, in the United States and Canada, thousands of people, both men and women and from all social classes, became amateur natural historians (Germany and continental Europe were in a period of insular conservatism following the Napoleonic wars). Almost every town boasted its own natural history society, of which anyone educated was a member. Several societies such as the American Philosophical Society and the Academy of Natural Sciences of Philadelphia emerged as preeminent institutions in the United States. The societies organized outings to collect local species of plants, animals, and insects, and arranged social gatherings where various aspects of natural history were the topics of discussion and debate. To go "botanizing" was a common pastime that fit nicely with the Victorian belief that pure leisure was somehow suspect and wasteful, and that it was morally superior to be advancing one's knowledge of the world. Natural history museums, botanical gardens, zoos, and aquariums were constructed in most cities; new books on natural history rolled off the presses regularly; and most newspapers ran natural history columns.

The dramatic rise in interest in the natural world was directly linked to natural theology—the belief that evidence of God could be found in the world he created. Natural theology, according to Lynn Barber, "made the study of natural history not only respectable, but almost a pious duty, and there was nothing the Victorians liked so much as a duty ... the purpose of studying Nature was to approach a closer knowledge of God." The divine urging to study and understand nature was a heady incentive for the average person to pursue natural history as a hobby.

Linnaeus and his classification system paved the way for natural theology and the natural history craze from the 1830s to the 1860s. By developing his great hierarchy of life he provided a template for collectors to fill. Once an accepted system for classifying species was in place, almost anyone could participate in the great hunt and expect to be published or achieve relative fame by being associated with the species that they discovered. Not only could a layman understand the basic principles behind this line of scientific reasoning, but he or she could hope to contribute something useful. Any Sunday bug hunter or seaside beach roamer might come across something new. Barber has pointed out that it was likely the lack of new theoretical scientific advancements in the mid-nineteenth century that contributed to natural history's popularity. There were no new complex ideas, and individuals could devote themselves to collecting and describing, comfortable in the knowledge that they were contributing a small piece to the great puzzle of life. Although many naturalists knew that the classification of species within an artificial hierarchy was not the ultimate objective of scientific inquiry, with the lack of contradictory theories in the mid-nineteenth century, classification became the prime objective of naturalists to the exclusion of other lines of reasoning.

Barber writes that "the facts that naturalists were most concerned with were those bearing on the description and classification of species. Finding new species was the highest goal to which they aspired; squabbling about names and priority was an occupational disease; describing, arranging and collecting ever more and more species was the business to which they devoted every minute of their working lives." Once a species was named, it was believed to be static and distinct from all others; and a certain degree of immortality could be achieved by affixing a name to a species since they were often named after the discoverer. Modern biologists have a much more fluid view of species, seeing them as changeable over distance and time—taxonomy and classification is now used mostly to give meaning by association. Knowing a species' name helps to understand its relationship to other similar organisms, but does not define it forever.

When most of the local species in Europe and the eastern United States had been collected and catalogued, the savants of the various scientific societies sent collectors on expeditions to distant and exotic lands—in the United States this merely meant travelling west into the scientifically unexplored lands on the far side of the Mississippi River. Like their earlier counterparts, these travelling naturalists wrote books that, in addition to describing the new species they had discovered, presented a romantic and fascinating view of the natural world that was a powerful stimulant to the imagination. New species from ever more remote and wild corners of the globe appeared with enough regularity to keep the public interested. Natural history books became a genre in themselves and enjoyed a wide readership. Barber has observed that an eager and interested public read voraciously anything new in popular natural history—which often meant the books of the scientific travellers. "Books on the subject," she wrote, "were only marginally less popular than novels of Dickens."

There was also a great market for collectors to sell their specimens to wealthy connoisseurs. Rather than being an abstract science for theorists, natural history was tactile and aesthetic. Many specimens were beautiful and interesting objects regardless of their scientific value and became de rigueur in the cabinets of the curious. Properly displayed, a collection of exotic birds, plants, or shells could enliven a sober drawing room. One's knowledge and learning could be displayed in an aquarium, a fern-case, or in a butterfly or beetle cabinet. A shell or mineral collection could be mounted on a wall, and a side table could be adorned with stuffed amphibians or snakes. The newest and most exotic specimens bestowed the greatest prestige and commanded the highest prices.

Scientific institutions also commissioned collectors to seek exotic plants and animals, offering funding in exchange for duplicate copies of anything they collected. Many field naturalists earned their living selling duplicate specimens from their collections. The more distant the location and the more detailed the description of how, and under what circumstances, a specimen was found increased its value.

It was throughout this period that the closet and field naturalists diverged so completely that they were essentially separate entities. The field naturalists of this era were professionals, not scientists or scholars at universities or museums, but professional collectors, dedicated to scouring the remotest regions with the specific task of bringing back everything new they could find. They all understood the principles of taxonomy, had a reasonable grounding in botany and zoology, and seemed willing to undergo great deprivation in the course of their duties. The closet naturalists were formally educated specialists, often of aristocratic descent or from families of great wealth and prestige, who laboured in museums or universities. Some naturalists tried to straddle both worlds, but very few were successful. Although the distinction was less pronounced in the United States, particularly regarding the social class of the individual, it was still difficult for a collector to join the ranks of the more formally trained laboratory naturalists.

The Royal Horticultural Society sent David Douglas on several collecting expeditions to North America beginning in the mid-1820s. As a professional collector, funded and salaried by his patron, he was searching specifically for plants that could be cultivated in England. Douglas, however, went far beyond his mandate and collected hundreds of new species of plants. He wrote detailed descriptions of them, including information about the climate in which they thrived and the type of soil in which they typically grew. He tried to classify them, but much of his work was incorrect and was renamed after his return. The wealthy beneficiaries of his dutiful collecting were nevertheless pleased with the multitude of new ornamental plants for their gardens. Although Douglas was well regarded as a collector by institutional scientists, he lacked the credentials and contacts to secure a scientific position at a museum or university. To compound his financial woes, his literary skills did not match his botanical ones, and he failed to turn his journal into a book, one of the prime sources of income for field naturalists during the golden age.

Like Douglas, John Kirk Townsend's great cross-continental trip in the 1830s was funded by institutions eager for new specimens from remote regions. He excelled as an ornithological collector, returning from the American West with dozens of new bird species. The reception of his descriptive work within the scientific establishment, however, was only lukewarm. It was on the verge of being too imprecise for the time. Later scientists dismissed him as a mere collector and stuffer of specimens, a quaint sentimental amateur who referred to birds as "feathered songsters" and rhapsodized about the glory of Nature without trying to understand it. As a pious Quaker, he was very much a believer in natural theology.

Natural theology was also likely a strong motivation for John Richardson, a deeply religious Presbyterian who began his career in the Royal Navy as a surgeon during the Napoleonic wars. Enlisting as a surgeon/naturalist in the navy may have been the only other way by which someone of modest means could earn a living while pursuing an interest in natural history. After the war Richardson had the good fortune to be selected by the navy for an overland expedition to the Far North of North America. Although the main objective of the expedition was geographical, he was able to devote a considerable amount of time to collecting and studying arctic and subarctic species. He had little formal training, but Richardson was one of the few professional collectors who was later accepted into the institutional scientific community. His distinguished military service and medical career likely helped turn his reputation as a collector into a reputation as a laboratory naturalist by lending credibility to his scientific career. Unlike some of his counterparts, he generally wrote in a sober and scholarly tone, the first audience for his writing being his superior officers in the navy.

Richardson was fortunate that his career coincided with the heyday of natural history in the mid-nineteenth century. The foundation of the collecting craze however—natural theology—would be dealt a mortal blow just before his death in 1865. Other later travelling naturalists would have to deal with a new set of principles, less absolute and certain, that governed the world.

CHAPTER FIVE

David Douglas

Such are the not unfrequent disasters attending such undertakings.
On the whole I have been fortunate, for considering the nature and extent of
the Country I have passed over (now eight years here) and the circumstances
under which I travelled, my accidents have been few.
—DAVID DOUGLAS,
Journal of North American Travels

David Douglas
(1799–1834), the Scottish
botanist who scoured the
Pacific Northwest of North
America for new plant
specimens for the Royal
Horticultural Society.

In 1834, in a forest in Hawaii, the thirty-five-year-old Scottish botanist David Douglas tumbled into a pit containing a wild bull and was gored to death. He had spent nearly a decade wandering and studying the flora and fauna of the Pacific coast of North America, from California to British Columbia, and was regarded as one of the great botanical and horticultural collectors of the era.

In his short career he had amassed a considerable repertoire of plants and animals, and had brought many from America to Britain and Europe for cultivation. He was originally sent to North America under the auspices of the Horticultural Society of London (later the Royal Horticultural Society), founded in 1804 with the general objective of encouraging and advancing the study and practice of the cultivation of plants new to the British Isles. One of the society's primary activities was to promote and fund collecting expeditions to remote regions of the globe where exotic plants were believed to grow. Requisite characteristics for a collector were a solid foundation in practical botany and a willingness to undergo extreme hardship and danger in pursuit of the society's lofty objectives. David Douglas was just such a man.

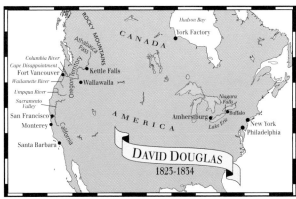

David Douglas's roamings in North America, 1823–1834.

Short, with large eyes, thinning hair, and a serious introverted countenance, his appearance reflected his personality. Douglas's 1947 biographer, George Harvey, notes that he was reputedly somewhat dour and single-minded, irascible and stubborn, driven by his strong will to unflagging lengths and victimized by almost comically severe deprivations in pursuit of his botanical quest. Douglas's own journal reveals a person who was both imprudent and impatient. When his Indian guides refused to lead him up a dangerous mountain in the Pacific Northwest, he chastised them for cowardice and set off alone, and when he was a guest of the Hudson's Bay Company, he provoked a trader into challenging him to a duel (and then declined to fight).

Douglas was born the second son in a humble family in the town of Scone, near Perth, Scotland, in 1799, the year Alexander von Humboldt sailed from Europe on his five-year expedition to South America. As a youth he proved to be so stubborn and ill-tempered that his mother sent him away for schooling at the tender age of three. Even his passion for roaming the open countryside and his interest in plants and animals could not keep him in school beyond the age of ten, however, and it was only a remarkable streak of good luck that enabled him to pursue his interest in nature. A position was available as an apprentice gardener at the estate of the Earl of Mansfield at Scone Palace, and Douglas's father, a stonemason, was acquainted with the head gardener. Douglas excelled as a gardener. He devoted himself thoroughly to his duties and persuaded the head gardener to tutor him in the rudiments of botany. Through a regimen of self-study, Douglas eventually became knowledgeable enough to secure a position at the prestigious Botanical Gardens in Glasgow.

The energetic youth began his duties at the gardens just as the respected botanist William Hooker (later the director of the Kew Gardens) assumed the professorship of botany at the University of Glasgow. The two became close friends, and Hooker brought the eager and diligent undergardener on many rambles in the highlands and islands while preparing *Flora Scotica*. It was on these long excursions across soggy moors, along the stony shores of the lochs, and up the windswept promontories of the islands, where conditions were primitive and food was simple, that Hooker came to appreciate Douglas's dedication to the study of the natural world. "His great activity," Hooker wrote, "undaunted courage, singular abstemiousness, and energetic zeal at once pointed him out as an individual eminently calculated to do himself credit as a scientific traveler." When Joseph Sabine, secretary of the Horticultural Society of London, sought a recommendation for a scientific collector in 1823, Hooker put forward Douglas's name, and the twenty-four-year-old began preparing for his first trip abroad—to North America, the continent where he would spend the better part of the remainder of his life.

When he arrived in New York on his first assignment, Douglas was slightly disappointed that he had been sent into the relative civilization of the eastern United States, instead of to the wilds of China, where the Horticultural Society had originally planned to send him. He was in America to acquire, by the cheapest means possible, the latest examples of American fruit and other interesting plants that might be cultivated in England. American horticulture was primarily focused on plants with a practical application, while European horticulturists favoured ornamental plants. Most of the wild plants of eastern North America had long been discovered and classified by early naturalists such as John and

Abies Douglasii

Douglas Fir   Sapin de Douglas.

Abies Douglasii—the Douglas Fir—was a distinctive tree Douglas encountered throughout his wanderings in the Pacific Northwest, from northern California to British Columbia. He described it as "one of the most striking and truly graceful objects in Nature."

DOUGLAS' SQUIRREL

Douglas first encountered this distinctive species of squirrel near the mouth of the Columbia River. John Bachman, Audubon's collaborator on *Quadrupeds of North America*, originally intended to name the species after John Kirk Townsend, who had furnished him with a specimen. Bachman learned, however, that several years earlier, in 1836, John Edward Gray of the British Museum had already named the species after Douglas.

PI. IV.

Sinclair lith.

Quercus Douglasii

Douglas's Oak.　　　　*Chêne de Douglas.*

Quercus Douglasii, Douglas's Oak, is one of the many species of plants that Douglas avidly collected during his tenure in North America.

Pl. CXIV.

Pinus Lambertiana.

The quest for *Pinus lambertiana*, the Gigantic Pine, was Douglas's greatest adventure. One fallen specimen was 215 feet in length and 57 feet 9 inches in circumference three feet from where it would have been rooted to the ground. Douglas wrote that these trees "are remarkably strait; bark uncommonly smooth for such large timber, of a whitish or light brown colour, and yields a great quantity of gum of a bright amber colour. The large trees are destitute of branches, generally for two-thirds the length of the tree; branches pendulous, and the cones hanging from their points like small sugar-loaves in a grocer's shop."

William Bartram, Thomas Nuttall, and Andre Michaux. Douglas would have to content himself with what was known to science, but new to British gardeners.

His first voyage across the Atlantic was an appalling fifty-nine-day nightmare in which storms tossed the vessel mercilessly and water and food were strictly rationed. Even tobacco had to be conserved—it was first chewed, and then re-dried and smoked in pipes. When he arrived in New York Douglas was sickly, bedraggled, and pale, and immigration officials refused him entry until he had purchased new clothes and cleaned himself up. Nevertheless, he was immediately struck with the wild and luxuriant vegetation on Staten Island, and was particularly impressed with the trees, "the oaks and maples growing spontaneously."

For the next several days, two American members of the Horticultural Society took him around the city's markets and orchards along the Hudson River, and he collected flowers in a nearby swamp. But even then, New York was a busy, chaotic, and dirty place, where trash was flung in the gutters and the civic sanitary policy consisted of a legion of scavenging pigs. Although Douglas was impressed with the plump fruits dangling from trees in the flourishing orchards, New York was not the place for a quiet country lad whose inclinations led him toward the productions of nature rather the productions of man. He rode the stage and steamer to Philadelphia, which was much more to his liking, with its orderly, clean streets, quiet and pious people, and Quaker heritage. With sixty thousand inhabitants, Philadelphia was only half as large as New York.

He toured Philadelphia's botanical collections, paying particular attention to the specimens Lewis and Clark had brought back from their cross-continental trek several decades earlier, and strolled through Bartram's wonderful herbarium along the Schuylkill River. It was here that he met the noted Harvard botanist Thomas Nuttall, who had by this time gone on extensive forays to collect plants along the Missouri River and in the Southwest, and would later cross the continent to the Pacific with John Townsend. Nuttall and Douglas had much in common, including a devotion to science so extreme that it set them apart from most of society. Both seemed to prefer the companionship of plants over people.

After his meeting with Nuttall, where he may have been inspired by the older man's myopic interest in the vegetable world, Douglas travelled north to Albany, Rochester, Buffalo, and, finally, to Amherstburg, which he called the "Eden of Upper Canada" for its profuse orchards of apples, pears, plums, peaches, and grapes. He studied plants in the wild as often as he could, but his duties kept him fairly busy. During a celebration of the grand opening of the Erie Canal in Albany, for example, when the "town was all in an uproar—firing of guns, music, etc.," Douglas remained in his hotel room arranging his specimens and updating his journal.

When the leaves changed colour and began to drop from the trees, Douglas boarded a ship and returned to London, arriving in early January 1824. His journey was considered a success by his patrons, for he had provided them with a huge sampling of American cultivated plants and had lived very frugally. He had met and discussed botany with most of the leading horticulturists, as well as scientific botanists, and had visited many of the most prominent gardens and nurseries, where he learned collecting techniques, and was exposed to new ideas. Douglas devoted the six months after his return to cultivating and organizing the seeds and plants he had brought back with him. He proved to be very shy and retiring, always preferring the study of his specimens to the company of people. After meeting with Douglas to discuss his American travels, the president of the Horticultural Society, Thomas Andrew Knight, noted that he was "the shyest being almost that I ever saw." After several months, Douglas was commissioned for another botanical expedition to America, this time to the distant, wild, and uncharted Pacific coast.[*]

The vast extent of the territory and the scarcity of botanical and zoological knowledge was an enticing prospect for a young man like Douglas, who chafed at the constraints of polite society and preferred to lose himself wandering far from cities and towns. He immediately accepted the offer and was no doubt pleased that he was assured the protection and patronage of the Hudson's Bay Company, which controlled the only settlements and employed virtually the only white people in the entire territory west of the Rockies from California to Alaska. Lest he anticipate a luxurious and safe journey, however, the company warned that "he will however find the fare of the country rather coarse and be subject to some privations." It was a warning that proved to be one of the greatest understatements in Douglas's life.

By July 1824, he was aboard the Hudson's Bay Company's annual supply ship bound for the Columbia River on the Pacific coast of North America. "I stood on deck looking on the rocky shores of Cornwall, burnished with the splendour of a setting sun—a noble scene. By degrees the goddess of night threw her veil over it, and my delightful view of happy England closed—probably closed for ever!" There was good reason for his melancholy musings. Although he never would have passed up the opportunity for such a grand adventure, the fates of other collectors recently sent out by the Horticultural Society could not have been far from his mind. Out of three, one had died in Africa, and another became ill in Bengal and China and withered away shortly after his return. Only one had somehow survived his journey to Asia.

[*] Although the region had been visited by naturalists before, such as David Nelson and William Anderson, who had sailed with James Cook in 1778, Archibald Menzies, who had sailed with George Vancouver between 1792 and 1794, and various members of the Lewis and Clark expedition of 1804–06, none were exhaustive or conclusive in their studies and served only to whet the appetite of the scientific community.

The tedium of the long voyage was enlivened by the companionship of an old school acquaintance from Glasgow University, John Scouler, who was the ship's surgeon and naturalist. Douglas and Scouler were similarly in thrall to the wonders of nature. During the six weeks crossing the Atlantic to Rio de Janeiro, the two naturalists captured jellyfish, birds, sea turtles, and flying fish. And during the two-week layover in Rio, they ventured ashore just long enough to timorously explore the fringes of the vast forest. Among their many treasures was a new species of orchid that Joseph Sabine later named *Gesneria Douglasii*, in commemoration of its first introduction to science. Nearing the treacherous and storm-shrouded Cape Horn, the giddy duo scooped up immense coils of seaweed that were swirling just beneath the surface of the water. The seaweed was, Douglas recorded with awe, sixty feet in length and its slimy roots were home to what Scouler called "a menagerie of marine animals."

Ten days of turbulent storm-lashed seas followed as they rounded the Cape, yet even here, after a succession of heart-stopping nights where no one could sleep in peace with the weight of possible annihilation upon them, Douglas speculated on the vegetation of the bleak and windswept rocks. "As to the geography of plants," he wrote, "it would be an interesting point to compare those found on the South extremities of the Southern continent with the very extensive and beautiful Flora of the northern in similar Latitudes. Gladly would I spend a few days on the shores of Tierra Del Fuego—many novelties are there no doubt, that for the present must be laid aside."

After a calm and pleasant cruise of several months north along the coast and a brief stop on the Galapagos Islands (the pristine ecosystem yet to be visited by Charles Darwin), the ship neared the mouth of the Columbia River. A tremendous storm spun the vessel, wind tore at the rigging, and the deck was buffeted by the foam-flecked spume of a wicked sea. The ship laid to and dared not approach the wild shore. "We were

Fort Vancouver along the Columbia River was the principal outpost of the Hudson's Bay Company in Oregon and Douglas's base for many years.

tossed and driven about in this condition for six weeks," Douglas wrote, "...we experienced the furious hurricanes of North-West America in the fullest extent a thousand times worse than those of the noted Cape Horn." A heavy fog wreathed the coast, and occasionally the lush forest appeared green and luxuriant, through the gray swirling mist. After months aboard ship, Douglas ached to set foot on shore. Just the sight of the forest made him proclaim that it was "one of the happy moments of my life."

On April 9, 1825, after eight and a half months at sea, Douglas was set ashore near Cape Disappointment (the ship still could not navigate up the river because of the fog) and he immediately spied a new plant sprouting from the muck along the river. "On stepping on the shore *Gaultheria shallon* [salal] was the first plant I took in my hands. So pleased was I that I could see scarcely anything but it." It was an auspicious beginning.

The chief factor of the Hudson's Bay Company's Pacific operations was John McLoughlin, a regal individual with piercing eyes and a great mane of white hair, who looked more like a tribal medicine man than a British gentleman. It so happened that he was visiting a small trading fort on the coast and warmly welcomed Douglas as he disembarked; McLoughlin "received me with much kindness. I showed him my instructions and informed him verbally of the object of my voyage, and talked over my pursuit. In the most frank and handsome manner he assured me that everything in his power would be done to promote the views of the Society."

In a great canoe, McLoughlin transported Douglas the seventy or so miles up the broad forest-lined river to Fort Vancouver, a large primitive palisade arranged on a patch of flat land near the confluence of the Willamette and Columbia Rivers. He offered Douglas the assistance of any of his employees in the interior and agreed that Douglas could accompany trading or trapping expeditions into the hinterland. Douglas happily made his base at Fort Vancouver, where up to several hundred English-speaking traders could be found at any time. "The scenery round this place is sublimely grand," he wrote, "lofty, well wooded hills, mountains covered with perpetual snow, extensive natural meadows, and plains of deep, fertile, alluvial deposit, covered with a rich sward of grass, and a profusion of flowering plants." He first settled himself into a tent within the walls of the fort, but soon upgraded to a deerskin lodge and, still later, to a cedar-bark hut.

During his first few weeks in the country, Douglas strolled delightedly through stands of evergreens that dwarfed anything he had ever seen. He came upon a grove of what would later be named the Douglas fir and was in awe. A fallen specimen stretched 227 feet along the ground and was 48 feet in circumference. It was, he wrote, "one of the most striking and truly graceful objects in Nature." Douglas predicted the future value of the Douglas fir to the forestry industry when he noted their uniform size, density, and quality of wood. All manner of evergreens flourished along the Pacific coast, and, in addition to the Douglas fir, Douglas collected and classified dozens of species including the Sitka spruce and the sugar pine. "You will begin to think that I manufacture Pines at my pleasure," he wrote in a letter to Hooker. England has only three native species of conifer: the yew, Scots pine, and juniper. Douglas's samples sent to the Horticultural Society were the first of many conifers that now grow in England. With their great variation in size, shape, colour, and interesting needles and cones, North American conifers were ideally suited to English ornamental gardens of the mid-nineteenth century.

Douglas spent the first summer reasonably close to Fort Vancouver, accompanying traders on their missions to local Indian tribes, through the lush and dripping foliage. It took a while, however, until he was comfortable sleeping under his canoe or under a tree. Noting that people in England "shudder" at the idea of sleeping with open windows, he was pleased when he acquired comfortable acceptance of the custom of Oregon. "Each individual takes his blanket and with all the complacency of mind that can be imagined throws himself on the sand or under a bush just as if he were going to bed." Soon, he was able to proudly write that "comfort seems superfluity."

And good it was that primitive conditions agreed with Douglas to such an extent, for during the next several years he had to endure hardships the most fertile mind could never have envisioned. "The luxury of a night's sleep on a bed of pine branches," he later wrote, "can only be appreciated by those who have experienced a route over a barren plain, scorched by the sun, or fatigued by groping their way through a thick forest, crossing gullies, dead wood, lakes, stones, etc." Douglas seemed to take a perverse pleasure in relating the woeful and deplorable conditions under which he laboured. "Indeed so much worn out was I three times by fatigue and hunger that twice I crawled, for I could hardly walk, to a small abandoned hut. I had in my knapsack one biscuit...."

On one horrible trip from Fort Vancouver down the Columbia to the coast in the summer, he stabbed his knee with a rusty packing nail and it became infected and badly inflamed, requiring three weeks to heal. Several weeks later the joint remained stiff and painful. Douglas pushed on over a portage during a tremendous rainstorm. The detritus-laden track wound over mud-slicked roots, slippery stumps, and rocks. Walking became difficult as his knee stiffened further and soon he was unable to walk; he was stormbound for two days, lying on the damp forest floor while hail and rain pummelled the ground. He could only light a tiny smouldering fire and had no food other than some berries and roots, and a piece of chocolate. He became "so broken down with fatigue and starvation, and my knee so much worse, that I could not stir out for the whole of the day." Fortunately he shot two ducks the next day and was rescued soon after by a small band of Indians. He recuperated at their camp for several days before setting out to return to Fort Vancouver.

On another journey, Douglas was so fatigued from portaging and walking through tangled underbrush in drenching rain without food that he could scarcely muster the energy to cook his dinner of boiled partridges. His two native guides were so exhausted that they ate a meagre meal, rolled in their blankets, and immediately fell asleep. "Before my birds were cooked," Douglas related, "Morpheus seized me also; I awoke at daybreak and beheld my supper burned to ashes and three holes in the bottom of my kettle." Undaunted, he emptied his tinderbox and boiled up some tea, "the monarch of all food after fatiguing journeys." Salmon—plump, pink, and delicious whether fresh or smoked—was one of his most reliable staples and he learned to catch them with nets almost anywhere in the Oregon Territory or purchased them from the natives. Douglas found salmon particularly tasty "cooked under the shade of a lordly pine or rocky dell far removed from the abodes of civilized life."

The rain in the early summer nearly ruined his botanical specimens, but nevertheless he returned to Fort Vancouver in August "richly laden with many treasures." In less than six months he had travelled over two thousand miles by foot and canoe and had collected an astonishing 499 species of plants. He had gathered between twelve and twenty-four specimens of each species and carefully preserved each in special botanical paper brought from England. He wrote a detailed description of each one and classified them as best he could without access to reference books. Although not all his specimens proved new to science, a good number certainly were. Trained as a horticulturist and sponsored by the Horticultural Society, Douglas was primarily interested in plants that could be cultivated in England in the gardens of the wealthy, who vied with one another for rare, new, and exotic plants. The Horticultural Society received the bulk of its financial support from wealthy individual patrons, and these patrons received many of the new plants for their gardens before they became generally available.

Douglas described hundreds of plants in his journal, such as the *Ribes sanguineum* with "flowers pink or rose colour, inside of the petals white, anthers white in long racemes.... This exceedingly handsome plant is abundant on the rocky shores of the Columbia and its branches, and in such places produces great profusion of flowers but little fruit." Most of his descriptions are in such a dense format, describing the minutiae of a plant's appearance and location and distribution, that reading about them is a tedious task. Douglas was a dedicated explorer, willing to undergo great hardships in pursuit of his objective, but his writing was not equal to his endurance. Nothing of William Bartram's descriptive poetry ever found its way into Douglas's journal. His eloquence increased only when describing his suffering and hardship.

During the winter Douglas remained close to Fort Vancouver. Since most plants were then dead or dormant, he spent his time reading, socializing at the fort, and copying out his journal. He packed and labelled boxes of specimens and seeds, including eight bundles collected on the voyage to the Columbia and sixteen bundles from Oregon. He also packed a massive chest with seeds, so that the plants could be reproduced in England, and shipped them on a Hudson's Bay Company vessel.

The winter of 1825–26 was miserable with rain and fog. "On the 24th December," Douglas wrote, "the rain fell in such torrents, without the least intermission, that my little hut of *Thuya* bark, which stood in a rather low situation, was completely inundated; 14 inches of water was in it." By New Year's he was in a despondent state. "Commencing a year in such a far removed corner of the earth, where I am nearly destitute of civilized society, there is some scope for reflection. . . . I am now here, and God only knows where I may be next. In all probability, if a change does not take place, I will probably be consigned to the tomb." That March it rained for twenty days without a break.

At the end of March, Douglas accompanied a fur brigade inland to the Spokane River and Kettle Falls. He dispensed with extra clothing and personal items and chose instead to haul along an astonishing 102-pound ream of botanical drying paper to protect any new species he might encounter. Through days of miserable rain and upriver paddling the brigade pressed on to Kettle Falls. The scenery was "grand beyond description, the high mountains in the neighbourhood which are for the most part covered in pines of several species, some of which grow to an enormous size, are all loaded with snow; the rainbow from the vapour of the agitated water, which rushes with furious rapidity over shattered rocks and through deep caverns producing an agreeable although at the same time a somewhat melancholy echo through the thick wooded valley; the reflections from the snow on the mountains, together with the vivid green of the gigantic pines, form a contrast of rural grandeur that can scarcely be surpassed."

The world was still and quiet in the wake of a spring snowfall. Branches of evergreens swayed with the weight of great globs of heavy snow. The smaller bushes and grasses were stooped under the burden and the trunks of trees and the stalks of bushes were crusted with windblown powder. The forest was a latticework of white and gray and brown, intermingling with the shadows, a forest of giant powdered matchsticks. Not a breath of wind was in the air, but as he pushed the burdened branches aside, snow fell silently from above, dislodged from its precarious perch, landing on his head, running down his neck, and soaking his clothes as it melted in the midday spring sun. As the brigade neared Kettle Falls, however, Douglas noted that the climate became drier and vegetation became more sparse. Along the river now grew sagebrush, and Douglas found and collected sixteen different varieties.

Upstream of Kettle Falls, the land was "destitute of timber. Dry gravelly and rocky soils, with extensive plains.... The whole herbage very different indeed from the vegetation on the coast." He was, nevertheless, able to collect several species of new shrubs "which were perfectly unknown." As he pressed on north, the spring sun was more frequent and soon it was very hot and dry, but the streams remained exceedingly cold. Douglas had to ford several of them, holding his precious specimens above his head as he waded, with benumbed legs, through the current. In June the sun blazed hot and the ground was dry and dusty. By this time, he had returned south to Wallawalla and decided to venture still farther south into the Blue Mountains.

In the mountains, Douglas spied an especially steep and forbidding peak and determined to climb to the summit. His native guides, however, being far more pragmatic, refused to accompany him, but agreed to wait in the valley for him to return. Douglas laboured upward alone from the hot valley bottom to where the snow still lay. Slowly, but surely, he ascended to the windswept peak, where he was treated to a view of the surrounding valleys that was "extensive and grand." But he was only able to enjoy it briefly because, with alarming speed, "the mountain was enveloped in dense black cloud." A vicious storm rattled the peak with blasts of lightning crackling all around "as if the heavens were in a blaze." The wind "was whistling through the low stunted dead pines accompanied by the merciless cutting hail." He realized that his "situation was not a desirable one for spending the night," and hastily retraced his steps down the face of the mountain, continually buffeted by the storm. By the time he reached the bottom he was shivering and wet, but had no dry clothes to change into; he might have died if his guides hadn't stoked a fire. Douglas spent a miserable night rolled in his blanket under a large pine. Around midnight he tried to get up and was unable to walk because of stiff knee joints. "If I have any zeal," he wrote, "for once and the first time it began to cool."

After several more months of wandering the grassy hills of the hot barren and dusty interior lowlands, he made his weary way back to Fort Vancouver in August, bedraggled and forlorn. When he crawled out of his canoe and stumbled to the fort, he was met with stares of horror and immediate inquiries. With clothes in tatters, beard wild and hair capped in a dirty straw hat, shoeless, scrawny, and limping, Douglas was presumed to be, as he noted—perhaps with a hint of pride—the sole survivor of a great calamity, and had somehow "escap[ed] from the gates of death."

Douglas's journal is laden with such a litany of woeful misadventures that it is impossible to relate them all. He was frequently laid up ill or recuperating for days, or even weeks, at a time from wounded feet, infected cuts, fevers, chills, afflictions of the eyes, swollen joints, or near starvation. On one occasion, after days of punishing travel without adequate water, food, or sleep, he collapsed on the floor of an "Indian Hall" in dire need of rest, "but was very shortly afterwards roused from my slumber by an indescribable herd of fleas." When he stumbled outside "to sleep among the bushes; the annoyance of two species of ants, one very large, black, ¾ of an inch long, and a small red one, rendered it worse, so this night I did not sleep and gladly hailed the returning day."

While he was in the interior, the fine sands and dusts irritated his eyes until they were bloodshot and watery. His vision grew dim, so he could only read or write early in the morning. And one evening a "herd of rats" scurried into his chamber, devoured many of his precious seeds, and began dragging off his personal toiletries. He was awakened when one beast overstepped the bounds of propriety by tugging at the inkstand near his bed. Douglas quietly grasped his pistol, "which is my night companion as well as day," and with a well-aimed shot, blasted it dead. In his tally of specimens forwarded to England later that year was listed "one curious rat."

So great were Douglas's deprivations and sufferings that even he, upon glancing over his journal, felt compelled to write "when my people in England are made acquainted with my travels, they may perhaps think I have told them nothing but my miseries. That may be correct, but I now know that such objects as I am in quest of are not obtained without a share of labour, anxiety of mind, and sometimes risk of personal safety."

Douglas's suffering was perhaps most extreme on a journey to the Umpqua River, far to the south, in search of a monstrous pine with eighteen-inch cones and seeds that were sweet when cooked and a great treat to the local people. He wrote to his friend Hooker about his great goal. "I rejoice to tell you of a new species of *Pinus*, the most princely of the genus, perhaps even the grandest specimen of vegetation." He joined a fur brigade for part of the journey, slogging through bramble-infested underbrush, and then elected to branch off on his own. His journey began with a storm. "Last night was one of the most dreadful I ever witnessed," he related on September 25, 1826. "The rain, driven by the violence of the wind, rendered it impossible for me to keep any fire, and to add misery to my affliction my tent was blown down at midnight.... Every ten or fifteen minutes immense trees falling produced a crash as if the earth was cleaving asunder.... My poor horses were unable to endure the violence of the storm without craving of me protection, which they did by hanging their heads over me and neighing." The next morning was cold and damp, and Douglas, not surprisingly, was "seized with a severe headache and pain in the stomach, with giddiness and dimness of sight."

A few days later he stumbled while hunting and slid down a steep rocky ravine, banged his head, bruised his chest, and lay stunned and unconscious at the bottom for five hours until a passing band of Indians revived him and helped him back to his camp. As a treatment, he bled himself in the left foot and then, after a fitful sleep, he purged himself of the lingering ill-effects with a morning dive into a freezing river. Apparently, his condition improved, though one wonders how it possibly could have been so. He pushed on in his quest for the "much-wished-for Pine." He purchased some dried salmon and got directions from another native man he encountered as he stumbled about the forest. Within an hour had reached his "most beautiful and immensely large tree"; the sugar pine, as it is now known, was his great prize. One fallen specimen was 215 feet in length and 57 feet 9 inches in circumference three feet above where it would have been rooted to the ground.

It was a monster, as were the others in the vicinity. Douglas recorded that, in general, the species now known as *Pinus lambertiana*, the largest of the ninety-six species of pine, "are remarkably strait; bark uncommonly smooth for such large timber, of a whitish or light brown colour, and yields a great quantity of gum of a bright amber colour. The large trees are destitute of branches, generally for two-thirds the length of the tree; branches pendulous, and the cones hanging from their points like small sugar-loaves in a grocer's shop." Unable to climb to such vast heights, Douglas began firing his rifle to dislodge several giant cones. Unfortunately his activity drew the attention of a band of ten heavily armed natives, and it was only after promising them some tobacco that he was able to flee back to his camp with three large cones. But he was to have no rest. Early the next morning three grizzly bears attacked his camp and ravaged his pack for food. He shot two of them before the third fled.

Exhausted and nervous, Douglas rushed to rejoin the fur traders who were camped several days travel away. He then set off to Fort Vancouver with them. Given Douglas's luck, it should be no surprise that even this journey proved to be a disaster. After stumbling through the underbrush and going hungry for several days, he and the others quarrelled about their location. "The fact plainly is this," he recorded, "all hungry and no means of cooking a little of our stock; travelled thirty-three miles, drenched and bleached with rain and sleet, chilled with a piercing north wind; and then to finish the day experienced the cooling, comfortless consolation of lying down wet without supper or fire. On such occasions I am very liable to become fretful." After reaching Fort Vancouver in mid-November, Douglas rested for only a few days before venturing off on one final expedition before winter set in. He almost starved on the return journey. His only food was a chunk of salmon caught during the spawning season. "When dried," he wrote, "it resembles rotten dry pine-bark. Having nothing but this to subsist on, I was seized with a most violent diarrhea which reduced me in four days unable to walk." After he struggled back to Fort Vancouver, he spent the next few months preparing to leave the country the following March with the eastbound fur brigade.

Although he was seemingly impervious to deprivation and suffering, the hardened Scot was overcome with emotion when he received letters from home. Letters "were grasped greedily and eagerly broken open.... There is a sensation felt on receiving news after such a long silence, and in such a remote corner of the globe more easily felt than described." He stayed up all night reading each letter again and again until he had it memorized. Tramping through a rugged and uncharted wilderness with only an Indian guide, who spoke imperfect English, for companionship was a lonely life.

Douglas would frequently go weeks, or sometimes months, without encountering traders. Natives from the various tribes were his more frequent companions, and he grew to consider many of them as his friends. They named him the "Grass Man" because he was always burdened with plants, and, on one occasion, invited him to attend a feast involving a stupendous five-hundred-pound sturgeon that was twelve feet long and seven feet around the middle and roasted over a bed of coals. Douglas was honoured with the choicest portions—the head and spine. It was, he related, "the most comfortable meal I had for a considerable time."

On March 20, 1827, Douglas left Fort Vancouver with the annual fur brigade following the Columbia River into the interior. He had mixed feelings about his departure from a "country so exceedingly interesting." The huge boat plied up the sluggish river to Great Falls, but Douglas declared in his journal that he walked instead of riding the boat, partly from overcrowding and partly to see the country one last time. "Not a day passed but brought something new or interesting either in botany or zoology," he reported, although his poor feet suffered tremendously and eventually became "very painful, blistered, and blood-run." When the river widened into a lake, near what is now called Lower Arrow Lake in southern British Columbia, they rigged a primitive sail and glided north until they came to a wild and turbulent whirlpool near the present-day community of Revelstoke. "Rapids, whirlpools, and still basins, the water of a deep dark hue, except when agitated. On both sides high hills with rugged rocks covered with dead trees, the roots of which being laid bare by the torrents are blown down by the wind, bringing with them blocks of granite attached to their roots in large masses, spreading devastation before them. Passing this place just as the sun was tipping the mountains and his feeble rays now and then seen through the shady forests, imparts a melancholy sensation on no ordinary description, filling the mind with awe on beholding this picture of gloomy wilderness."

After crossing the rapids, they paddled northeast toward the Big Bend of the Columbia, where the imposing Rocky Mountains first came into view. The scene, Douglas wrote, "impresses on the mind a feeling beyond what I can express. I would say a feeling of horror." Certainly the route to the base of Athabasca Pass proved to be horribly rugged and tiring. At Boat Encampment (now flooded by the Mica Dam) they abandoned the boat, hoisted bone-crushing packs, and began labouring up the steep incline. The trail through the lower reaches of Athabasca Pass wound through a partially frozen swamp where they sank to their knees, and then through snow that was up to seven feet deep. The long line of hunched, weary pack-bearers crossed a freezing mountain stream fourteen times in a single day, wading up to their waists until half their bodies were numb from the cold.

The pass itself was steep and wicked, and on several occasions Douglas fell, tangled in his snowshoes "like a broken-down wagon-horse entangled in his harnessing, weltering to rescue myself." By noon they were too worn out to press on and camped midway up the pass, boiling snow for tea and devouring the food in a ravenous frenzy—"no fault with the food," Douglas wrote, too tired to criticize, "glad of anything." During the next day's struggle, one of the voyageurs shot "a most beautiful partridge" and would have kept it for dinner, a blessed respite from the dried rations, but Douglas ran up and claimed it. It was a new species, and he "could not resist the temptation of preserving it." He blithely strapped it to his already overburdened pack and continued struggling up through the snow.

The pass was a wonder of desolation. Winds whistled along a ridge of icy jagged spires that ran the length of the valley like the jawbone of an ancient beast. To one side was a craggy lump of rock like a giant tooth bursting through the crust of the earth. And on another peak a great glacier hung like a tongue, blue and forbidding, strapped to the lifeless rock. Mottled green lichens covered the barren stones in the valley bottom and a wind blew down from the towering peaks. Across the valley was a weeping wall of dark rock, water streaming down the face and shining against the fading sun, a cap of snow perched atop it.

During the afternoon Douglas found himself several miles ahead of the others and veered from the path "with a view of ascending what seemed to be the highest peak on the north." Looming overhead was the mountain, hunched ogre-like above the valley. Its snow-dusted stony face was grim and brooding, and rivulets of snow trickled down into the shadowy woods. It was an ominous spectacle. For several hours he thrashed his way up a steep, heavily forested slope. About halfway up, the trees withered into shrunken, wind-lashed and contorted dwarfs and "one third from the summit it becomes a mountain of pure ice." After nearly five hours he struggled to the top of the peak and beheld a dizzying scene in an arc from his lofty prominence. "Nothing as far as the eye could perceive, but Mountains such as I was on...some rugged beyond description....The aerial tints of the snow, the heavenly azure of the solid glaciers, the rainbow-like hues of their thin broken fragments...the snow sliding from the steep southern rocks with amazing velocity, producing a crash and grumbling like the shock of an earthquake, the echo of which resounding in the valley for several minutes." Douglas diplomatically named the peak he had ascended Mount Brown after an "illustrious" botanist and another rugged peak off to the south Mount Hooker "in honour of my early patron, the enlightened and learned Professor of Botany in the University of Glasgow." He then made his weary way down, arriving in the dark.

The next morning Douglas found that his "ankles and feet pained so much from exertion that my sleep was short and interrupted." He rose before dawn, stoked a blazing fire, warmed himself, and set off through the remainder of the pass alone. On the eastern side of the Continental Divide, descending along the Whirlpool River, the weather was much milder, there was much less snow, and the vegetation was strikingly open and dry-looking. The trees were smaller and scraggly and the underbrush was more wiry and stunted. "The difference of climate and soil," Douglas wrote, "with the amazing disparity in the variety and stature of the vegetation, is truly astonishing; one would suppose it was another hemisphere, the change is so great."

Heading down the eastern slope, they were met by Jacques Cardinal, a guide leading a string of eight horses to help haul the bundles of furs. Douglas spent an entertaining evening as a guest at Cardinal's camp. After feasting on "a shoulder of *Mouton gris*," Douglas noted that, while Cardinal boiled tea in a patched copper kettle, he must have seen Douglas eyeing the kettle and thought he had a thirst for rum. Cardinal "observed he had no spirit to give me, but turning around and pointing to the river he said 'This is my barrel and it is always running.'" The next day they loaded their burdens onto the horses and descended into the valley, where they eventually came to the Athabasca River, transferred the loads into boats, floated past present-day Jasper, and were propelled from the mountains onto the prairie. They travelled east across half the continent ("seeing one mile gives an idea of the whole," wrote Douglas of the botanically uninspiring terrain) to York Factory on the shores of Hudson Bay. During a brief stopover at Cumberland House in present-day Saskatchewan, Douglas met up with Dr. John Richardson and Thomas Drummond who were returning from their own expedition to the Canadian Arctic. They discussed natural history and shared their opinions on various specimens. Douglas boarded a Hudson's Bay Company ship at York Factory and sailed across the Atlantic to England, where he arrived on October 11, 1827.

For the next two years he proceeded to offend and alienate most of his friends in England. Celebrated and lionized for his achievements, which were far in excess of even the wildest dreams of the Horticultural Society, Douglas was elected a Fellow of the Linnean Society, the Zoological Society, and the Geological Society, without the obligation of paying the hefty membership fees. Unfortunately, he was ill-suited to admiration and the fruits of success. He tried to write up his journal and failed, after turning down a generous offer of assistance from his colleagues and a well-known publisher of natural history books, John Murray and Co. And he grew bored, offensive, and ill-behaved. His biographer, Harvey, wrote in 1947 that "he was surfeited with the monotonous praise of the fashionable society, and, like many another who has come under the spell of the wilderness, he was irked by the restraints and congestion of the metropolis and disgusted with the smells, smoke, and grime." Douglas also realized that he had no career prospects. Without formal education and with a humble social station, he had a future that looked bleak. "His temper became more sensitive than ever," wrote his mentor, William Hooker, "and himself restless and dissatisfied; so that his best friends could not but wish as he himself did, that he were again occupied in the honourable task of exploring north-west America."

Through the influence of Hooker, the Horticultural Society laid plans to send Douglas on a second trip to the North American West. In addition to collecting plants for the Horticultural Society, he was asked by the Colonial Office to take measurements for accurate maps. On this journey he was also instructed to explore California, a land that was then part of the Mexican Republic. Douglas threw himself into his task, spending the months until his departure locked in study. His eyesight, however, had progressively worsened, so that by 1829, he could not read small print even if he squinted.

He arrived at Fort Vancouver in June 1830 and spent the summer exploring the Columbia region again before sailing for California. Mexican authorities kept him waiting for his passport for several weeks, and then sternly warned him not to sketch military fortifications. Douglas found the people around Monterey to be immensely pleasant and helpful, and perhaps he was secretly pleased when they referred to him as "Don David," an *hombre de educacion*—a distinction he craved, but was not really possible for him in the stratified world of the pre-Victorian scientific community. In California, he was respected and called a doctor on account of his learning, and was pleased with the reception he received from the Franciscan friars who had missions throughout the territory. He observed that they "loved the sciences too well to think it curious to see one go so far in quest of grass," and offered him hospitality throughout the country. After he had travelled north as far as San Francisco, which he described as "a few dilapidated buildings," Douglas's opinion of the government contrasted with his opinion of the people. "The Mexican territorial govern-ment," he wrote, "as applied to California is abominable, and that is the mildest word I can use."

The collecting was as productive as the Columbia region had been. "Nothing can exceed the beauty of a California Spring," he wrote, and lamented the short season for botaniz-ing. "The intense heat set in about June, when every bit of herbage was dried to a cinder...were it not for the intense drought of July and August, the soil would be very produc-tive." He was also impressed with the region's vineyards, noting that "the wine is excellent, indeed, that word is too small for it; it is very excellent." After nearly two years in California he had amassed a thorough collection of the region's flora, including hundreds of new species of plants, seaweeds, and mosses, and detailed descriptions of their appearance and where they were found.

Douglas sailed from Monterey and returned to Fort Vancouver in the late fall of 1832. He wintered there, and the next spring made a disastrous expedition north, where he planned to reach Alaska and return to Europe via Russia. He paddled north along the Columbia, crossed into the Okanagan to Fort Kamloops, and then travelled north along the Fraser, the Nechaco and Stuart Rivers as far north as Fort St. James. It was a rugged and harsh country where the climate and temperature varied wildly and food was scarce. By now, he was blinded completely in his right eye from the intense sun of California. It was "as dark as midnight," he wrote, and it must have made movement in such wild terrain difficult. At Fort St. James, after nearly 1,150 miles of travelling, Douglas realized that it would be certain death if he continued with his plan of heading to Alaska, still hundreds of miles distant. For the first time in his recorded journals, he succumbed to fatigue and good judgment and retraced his route to Fort Vancouver. Before he reached the fort, however, his canoe was dashed to pieces in treacherous rapids and Douglas was sucked down into a whirlpool that spun him mercilessly for an hour and a half before spitting him onto the gravelly shore, beaten and defeated. He had lost everything, including food and blankets, about four hundred plant specimens and his daily journal, of which he had no other copy. "This disastrous experience has broken my strength and spirits," he related in a letter to Hooker, after glumly returning to Fort Vancouver in August. He devoted the next several months to preparing a final shipment of specimens and seeds.*

With his eyesight failing and his health now waning, he knew his days as an itinerant botanical collector were over. In October 1833, he boarded a ship for Hawaii, where he hoped to recuperate from his trials before returning to England. Perhaps he should have remained at Fort Vancouver where he had many friends, or returned to California where he was highly regarded by the people. With his bad eyes to blame as much as his inherent curiosity, he accidentally slipped and

---

* The collected scientific discoveries of Douglas were not prepared for publication until the first volume of Hooker's *Flora Boreali-Americana; or, the Botany of the Northern Parts of British America* was published in 1829, which also incorporated the collections of John Richardson and Thomas Drummond in the sub-arctic and arctic.

stumbled to his death in a Hawaiian bull pit on July 11, 1834, just before his thirty-fifth birthday.

It may be that Douglas's early death saved him from a life of lingering resentment, sorrowful reminiscences, and, perhaps, poverty. In the previous few years his eyesight had degenerated so that he was almost blind in one eye, and sensitive to bright light in the other. He was compelled to wear a pair of purple-tinted spectacles to ease the pain in his other still-functioning eye, but as he noted himself, he wore them "most reluctantly, as every object, plants and all, is thus rendered of the same colour." It was quite a handicap for a botanist. Although Douglas named many of the specimens he collected in the American West, he sometimes confused species, and many of his classifications and observations subsequently proved incorrect and were later altered by specialized closet naturalists. He was an excellent collector and an excellent horticulturist, but he didn't have the scientific background to accurately classify his specimens. And although he was revered as a botanical collector of the highest order, an institutional posting, without formal education or influential contacts, would have been beyond his grasp. He was a collector of specimens that others would study, and he knew that the novelty of his discoveries would eventually fade, leaving him blind and in broken health. He would have been swept aside by the tide of time to the fringes of the scientific community, and there, possibly, forgotten.

Several years after Douglas's death, William Hooker wrote a memorial to him that alluded to the source of Douglas's bitterness when he returned to England after his second expedition, and the bitterness that likely would have continued to be a source of disillusionment for him had he survived the third. Douglas's ambition was to be far more than a common gardener, but when his travelling days ended, so did the source of his acclaim. "Unfortunately for his peace of mind," Hooker wrote, "he could not withstand the temptations (so natural to the human heart) of appearing as one of the Lions among the learned and scientific men in London.... Flattered by their attention, and by the notoriety of his botanical discoveries...he seemed for a time as if he attained the summit of his ambition. But alas; when the novelty of the situation had subsided, he began to perceive that he had been pursuing a shadow instead of reality."

During the 1830s, the number of naturalists exploring remote regions increased dramatically. The study of natural history was becoming a common pastime in all levels of society, particularly in Britain and the United States, and the demand for exotic specimens prompted other professional collectors to embark on journeys. Around the same time that Douglas was concluding his explorations west of the Rocky Mountains, another naturalist named John Kirk Townsend was just setting out from Philadelphia to cross the North American continent, seeking renown as a naturalist by collecting species of birds and mammals from the remote regions along his route.

CHAPTER SIX

John Kirk Townsend

The wild forest, the deep glen, and the rugged mountain top, possess charms for
[the naturalist] which he would not exchange for gilded palaces; and . . . to
acquaint himself with nature he gladly escapes from the restraints of civiliza-
tion, and buries himself from the world which cannot appreciate his enjoyment.
—JOHN KIRK TOWNSEND,
Narrative of a Journey Across the Rocky Mountains to the Columbia River

A map of North America from the 1830s shows a strange patchwork of nationalities. Britain in the north, the United States in the south, and Mexico in the southwest. Alaska was Russian, the United States had only recently purchased Florida from Spain, and the Oregon Territory—the present-day states of Washington, Oregon, and Idaho—and the Canadian province of British Columbia was a jointly occupied no-man's land effectively under the control of the British fur monopoly, the Hudson's Bay Company. Most of what lay west of the Mississippi and east of the Rocky Mountains was considered the "Free Indian Territories." It was a land ripe for adventure.

John Kirk Townsend was already a physician and an ornithologist recently elected to the Academy of Natural Sciences of Philadelphia when he was invited by Thomas Nuttall, the renowned Harvard naturalist and curator of the botanical gardens, to join an overland collecting expedition to the distant West in 1834. Born the second of four children in 1809 to an upstanding Quaker family in Philadelphia, the

Thomas Nuttall, the famous botanist who travelled across the continent with John Kirk Townsend, was a Harvard professor of botany before resigning and heading west in 1834. No known portrait of Townsend exists.

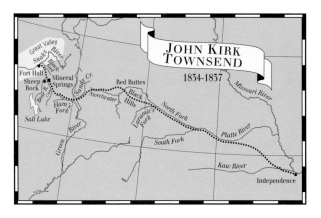

JOHN KIRK
TOWNSEND
1834-1837

John Kirk Townsend's cross-continental trek, 1834–1837.

energetic and curious Townsend was well educated at the boarding school at Westtown. Like many other members of his family and the Quaker community, he had a lifelong interest in natural history. And, like the wandering naturalist William Bartram who had died in 1823, Townsend believed, as a Quaker, that the study of nature was a way of knowing God through "creation." Several members of his extended family were amateur ornithologists and members of the local natural history society. He was a crack shot with a rifle and an able taxidermist—both prime skills for a naturalist in the days when acquiring and stuffing specimens for later study were at the forefront of scientific advancement.

Townsend received commissions from both the Academy of Natural Sciences of Philadelphia and the American Philosophical Society for his journey. Each had given him a stipend of $125 to outfit himself on the condition that he present them with a duplicate collection of his natural history specimens, including rocks and minerals, when he returned. Townsend and Nuttall's destination of Old Oregon and the Pacific coast coincided with the mercantile objectives of the optimistic Boston merchant Nathaniel Wyeth. Wyeth planned to do business with the independent fur traders, the mountain men, in the Rocky Mountains and then continue west to the coast and establish a permanent outpost in competition with the Hudson's Bay Company. In addition to the two prominent naturalists, Townsend and Nuttall, Wyeth invited a group of Methodist missionaries to tag along, perhaps to lend an air of greater purpose to what was essentially a commercial venture into a politically volatile region. Neither Nuttall nor Townsend had any interest in or understanding of Wyeth's risky commercial enterprise, but they were pleased to benefit from the security of travelling with a large, well-provisioned, and presumably well-organized pack train of seventy men, mostly French-Canadian trappers and hunters, and 250 horses. For Townsend, a young naturalist at the start of a promising career, it was a perfect opportunity to earn a reputation while collecting specimens in a land that had seen few visitors and no professional scientists.*

EXCURSION TO THE OREGON.

Townsend and Nuttall left Philadelphia together on March 13, riding the stage to Pittsburgh and then the steamer to St. Louis, where they met up with Wyeth while he was outfitting his caravan. Impatient to get on the road, they agreed to rendezvous in Independence, farther north along the Missouri, at the end of April.

This page from Townsend's *Narrative of a Journey Across the Rocky Mountains to the Columbia River* shows the hunting of the Great American Bison, a magnificent animal that could be six feet in height at the shoulder and could weigh two thousand pounds.

The two naturalists, a jaunty youth with eyes trained to the sky for birds, and a short, balding, bookish, and unkempt fiftyish man squinting at the ground for plants, set off on foot along the rudimentary road to Independence, ahead of the bulk of Wyeth's party. It was a journey of nearly three hundred miles, but they were flush with excitement over the new landscape and new life forms. Birding and botanizing were the order of the day, and the two seem to have had a remarkable rapport—working together to discover the greatest possible number of specimens. Although the season was plentiful for birds, a boon for Townsend, Nuttall noted sadly that many of the plants "a number of which are rare and curious" were not yet blooming. Both had read extensively about

---

* David Douglas was the only professional naturalist to explore western North America. Although he had travelled along the Pacific coast from California to what is now British Columbia, he never ventured east of the Continental Divide, leaving a vast territory scientifically unexplored.

the latest discoveries in natural history before embarking on the journey. Because their capacity for transporting specimens would be limited by the constant travel through wild terrain, a thorough knowledge of what had already been discovered and classified was required to guide them in collecting only what was new or intriguing.

The peripatetic pair meandered slowly along the shore of the Missouri River, stopping at farmhouses along the way for food and shelter. The terrain was alternately flat grassland and heavily wooded rolling hills with farms carved out of the forest. There were no major cities and few towns. Townsend observed "large flocks of wild pigeons," "thousands of golden plovers," prairie hens, pileated woodpeckers, flocks of "splendid green and red" plumed parrots, and many other exotic avian attractions. The crack of his rifle echoed frequently along the road. He shot many birds for study and stuffing, but others, such as the wild turkeys that occasionally perched squawking in the treetops, filled their bellies in the evenings.

It was a pleasant journey through a prosperous land populated with friendly, industrious people, much to Townsend's liking. Nuttall, on the other hand, rarely took note of anything unrelated to natural history. But they both found the inhabitants "exceedingly inquisitive, propounding question after question, in such quick succession as scarcely to allow you breathing time between them" and they soon wearied of answering the same questions repeatedly. The resourceful Townsend solved the problem with an elaborate introduction: "We come from Pennsylvania," he would announce, "our names are Nuttall and Townsend; we are travelling to Independence on foot, for the purpose of seeing the country to advantage, and we intend to proceed from thence across the mountains to the Pacific. Have you any mules to sell?" When the answer was invariably no, they lamented the sad state of affairs and continued on their way.

Near the end of April they caught a steamer that took

them the remainder of the way to Independence, where they met with Wyeth and his eager congregation. Soon the sprawling caravan was winding its way west across rolling plains in the golden sun, and Townsend could "scarcely contain" his excitement at the prospect of the adventure that lay before him. A few days later, however, a deluge of rain and hailstones "as large as musket balls" tumbled from the purple, forbidding sky, turning the merry band into a morose train of sodden, sullen, and solitary travellers. Soon, even moping was denied them. The hail grew more fierce, panicking the horses until they "plunged and kicked, and many of them threw their loads, and fled wildly over the plain." It was the first of many misadventures they were to endure in the coming year. But all was not bad. Townsend frequently woke early in the morning to enjoy the glorious silence of sunrise, marvelling as the first tendrils of light spread along the golden-green grasses swaying in the wind. The smell of sage was strong in the air.

Although the many Indians they encountered failed to live up to Townsend's notion of the "romantic savage" popularized in Fenimore Cooper novels, he was nevertheless excited on the few occasions that they encountered them on the plains. But his interest in natural history far overshadowed any other aspect of his adventure. He was enthralled by the variety and antics of the birds. "My favorites, the birds," he wrote, "are very numerous in this vicinity, and I am therefore in my element." The birds sang "joyously amongst themselves, grosbeaks, thrushes, and buntings, a merry and musical band." Others caught his eye as well, and he shot and collected specimens of any that seemed unknown, interesting, or odd—yellow-headed blackbirds, pipits, lark sparrows, chestnut-collared longspurs, bobolinks, and ravens. The prairie was an ornithologist's dream, although in his *Narrative* Townsend does not describe in detail the behaviour, preferred foods, mating rituals, method of rearing young, or migration patterns of any

AMERICAN BISON

John James Audubon and John Bachman included the American Bison in *Quadrupeds of North America*. Although Townsend supplied them with many unknown bird and small mammal specimens, a specimen of the bison was too large and bulky to transport. Bison were numerous and common and could easily be shipped by train east to Philadelphia.

species of birds. And he had no idea what they ate during the winter or if they migrated. The caravan travelled too fast for this type of observation. His bird skins, however, were perfectly preserved.

While Townsend was content to wield his own rifle with impunity in the pursuit of science, he lamented the senseless slaughter of antelope by the men of his troupe. The hunters frequently fired away at the creatures for sport, leaving the carcasses to rot in the prairie sun. "A number [of antelopes] are...slaughtered every day, from mere wantonness and love of killing, the greenhorns glorying in the sport like our striplings of the city, in their annual murdering of robins and sparrows."

Nuttall quickly earned the name *le fou* from the earthy French-Canadian trappers and hunters. He was far too studious and abstract for their respect—an eccentric and introverted little man who rushed ahead of the cavalcade, gathering plants from the path and casting reproachful glances at the advancing column. Although Townsend undoubtedly learned and benefited greatly from the older man's knowledge, Nuttall's peccadilloes were too much even for him at times; "Left Nuttall dreaming of weeds," he wrote in his journal one day.

After a month on the open plain, Townsend had his first view of bison. It was a "sight which seemed to astonish even the oldest amongst us.... The whole plain, as far as the eye could discern was covered by one enormous mass of buffalo." For ten miles a great undulating herd of shaggy, lumbering beasts surged across the land. When they moved, a great cloud of dust billowed into the air and the earth trembled under the weight of tens of thousands of hooves. It was, he marvelled, a sight that "would have excited even the dullest mind to enthusiasm."

For the next few weeks they feasted exclusively on the choicest portions of the huge beasts, the tender humps and the great ribs, roasted slowly over smouldering fires. The remaining portions of the great animals were left "to feed the revenous maw of the wild prairie wolf, and minister to the excesses of the unclean birds of the wilderness." They were, according to Townsend, "in truth living upon the fat of the land, and better feeding need no man wish." Although Townsend was appalled at the waste, he asked philosophically, "when are men economical, unless compelled to be so by necessity?"

Food was never a problem, yet as they approached the Platte River near the end of May the land became very arid and rocky with little water. One day, in what was evidently a vivid experience for Townsend, he was introduced to the ways of the wild, or at least the ways of the French-Canadian trappers. One of the hunters shot a buffalo, and after heaving it onto its side, slit its belly open exposing the "still crawling and twisting entrails." He then plunged his knife into the swollen gut, "from which gushed the green and gelatinous juices, and then insinuate[d] his tin pan into the opening" and strained off some of the murky liquid. After Townsend, staring in horror, declined the proffered mug, the man guzzled the turgid draught "smacking his lips, and drawing a long breath after it, with the satisfaction of a man taking his wine after dinner."

Although Townsend was shocked, his burning thirst from a day's dusty and sweaty travel momentarily liberalized his notions of propriety. The man urged him to drink a little blood to quench his thirst. "Immediately as it touched my lips," Townsend recounted, "my burning thirst, aggravated by hunger got the better of my abhorrence; I plunged my head into the reeking ventricles, and drank until forced to stop for breath." He then smiled a ghastly grin at his companions, and admitted to being "somewhat ashamed" at "assimilating myself so nearly to the brutes." Later that night, however, after drinking fresh water from the Platte River, his stomach convulsed and the blood issued forth from his mouth in a diluted stream. "I never drank blood from that day," he reported.

As the troupe continued west across the prairie, Townsend wondered at, and then shot, dozens more birds and small mammals for his collection. There was one occasion on which he was saddened by his own behaviour. As he lagged behind the brigade, a young antelope trailed him for a while. His "evil genius and love of sport prevailed" and he fired at the creature, blasting it in the belly. As he approached, it tried in vain to drag itself into the bushes, but he soon "stood over her, and saw her cast her large, soft, black eyes upon me with an expression of the most touching sadness, while great tears rolled over her face, I felt the meanest and most abhorrent thing in creation." After driving his knife through her heart to end the suffering he rode back to the camp quiet with "feelings such as I hope never to experience again. For several days the poor antelope haunted me, and I shall never forget its last look of pain and upbraiding."

On May 24, they led their train of pack animals across the ford of the South Platte River into new terrain, "a great sandy waste, without a single green thing to vary and enliven the dreary scene.... The soil was poor and sandy, and the few straggling blades of grass which found their way to the surface were brown and withered." The change of scenery, however barren, was a relief after a month on the plains. Townsend had been disconcerted by the disc-like horizon extending around him, being used to the mixed forest and rolling hills of the east. Just as he was commenting on the agreeableness of this new terrain, however, they were

Pl. XLIV.

Cratægus sanguineus.

Red Thorn.

Alizier rouge.

From *North American Sylva*, *Crataegus sanguinea*, the Red Thorn or hawthorn, beautifully illustrates how in the 19th century natural science and art were blended. Nuttall first spied the plant while entering the Rocky Mountains, and after tasting a few berries, called them "a welcome food."

PRONG-HORNED ANTELOPE, or PRONGHORN

Prong-horned antelope were common on the great plains in the 1830s. When Townsend wantonly shot and killed one, he was overcome with remorse. "For several days the poor antelope haunted me," he wrote, "and I shall never forget its last look of pain and upbraiding."

This bird medley painted by Audubon was based on specimens brought back by Townsend from the Far West. One of the birds is named after Townsend and another after Audubon.

Pl. XCVII.

Cornus Nuttallii.

Large-flowered Dogwood.   Cornouiller de Nuttall.

Nuttall first spied the Large-Flowered Dogwood, or Nuttall's Dogwood, near the Columbia River.

"suddenly assailed by vast swarms of the most ferocious little black gnats; . . . they dashed into our faces, assaulted our eyes, ears, nostrils, and mouths, as though they were determined to bar our way through their territory. . . . their sting caused such excessive pain that for the rest of the day our men and horses were rendered almost frantic. . . ."

In the following days, Townsend saw nests of eagles on the rocky outcroppings and was fascinated by the multitude of burrowing moles and gophers that pocked the earth. The next week was spectacular for collecting, perhaps the best on the entire trip. "The birds thus far have been very abundant," he recorded, "there is a considerable variety, and many of them have not before been seen by naturalists," such as blue grosbeaks and lark buntings. He and Nuttall finally flung aside their "useless and superfluous" clothing and equipment to make room for more specimens.

The party continued on through the narrow gorges between the bluffs of La Platte, a weathered mesa of layered limestone with a startling resemblance to a "dilapidated feudal castle." The road was barely a scratch in the dry earth, winding through three miles of twisting canyons lined with a brilliant array of wildflowers—"Beautiful. Beautiful!" wrote Townsend in awe. They camped along the North Platte in a grove verdant with cottonwoods. The spring birds were out in full and Townsend and Nuttall woke early in the morning and "stroll[ed] through the umbrageous forest, inhaling the fresh, bracing air" and blasting birds in all directions. "The lovely tenants of the grove flew by dozens before us. I think I never saw before me so great a variety of birds within the same place. All were beautiful, and many were new to me; and after we had spent an hour amongst them, and my game bag was teeming with its precious freight, I was still loath to leave the place, lest I should not have procured specimens of the whole."

By early June the plains receded and they struggled over a rugged cluster of stony outcroppings "dreary and forbidding," laced with "deep and craggy fissures" and precipitous cliffs (now called the Laramie Mountains). Here Townsend shot Say's phoebe, mountain bluebird, and sharp-tailed grouse. They followed the Sweetwater River west to South Pass, a common fur trade route across the Continental Divide. In addition to bighorn sheep and grizzly bears, Townsend recorded a few less frightening creatures, such as a new whippoorwill, mountain plover, sage thrasher, violet-green swallow, yellow-crowned sparrow, Lewis's woodpecker, arctic towhee, and black-headed grosbeak—all of which were a delight, and quite different from the birds of the plains. One day, while strolling along a pine-clad hillside approaching the mountains, Nuttall was astonished to hear a "distinct bleat, like that of a young kid or goat." After casting his eyes about he spied only a tiny mouse-like creature scurrying into its hole. "I may almost say," he remarked later in a rare display of humour, "the mountain brought forth nothing much larger than a mole."*

After a few days of following a pine-covered valley beneath a range of lofty snow-smothered peaks, they led their horses across the Green River (Siskakee) and continued on to the broad plain at Ham's Fork for the annual rendezvous of the mountain beaver trappers, where Wyeth planned on dispersing his caravan of supplies. Although they made their camp about a mile from the main congregation, they were pestered by many peculiar visitors, and for once, Townsend was more intrigued with the chaotic antics of the humans than the birds. Many of their visitors, were "Indians, of the Nez Perce, Banneck and Shoshone tribes, who come with the furs and peltries which they have been collecting at the risk of their lives during the past winter and spring, to trade for ammunition, trinkets, and 'fire water.'" But it was the French

---

* It was a pika, or little chief hare, that had, unfortunately for Townsend, already been collected by Thomas Drummond, an assistant collector to the British naturalist and surgeon John Richardson, farther north in the Rockies in 1829.

Canadians who stimulated his greatest sense of incredulity. "These people," he reported, "with their obstreperous mirth, their whooping, and howling, and quarreling, added to the mounted Indians, who are constantly dashing into and through our camp, yelling like fiends, the barking and baying of savage wolf-dogs and the incessant crackling of rifles and carbines, render our camp a perfect bedlam....I am compelled all day to listen to the hiccoughing jargon of drunken traders, the sacré and foutré of Frenchmen run wild, and the swearing and screaming of our own men who are scarcely less savage than the rest."

They remained at the rendezvous until early July, when Wyeth, unable to dispose of any of his goods because a rival trader had beat him to the scene by one week, optimistically decided to push on to the Snake River, where he planned to build a fort and hunker down for the season. The diminished group of twenty-seven followed the valley west and crossed over the ridge to the watershed of the Columbia River. The spirit of the rendezvous seized the traders as they travelled along this circuitous route and they had one final hurrah on July 4. "This being a memorable day," Townsend wrote, "the liquor kegs were opened. We, therefore, soon had a renewal of the coarse and brutal scenes of the rendezvous. Some of the bacchanals called for a volley in honor of the day. We who were not 'happy' had to lie flat on the ground to avoid the bullets which were careening through the camp." The two naturalists, undeterred by the final flurry of debauchery, celebrated in their own manner, shooting and inspecting a few "rare and valuable" birds near the camp, and admiring the fishes in the stream. "The fish probably average fifteen or sixteen inches in length," Townsend recorded for posterity.

Soon after they descended from the highest passes of the Rockies, the terrain became lava-strewn and parched, with "large sunken spots, some of them of great extent, surrounded by walls of lava...." After a few days crossing this bleak terrain the Teton mountain range came distantly into view, crisp stone spires jutting ice-encrusted into the blue sky. It was rough travelling, and although they must have suspected that Wyeth was in serious financial trouble, the two naturalists remained concerned only with matters in the "pursuit of science." While Wyeth pondered his predicament and the travellers grumbled about the conditions, Nuttall excitedly noted a new whippoorwill and Townsend matched it with an unclassified mountain plover.

On July 15, on a grassy plain along the upper Snake River, the dispirited Wyeth and his remaining men hacked down some trees and constructed a ramshackle palisade. They named it Fort Hall and began trading with the local Indians and freelance trappers. During the three weeks of construction, while Townsend was away with a party of hunters, Nuttall, although remaining close to camp for fear of encountering Blackfeet Indians (who usually tried to kill invaders in their land), observed the furtive Western marsh wren. He described it as if he was preparing a pamphlet for a local zoo: it was a "remarkably active and quaint little species, skipping and diving about with great activity after its insect food and their larvae among the rank grass and rushes."

During his three-week foray with the hunters, Townsend had added no new species to scientific knowledge and English lexicography. But he had met with "a grizzly bear of the largest kind" rearing up a dozen yards in front of him in a copse of berries. "His savage eyes," Townsend wrote in a furious burst of purple prose, were "glaring with horrible malignity, his mouth wide open, and his tremendous paws raised as though ready to descend upon me." Fortunately he and the bear parted company in mutual fear, unlike many other bears that the expedition had encountered, which were hunted with a tenacious glee and, with a single exception, pursued to the bitter end. One massive bear that was flushed from a berry patch, weighing perhaps seven hundred pounds, received upward of thirty rifle shots before it finally roared in pain and slumped into a nearby stream. The slaughter of vast numbers of animals for no particular reason was common at the time.

When Fort Hall was complete, Wyeth rode west with a small contingent of men (including Townsend and Nuttall), to the Hudson's Bay Company's Fort Walla Walla on the Columbia River. A few days into the journey they began crossing the dreaded Snake River lava beds—a vast plain of tumbled volcanic rock, fissured with chasms and cracked and barren with occasional twisted wormwood bushes pushing up from the bleak earth. "The air feels like the breath of a sirocco," Townsend wrote, "the tongue becomes parched and horny, and the mouth, nose, and eyes are incessantly assailed by the fine pulverized lava, which rises from the ground with the least breath of air." Crossing it was a humourless endeavour for most of the men, strung out in a weary, despondent mile-long line with the "poor horses' heads hanging low, their tongues protruding to their utmost extent, and their riders scarcely less drooping and spiritless." There were no intriguing species of birds to distract Townsend; only Nuttall had the energy to note "beautiful pebbles of chalcedony and fine agate." And as they shambled on, his squinting eyes caught "the sweet berries of a hawthorn which occurred sporadically from the Rockies westward." A "welcome food," he commented, after tasting a few.

It was a gruelling four-week trek. In addition to land "where nothing meets the eye but desolation and awful

GRIZZLY BEAR

Audubon and Bachman painted the grizzly bear for their *Quadrupeds of North America*. Although Townsend didn't himself shoot one, the men he travelled with killed any they found.

waste," they had to traverse "some of the highest mountains we have yet seen ... capped with enormous masses of snow." It was treacherous, rugged, and unrewarding. At one point, Wyeth recorded that they reached their camp only after a nocturnal tramp "through an infernal rough rocky prickly Bruisy swampy woody hole." Hardly the pleasurable jaunt they had had traversing the prairies in the spring.

By August 18, they had been "living for several days on a short allowance of wretched, dry meat," and their horses were dying. Luckily, the next day they reached the Boise, or Big Wood, River, "literally crowded with salmon, which are springing from the water almost constantly." Although their mouths were watering, they had no means of catching any of the plump fish and so pressed on with empty bellies and dark thoughts. When they did manage to purchase some fish from a band of friendly Snake Indians on August 24, the sudden change in diet caused them to be violently ill and unable to travel for a few days.

Another week of travel brought them close to Fort Walla Walla, and Wyeth rode ahead while the remainder of the column followed at a more dignified, or road-weary, pace. Townsend and Nuttall, wishing "to appear like fellow Christians" at the fort, burrowed amongst their by-now bloated bird and plant sacks for a razor to remove their "heathenish badges." Townsend was quite amused at his multi-hued complexion: "the lower portion being fair, like a woman's, and the upper, brown and swarthy as an Indian." As he later strolled along the river collecting rosebuds for his meagre repast, he surprised Nuttall and another man "picking the last bones of a bird which they had cooked." Upon inquiry he was startled to discover that the bird was an "unfortunate owl which I had killed in the morning and had intended to preserve as a specimen." The poor bird of wisdom, consumed to fulfill the mere prosaic needs of the two epicures, had now "lost the immortality which he might otherwise have acquired" (by being stuffed, presumably).

Within a day of relatively easy travel over "regular undulating country," they came upon the Walla Walla River. By evening, "on rising a sandy hill, the noble Columbia burst at once upon our view...I gazed upon the magnificent river,... and reflected that I had actually crossed the vast American continent, and now stood upon a stream that poured its waters directly into the Pacific." The fort, a rudimentary fur outpost, was in the distance near the river, a hub of activity with horses and horned cattle roaming about the nearby pasture. The two naturalists were heartily received and dined that night on a tempting dish of stewed hares. It is "needless to say," observed Townsend, perhaps remembering his rosebud salad and the bones of his prized owl, "that we did full justice to the good men's cookery." Around this time he obliquely noted in his journal that some of the Indian women were "rather handsome," despite being clothed "in truly savage taste."

After a few days recuperating at the fort, they followed the Columbia downstream to the Dalles, where the broad river was transformed into a malevolent foaming channel. As they set out in canoes a vicious storm almost swamped them and destroyed their priceless collection of specimens, by now weighing several hundred pounds. Although Townsend's "bale of birds...escaped without any material injury," Nuttall's "large and beautiful collection of new and rare plants was considerably injured by the wetting it received." While the drizzle continued unabated the following day, Nuttall, "exhibiting a degree of patience and perseverance truly astonishing," opened each packet of plants and carefully dried them in the heat of an enormous fire.

They reached Fort Vancouver on September 16, and were cordially greeted by Chief Factor John McLoughlin, who graciously assigned them a comfortable room and a servant. Here they remained until late in the season, dining as honoured guests among the Hudson's Bay Company officers in the evenings, with all the predictable rituals of an outpost of the British Empire—fine china, silverware, and proper cere-mony. Although they scoured the nearby land for new species (including a trip into the Willamette Valley to help Wyeth and the missionaries select a good site for a farm), the terrain had been thoroughly explored by David Douglas in previous years. They also received word of Douglas's death in Hawaii the previous July.*

By now they had together procured several thousand specimens of plants and hundreds of flayed, preserved bird skins, as well as numerous amphibians, reptiles, mammals, invertebrates, and even some weighty mineral samples. The effect of the dank, clammy winter weather of coastal Oregon on their collections began to worry them, and in November they caught a ship to Hawaii for the winter. They both returned in the spring for some final collecting on the coast before going their separate ways.

Nuttall eventually made his way home around the Cape Horn, arriving in Boston to the acclaim of the scientific community in September 1836. Due to his dwindling per-sonal fortune, he reluctantly retired to an inherited estate at Nutgrove in England, where he continued to study plants, nostalgically cultivating many of the specimens he had col-lected in America, until his death in 1859.

Townsend, however, spent an additional year in Oregon, working as a physician for the Hudson's Bay Company at Fort Vancouver, before he too sailed east after a life-threatening bout of yellow fever. He arrived in Boston in November 1837, and presented most of his bird and animal specimens to the Academy of Natural Sciences of Philadelphia in accordance with his prior agreement. His

---

* Although Wyeth's business ventures completely unravelled, and his personal losses were doubtless extensive, the settlements in Oregon resulting from his expeditions were probably the greatest single determining factor that secured the forty-ninth parallel as the boundary between Britain and the United States, instead of the Columbia River, according to the Oregon Treaty of 1846.

other sponsor, the American Philosophical Society, also expected a full complement of specimens from his collection, however, and was greatly disappointed with the "trifling" specimens presented to them. A committee report officially expressed dissatisfaction with his

TOWNSEND'S GROUND SQUIRREL

work, even though, in a letter written from Fort Vancouver two years earlier, Townsend had apologized for not collecting rocks and minerals, explaining that he was unable to do so as a member of a fast-paced trading caravan. He appears to have had no further dealings with the society. Specific details of Townsend's professional and personal life after his return from the West are sketchy and no full-length biography has ever been written, perhaps due to the scarcity of material.

Townsend's Ground Squirrel was a species Townsend encountered on his cross-continental trek in 1834.

Townsend described many of his newly discovered species in the *Journal of the Academy of Natural Sciences of Philadelphia* in 1837 and 1839. John James Audubon used a number of Townsend's specimens to complete his great work, *Birds of America*, which was lacking in species from the Western prairies, the mountains, and the Far West. Audubon and John Bachman also used Townsend's mammal specimens, describing and painting them in their *Viviparous Quadrupeds of North America* in 1845–49. In 1839, Townsend published an account of his adventures crossing the continent, *Narrative of a Journey Across the Rocky Mountains to the Columbia River*, and in 1840 he produced one part of a projected series entitled *Ornithology of the United States of North America*. The series was abandoned because it was overshadowed by Audubon's *Birds*, just as he himself was overshadowed as an ornithologist by the dominant personality and fame of Audubon.

Townsend supplied many of his bird specimens from the Far West to Audubon who used them for his monumental *Birds of America.*

Townsend worked in Washington for three years for the National Institute (a forerunner of the National Museum), classifying and mounting bird specimens and organizing their collection, before returning to Philadelphia to study dentistry. His health began to deteriorate in the late 1840s for unknown reasons, and although he planned one final expedition as a naturalist on a naval vessel bound for the Cape of Good Hope, he died in February 1851 at the age of forty-two, before the ship departed. He left behind his wife, Charlotte, whom he had married sometime after returning from Oregon, and a young child about whom little is known.

The two years Townsend spent scouring the Western frontier for new scientific specimens were his glory days, and he is known as the first naturalist to discover and collect many of the birds and mammals of the northwestern United States and the first trained zoologist to cross overland to the Pacific Ocean. He added hundreds of species and subspecies to the world's known roster of plants, mammals, and, especially, birds. Quite a few bear his name. The sentiment he expressed while resting by a river in the foothills during his great trek conveys some of his dedication to science and his willingness to disregard hardship in pursuit of what he evidently considered his life's calling. "None but a naturalist," he suggested, "can appreciate a naturalist's feelings—his delight amounting to ecstasy—when a specimen such as he has never before seen, meets his eye, and the sorrow and grief which he feels when he is compelled to tear himself from a spot abounding with all that he has anxiously and unremittingly sought for."

While Townsend's accomplishments were cut short by his illness and early death, another naturalist who began his career in the Royal British Navy was beginning a thorough and systematic study of the Far North that would prove to be accurate and reliable and would be the foundation of subarctic and arctic botany and biology for years to come.

CHAPTER SEVEN

John Richardson

*With the decay of our strength our minds decayed, and we
were no longer able to bear the contemplation of the horrors that surrounded
us. . . . Yet we were calm and resigned to our fate, not a murmur
escaped us, and we were punctual and fervent in our
address to the Supreme Being.*

—JOHN RICHARDSON, *Journal 1820–1822*

John Richardson
(1787–1865) was a
celebrated explorer and the
foremost naturalist on the
regional zoology of the subarctic and arctic.

I put an end to his life by shooting him in the head with a pistol," reported Dr. John Richardson on October 20, 1821, after killing a demented and cannibalistic voyageur named Michael Teroahaute. Richardson, a thirty-three-year-old Scottish medical doctor, naturalist, and veteran of the Napoleonic wars, was stranded in the desolate arctic tundra north of Great Slave Lake in what is now the Northwest Territories in Canada. He was part of an ambitious but ill-conceived British expedition to chart the northern coastline of North America and collect specimens of natural history from the little-known region. All did not progress as planned, however, and a combination of bad luck and an underestimation of the difficulty of their task left the twenty-one-member expedition far from their food cache at Fort Enterprise on the Coppermine River, north of Great Slave Lake, as an early winter tightened its grip on the wind-lashed barrens.

While the main contingent of the starving band pushed on to their primitive fort south of the treeline, Richardson and British seaman John Hepburn remained behind in a copse of stunted spruce to nurse twenty-year-old Robert Hood, a naval officer and artist who was dying from exposure and starvation. The main party promised to send aid to the trio after reaching the fort. A day later Michael Teroahaute returned alone, with a hastily scrawled note from the commanding officer John Franklin. The note suggested a better resting spot for the three men not too far distant; it also reported that Teroahaute, who could not read, had been accompanied by another voyageur when he departed. When questioned concerning the whereabouts of his companion, Teroahaute brusquely claimed that the man had become lost and was presumably dead.

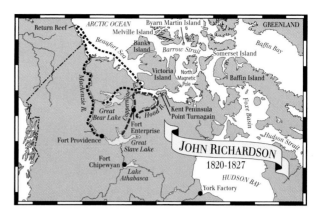

John Richardson's exploration in the Arctic and Subarctic, 1820–1827.

In the following days, Teroahaute's behaviour became erratic and crazed and he lingered about the camp, eyeing the three, yet refusing to hunt or collect firewood. He frequently murmured his opinion that he would rejoin Franklin alone if he only knew the direction. He also suggested that to save their own lives they should abandon Hood to his fate and rush to the fort before they all perished. "Mr. Hood endeavored to point out to him…the cruelty of (his recently announced decision to depart on his own)," wrote Richardson, "without leaving something for our support; but the discourse far from producing any beneficial effect, seemed only to excite his anger, and amongst other expressions, he made use of the following remarkable one: 'It is no use hunting, there are no animals, you had better kill and eat me.'" Soon after, Teroahaute returned to camp with a chunk of frozen meat he claimed he had hacked from the carcass of a recently slain wolf. The men roasted it over the fire and devoured it. Richardson later theorized darkly on the true nature of the meal. "We implicitly believed the story then," he reported, "but afterwards became convinced from the

Crossing the barren lands was a task far more difficult than the members of the expedition could ever have imagined.

circumstances, the details of which may be spared, that it must have been a portion of the body of Belanger or Perrault."[*]

Several days later, on October 20, while scraping *tripe de roche* lichens from weathered stones for a meagre repast, Richardson heard an argument between Hood and Teroahaute, followed by a gunshot. He rushed back to the camp and found Hood slumped on the ground near the tent. Although both he and Hepburn initially assumed that the man had taken his own life, the abnormal behaviour of Teroahaute and a closer inspection of the body convinced them that Hood had been murdered. Richardson "discovered that the shot had entered the back part of the head, and passed out at the forehead, and that the muzzle of the gun had been applied so close as to set fire to the night cap behind. The gun, which was of the longest kind supplied to the Indians, could not have been placed in a position to inflict such a wound, except by a second person." Richardson and Hepburn laid Hood's stiff body on the frozen ground in a

---

[*] However disgusted he was later, the added protein from the ill-tasting meat may well have saved his life. Teroahaute had probably been feasting on the flesh of one or more of his comrades. It will never be known whether Teroahaute murdered them to sustain his own waning life or if they perished from starvation and exposure.

copse of stunted willows, said their prayers, and then shambled south across the lumpy ground to Fort Enterprise. Teroahaute accompanied them, frequently denying that he had killed Hood, though no accusation had been openly made, and warning the others against accusing him of the deed. He seemed much stronger than either Richardson or Hepburn, who were wasting away on a protein-deficient diet.

Tripe de Roche.

Stone near Fort Enterprise.

A species of lichen called *tripe de roche* was abundant in the region north of Fort Enterprise and for several weeks was virtually the only food eaten by members of the expedition.

Two days later, Teroahaute lingered on the fringe of the camp, allowing Richardson and Hepburn to speak freely for the first time since Hood was shot. Now truly fearing for their lives, Richardson and Hepburn formulated a plan to kill Teroahaute when, or if, the opportunity arose. It did. Richardson shot him in the head as he returned to camp through the bushes. According to Richardson's report, Teroahaute's rifle was loaded, perhaps with the intention of killing them and returning to Fort Enterprise alone.

For several more days, the two trudged south through the lonely land, following the frozen river where only the summer before caribou herds grazed and birds were abundant. Richardson and Hepburn subsisted on little more than boiled buffalo-skin robe and acrid lichen broth, which produced "severe bowel complaints" and was "inefficient in recruiting our strength." They stumbled into the clearing around the fort only to discover the appalling destitution of their comrades. It was 20 degrees centigrade below freezing and an icy wind tugged at the clothes of John Franklin and five voyageurs, swirling snow around the dirty floor of the gloomy hut that had been partially pulled down to keep a feeble fire in the corner. "Our own misery," Richardson remembered, "had stolen upon us by degrees, and we were accustomed to the contemplation of each other's emaciated figures, but the ghastly countenances, dilated eyeballs and sepulchral voices of Captain Franklin and those with him were more than we could bear."

It was the end of October 1821, a bitter nine-month winter lay ahead of them, and they had no provisions other than a heap of old charred bones and mouldering deerskins hauled from the previous year's refuse pits. With the shooting of Teroahaute and the starvation of nearly a dozen voyageurs on his mind, Richardson settled in to wait for aid. The bone-chilling horror of the past three weeks and the realization of his more-than-likely eventual starvation must have been hard to bear. Although Lieutenant John Franklin, the commanding officer, tried to dispel the "gloomy apprehensions of approaching death," he soon collapsed from his exertions, barely able to collect a few sticks for the fire. They waited for their fellow officer, George Back, and several voyageurs to return from a desperate cross-country trek in search of a band of natives who had promised to provide them with food. Several emaciated men lost hope and expired in their bunks, their teeth huge in their shrunken faces. Richardson wrote that it was only fervent and frequent prayers that kept his spirits up and he definitively stated his opinion that it was the lack of Christianity that let the Indians and voyageurs perish.[*]

They had spent eight days languishing in the gloomy hut with barely the strength or will to move when, on November 7, George Back returned with a band of Copper Indians and lifesaving provisions. The skeletal explorers, including Richardson, acting against his own orders, gobbled down stewed caribou until they became violently ill, as their stomachs were unaccustomed to the intrusion of food. They were

---

[*] Although Richardson was fairly open-minded when it came to appreciating native culture and traditions, his nineteenth-century British sense of cultural and religious superiority remained undiminished and untempered by empathy and imagination. He believed that missionaries would be a positive influence on the native peoples. "I should like to see the torch of truth carried into the dark regions of the north," he wrote later in life.

painfully nursed back to health over several weeks—their bodies filled out, their minds cleared, and the aching of their swollen joints subsided. Only nine out of twenty survived.

During the following months they travelled overland to York Factory on the western shore of Hudson Bay. Before leaving for England in the spring of 1822, Richardson wrote to his wife of his miraculous deliverance from what seemed to be certain death. "I have, through plentiful fare," he proudly recounted, "become fatter than ever I was before, and have recovered from every painful effect of my late sufferings; but you must be prepared to behold traces of age upon my face that have been impressed since we parted. This, however, is the common lot of humanity, and I have only taken a sudden start of you by a few years; hereafter I hope we shall grow old together."

The British Admiralty, who had funded the expedition, was almost as pleased with the explorers' return as were their families. Despite starvation, cannibalism, and murder, the Admiralty did not consider the expedition a failure. They had charted nearly five hundred miles of arctic coastline east from the Coppermine River, had kept accurate records of the climate and terrain, and had amassed a considerable cache of natural history specimens, dried plants, and skins and skeletons of fishes, small mammals, and birds. Richardson had been well equipped with dozens of notebooks, presses for plant and insect preservation, a few jars with spirits for preserving animal specimens, and "paste for preparing skins of quadrupeds & birds." During the first segment of the two-and-a-half-year ordeal, Richardson had plenty of time to collect and study the flora and fauna along the route of his travels—six hundred miles by canoe from York Factory to Cumberland House on the Saskatchewan River, and then on to Fort Chipewyan on Lake Athabasca, and Fort Providence on Great Slave Lake. It was a huge distance and they had travelled fast, but Richardson had used the winters of 1819–20 and 1820–21 to collect specimens of the natural world.

After the defeat of Napoleon in 1815, the Admiralty was actively promoting exploration and scientific study. With hundreds of officers and mariners, and dozens of ships in need of a purpose, the Admiralty cast its eyes north to where geographers and cartographers had mysteriously scrawled *Terra Incognita* across the vast tract of land along the northern half of North America. It was a land in which for centuries British sailors had searched for the Northwest Passage to the Orient; it was one of the most remote, inaccessible, and little-known regions of the planet, where the freezing winter could linger for nine months of the year—much of it under a melancholy dome of perpetual darkness. In some regions the sailing season was limited to a single treacherous and fickle month. What mysteries the North contained remained unknown, but early travel tales hinted at something spectacular—perhaps hidden gold deposits or copper mines, the shores of a vast inland sea, a sea route to the spice islands, even a hidden temperate country near the North Pole.

The Admiralty was not particularly interested in the study of natural science, but it was a service that secured the support of the prestigious Royal Society and the scientific community. And, by extension, it generated greater public appreciation for the navy's role, not only as heroic vanquishers of Britain's foes, but also as participants in the quest for scientific truth and the accurate cataloguing of all of nature. It gave an elevated sense of purpose to this and other expeditions, a lofty diversion from the more prosaic responsibilities of the navy. Part of the role of a natural historian, in the navy's eyes, was to help ascertain the value of unexplored land to British commercial and military interests.

For a young navy veteran fascinated with the natural world, the Arctic land expedition was an unparalleled opportunity to advance his naval and scientific careers. "I consider this appointment," he wrote to his brother before he set off in 1819, "as affording a fairer prospect of advancement than any I have hitherto held, and as it will bring me into acquaintance with many scientific men, and those at the head of naval affairs, I am much pleased with it."

Born on November 5, 1787, Richardson was the eldest of twelve siblings, the children of prosperous brewers in Dumfries, Scotland. The precocious lad was reputedly reading by age four and began his medical apprenticeship, under the tutelage of his uncle in Edinburgh, at the age of thirteen. He attended the University of Edinburgh, studying medicine, ancient languages, chemistry, and, most important for the Arctic land expedition, natural history. The Royal College of Surgeons in London graduated him before his twentieth birthday and he immediately signed on as an assistant surgeon in the navy, just in time to join Horatio Nelson as he led the British fleet in the spectacular and violent bombardment of Copenhagen in 1807.

Surgeons were in great demand during the bloody battles of the Napoleonic wars and, for a young doctor, it must have been a rude introduction to the world—in the dank, sunless bowels of the rolling warships, he crudely amputated the mangled limbs of dying mariners or carved into flesh to retrieve chunks of metal or wooden shrapnel. He ministered to those burning with dreaded yellow fever or suffering from battle-induced dementia. The survival rate for serious injuries was very low, anesthetic and sterilization nonexistent, and surgical techniques in their infancy. He must have had a stable and level-headed temperament to thrive in such an environment.

For over twelve years, Richardson served on various ships travelling near Halifax, Montreal, Quebec, and the Florida/Georgia border before being discharged after the war. Aside from naval records and Richardson's own travel accounts, almost all other information on his life comes from an 1868 biography written by his son-in-law, the Reverend John McIlraith. McIlraith, not surprisingly, has nothing negative to say about his father-in-law, and true to the Victorian sense of propriety, seldom comments on Richardson's personal life. Robert E. Johnson's 1976 biography is not much more illuminating, concentrating on Richardson's scientific accomplishments. From these sources it is apparent that Richardson wasted little time joining civilian society after his discharge, and married Mary Stiven of Leith, of whom little is written, on June 1, 1818, in Edinburgh. Ambitious and studious, the young doctor then augmented his officer's half-pay with a private practice in medicine while he continued his studies in natural history under Professor Robert Jameson at the University of Edinburgh.

The sleepy life of a provincial surgeon did not hold his interest long, however, and when he heard of the Arctic land expedition, he immediately applied for the position of surgeon/naturalist. He probably knew that he would be gone for at least two years, so one wonders what his wife thought of the arrangement, considering they were newlyweds of only nine months when the idea came to his mind. The staid and secure was never for Richardson, though his demeanour and appearance suggested otherwise. According to Jane Griffin, who would later marry John Franklin, he was "a middle-sized man...not well dressed—looks like a Scotchman as he is—he has broad & high cheekbones, a widish mouth, gray & brown hair—upon the whole rather plain, but the countenance thoughtful, mild and pleasing."

In May 1819, the otherwise responsible doctor took leave of his new bride and comfortable life in private practice and set out, with high hopes for success and perhaps fame, to chart the Arctic coast in the Barren Lands of North America and make his mark in the world of science. In addition to his role as surgeon, he hoped to create an intelligent and definitive collection of minerals, plants, fishes, lichens, mammals, and other northern exotica unfamiliar to denizens of the green and pleasant British Isles. "The country has never been visited by a naturalist," he explained to his father before departing London, "and presents a rich harvest."

It turned out to be a rich harvest, indeed, although a good portion of his collections from the Arctic coast were jettisoned in the desperate dash south in the early winter of 1821. After returning to England as a national hero, he had ample time to prepare his notes for publication and arrange his specimens for study. In addition to contributing chapters to John Franklin's *Narrative of a Journey to the Shores of the Polar Sea in the Years 1819–20–21–22*, Richardson contributed almost all of the material for the seven appendices relating to the natural history of the Subarctic and Arctic—with special attention to botany, geology, fishes, and the aurora borealis. He also wrote numerous journal articles about his northern observations and collections. Not long after his return, he was considered the foremost natural historian of the Far North in North America—his descriptions and observations were the first reasonably accurate information concerning the flora and fauna of the region.

Richardson had encountered species that were previously unknown to science, and he went to painstaking efforts to observe them and wrote detailed descriptions of their characteristics. "Several beautiful fish," he wrote, "were taken today with the rod and artificial fly at a small rapid at the commencement of Winter River. They belong to a species of the genus Salmo.... The stomach of this beautiful fish is generally filled with gravel or black earth. It bites eagerly at the artificial fly and deriving great power from its large dorsal fin, affords much sport to the angler. Its rectum is filled with black faeces." He named the fish Back's Grayling after his travelling companion and fellow officer, George Back.

Richardson's fish descriptions reveal that he regarded them as much more than scientific specimens. In addition to his descriptions, he wrote that "the burbot is found in every river and lake in the country, and is so little esteemed as food as to be eaten only in cases of necessity.... When well bruised and mixed with a little flour," however, "the roe can be baked into very good biscuits which are used in the fur countries as

Poisson inconnu was found to the north of Athabasca Lake (Alberta), in 1822. The study of fish, ichthyology, was one of Richardson's specialties. He also loved eating fish.

tea-bread." Of the walleye, or pickerel or dore, he wrote that "it is a well-flavoured, delicate fish, though being too poor to please the palates of those who have been accustomed to feast upon the Whitefish ... or Sturgeon, it is often abandoned to the dogs, with whom, for the same reason, it is no favourite. Even an Epicurean ichthyologist would relish it when fried; but from the scarcity of lard, butter or suet, this is not a usual mode of cooking in the fur-countries." The Pacific Herring, he reported, "has been compared to the common herrings brought to the London market in January, and found to agree exactly." The white sucker was "a very soft watery fish ... considered to be one of the best in the country for making soup." And the whitefish, "though it is a rich, fat fish, instead of producing satiety it daily becomes more agreeable to the palate; and I know, from experience, that though deprived of bread and vegetables, one may live wholly upon this fish for months, even years, without tiring." Culinary considerations aside, Richardson remained interested in ichthyology (the study of fish) throughout his long life, extending his interest and knowledge in the subject beyond that of a collector and becoming one of the foremost scientific experts on the subject.

He also had ample opportunity to observe lichens, sometimes his only food for days at a time. Richardson identified and collected forty-two distinct species and provided, in addition to a description, the most practical knowledge he could think of at the time—instructions on where to find them: "in moist places," in "rein-deer tracks," in "the shady clefts of rocks," or "at the roots of bushes near the summits of hills." Others he simply described as being "on the ground. Abundant." He didn't, however, give an assessment of their relative flavour or preferred cooking methods.

Richardson also studied and recorded all he could of the

common northern mammals such as reindeer, foxes, muskoxen, bears, and wolves, noting their seasonal migrations, preferred foods, mating rituals, behavioural characteristics, and habitat distribution. He singled out the meadow mole for a wry comment. "It shows a strong inclination to domesticate itself," he wrote, "many of them already frequenting the house." He wrote the first-ever descriptions of the yellow-billed loon, the hawk owl, the willow ptarmigan, the green-winged teal drake, and the red-necked grebe, to name but a few—very precise lengthy descriptions accounting for every detail of colouring, feathers, skin, feet, wing length, beak, and the difference between the males and females. His reports make for dense, turgid reading, but were no doubt of great interest to naturalists who had until then no reliable information concerning any but the most obvious and common subarctic and arctic creatures. Richardson's precise descriptions and observations, and later his accurate classifications and anatomical and physiological studies, set him above most other field naturalists.

Overall, however, Richardson was not satisfied with the information he collected. He felt his information was sketchy and haphazard, based on chance-encountered specimens picked up along the route. He believed his collection was a good start, but it was neither comprehensive nor definitive, and he hoped for the opportunity to continue his career as a natural historian in the North.

The Admiralty was also interested in continuing its explorations of northern North America and, in mid-1824, Richardson was offered the position of second-in-command and chief natural historian of a second, more ambitious but better planned, expedition to the polar sea where he would have much more time to study the natural world and collect specimens. To Richardson, this was exciting news and he spent the next year studying all he could in preparation for the journey.

Richardson, Franklin, Back, E. N. Kendall, and an

Pelican Portage on Slave River. Overland travelling on the Barren Lands required numerous unpredictable portages over difficult terrain.

assistant naturalist, Thomas Drummond, sailed to New York in the early spring of 1825, took a steamer up the Hudson River to Albany, and then rode a stagecoach to Niagara Falls. Richardson, like many others before and since, was amazed by the falls. "The grandeur of the scene far exceeded my previous conceptions of it," he admitted. "On comparison with this all other cataracts which I have seen dwindle into perfect insignificance." Eager not to miss any of the short northern summer, the party did not linger and pressed on along increasingly rough and primitive roads through Upper Canada to Penetanguishene, where they were joined by a large crew of voyageurs from Montreal. The voyageurs took them west in two huge canoes along the northern coasts of Lake Huron and Lake Superior. By mid-May, they had arrived at the fur-trading outpost of Fort William, and Franklin and Richardson pushed on to Cumberland House while the others brought along the supplies at a slower pace. After paddling from Cumberland House, the two caught up with twenty British seamen who had sailed from England the year before, and they completed the final portage together en route to Fort Chipewyan on Lake Athabasca.

Scarcely pausing for a rest, Richardson and half the British seamen loaded four boats and continued north along the Mackenzie River to Great Bear Lake, where they constructed a semi-permanent base for the next two years of exploration—and politely named it Fort Franklin. Learning from past mistakes, they selected a site well below the treeline and near plentiful food sources. Although it was a considerable improvement on the dilapidated cabin named Fort Enterprise, Richardson was still critical of the huts. "The miserable log houses in which we dwell," he wrote, "are scarcely to be distinguished, in their winter dress, from the fallen trees with which the woods abound."

Arctic Flora painted by George Back in 1818 shows the first plants collected by Richardson during the expedition's first season in North America.

After securing Fort Franklin, Richardson set out on a month-long canoe survey and specimen-collecting expedition of two hundred miles of the northern coast of Great Bear Lake before returning to join the others in September. By October, winter had settled upon the land. The fort was in a sheltered bower amidst a forest of dwarf pines, crooked and bent, struggling against the incessant wind, their twisted roots boring into the rock and permafrost. With fifty inhabitants for the winter, the fort was a crowded and social abode. Game and fish were plentiful, and the dark season passed in boredom, but not hardship. Richardson had plenty of time to prepare his collections and work on his journal.

He described the feasts at Christmas and New Year's in letters to his wife. "There were also some Indian dames," he wrote, "decorous spectators of the scene, their raven hair dripping with unguents prepared from the marrow of the reindeer, and their expanded countenances ornamented with twin rows of ivory teeth, gracefully contrasting with their lovely bronze features whereon streaks of lampblack and rouge were harmoniously blended." In the darkest days of winter, he seldom ventured far from the encampment. In

Portrait of Stoney Indian at Carleton House and Sketches of Indian Pipes, 1820. Without the help of the native peoples Richardson and his companions never would have survived their terrible ordeal.

addition to his naturalist work, Richardson spent considerable time reminiscing on his life. He had developed, he claimed, "that romantic attachment which a Scotchman, in his wanderings, feels towards the land of his birth."

As the snow melted in the spring, it released them from months of forced indolence and lifted palpable weight from their spirits. They eagerly prepared for some hard travelling through unknown arctic terrain. The entire party loaded their massive canoes with vast quantities of dried food and floated down the Mackenzie River to the coast. At the Mackenzie delta they split up. Franklin and his party proceeded west along the windy, perpetually frozen coast, while Richardson travelled east, charting the territory between the Mackenzie and Coppermine Rivers. "Everything," wrote the religious doctor, "wears a favourable aspect, and trusting in the all-powerful protection of the beneficent Ruler of the Universe, who has hither-to sustained us, we hope to return successful and in safety."

As part of the British Admiralty's ambitious plans, ships had been dispatched to sail into the Arctic Ocean to meet up with the two land expeditions and bring them home by way of the Northwest Passage, which they were sure of locating. The explorers prudently allowed plenty of time to return to Fort Franklin in the event the ships failed to show up by the end of the season (which they didn't). The Arctic coast was barren and rocky, with chilling gusts of wind blowing off the Beaufort Sea, icebergs colliding on the choppy open water, and a lumpy land of moss, lichens, and grasses stretching to the southern horizon, pockmarked with a seemingly infinite number of tiny lakes, ponds, and rivulets. Sailing and rowing their large boats close to shore proved tiring and frustrating as they dodged ice chunks and dealt with erratic currents and unpredictable winds. Richardson rowed up to familiar territory at the mouth of the Coppermine River without any major disasters. He built a large cairn and stuffed it with preserved supplies before heading south along the Coppermine. At the Dease River, he ditched the largest boats and continued paddling west to the eastern shore of Great Bear Lake, arriving on August 18, 1826. The group pressed on to Fort Franklin, arriving on September 1.

Beavers and muskrats were abundant throughout the near north and were the foundation of the fur trade and the Hudson's Bay Company's wealth.

Richardson scrawled a note to his commanding officer, in case he too returned to the fort, and then canoed south along the broad Mackenzie River to Great Slave Lake. He circumnavigated the lake in his canoe, describing the geology and collecting specimens of the flora and fauna. It was a pleasant month of travel for the doctor, freed as he was from the duty of charting and exploring. "The trees have assumed the livery of autumn," he wrote, "and the leaves are falling fast; but the scenery in its present dress looks delightful, and the fall, as it is termed, is in fact the only season of the year, when, from the absence of mosquitoes and other winged pests, travelling in this country is pleasant." He remained at Fort Resolution on Great Slave Lake for part of the winter.

When he learned that Franklin had returned safely to Fort Franklin, Richardson left for Carlton House on the Saskatchewan River to continue his studies. In the spring of 1827, his assistant naturalist, Thomas Drummond, who the previous year had travelled west while Richardson went north, rejoined him at Carlton House and the two compared notes. With the aid of Hudson's Bay Company traders, Drummond had canoed and hiked from Cumberland House along the Athabasca River, across the Rocky Mountains to the Fraser River, and into what is now British Columbia. He had hauled back to Carlton House, perfectly preserved and labelled, 1,500 species of plants, 150 species of birds, 50 species of quadrupeds, and 25 species of insects. The combined collections and observations of Richardson and Drummond were to become the foundation of the first comprehensive compendium of northern North American life. Because of the relatively small number of plants and animals that lived in the harsh environment of northern North America, it was much more feasible for naturalists to develop a definitive collection for this region than it was, for example, for them to do the same in Brazil.

The return to England was quick and uneventful. Franklin and Richardson retraced their route to New York and boarded a sailing ship to Liverpool, arriving in mid-September, while the others canoed east to York Factory on Hudson Bay and took a ship to Portsmouth, arriving a month later. The Admiralty was most pleased with their geographic discoveries and charting of over eight hundred miles of Arctic coastline (about half the Arctic coast of Canada and a good portion of Alaska). There were only two accidental deaths during their two and a half years in the Arctic, and the success of the expedition contributed to the advancement of all their careers. During the next several years, Richardson settled into a quieter life, concentrating his time on preparing his manuscripts for publication, particularly the appendices on natural history in Franklin's narrative of the second expedition. Electing to remain with the navy, Richardson was placed in charge of the Naval Hospital at Chatham. His duties as chief surgeon, however, did not keep him from working on his most ambitious project, *Fauna Boreali-Americana*, a four-volume catalogue of Arctic biology that established the concept of regional ecology—the idea that certain zones of the world had distinct ecosystems, and that the species of a given region should be studied as an interrelated group independently from similar species in other climate zones.

Richardson laboured on the four volumes of *Fauna Boreali-Americana*, supported by the Admiralty, for nine years, sometimes in collaboration with other naturalists. In the first volume, published in 1829, he described dozens of mammals, from the tiny deer mouse to the large plains bison, while subsequent volumes, published every two years, were devoted to birds, fish, and insects. Partway through this work, Richardson's wife, Mary, became seriously ill with tuberculosis; she died in 1831 just before publication of the second volume. With no children from their union, Richardson threw himself into his work and studies during his period of mourning, labouring incessantly on his magnum opus and attending to his duties at the naval hospital. Two years later, he married Mary Booth. They eventually had seven children, five of whom survived to adulthood.

After the publication of the first several volumes of *Fauna Boreali-Americana* Richardson's position within the scientific community was secure. He had crossed over from being a professional collector to being a scientist, a closet naturalist. Respected for his role as an explorer and acknowledged as the foremost naturalist on the regional zoology of the Subarctic and Arctic, he continued to write journal articles, collaborated on books, and wrote the natural history appendices in other Arctic explorers' journals. In 1835 he was elected to the prestigious Royal Society in London and in 1856 he was honoured with a Gold Medal, its highest award. His career in the Royal Navy was also on the rise. He was eventually appointed Physician to the Fleets and was stationed at the Royal Naval Hospital at Haslar. There he pushed to improve nursing care for wounded sailors, experimented with the then-new concept of using general anesthesia in surgery, and made suggestions for the improvement of the treatment of mental disease among sailors.

Never tiring of natural history, Richardson became one of the most respected and foremost ichthyologists in the country. He was never a theorizer, but an anatomical specialist.

Fort Franklin, near the shores of Great Bear Lake, was the expedition's base for the two winters 1825–1826 and 1826–1827.

Fish specimens from all over the world were forwarded to him by naturalist/surgeons on navy ships, preserved in strong alcohol—which in the navy meant rum. Occasionally, strange fishes and other marine creatures arrived in empty casks, wrinkled and mouldering in the dregs—the sailors having secretly siphoned out the tainted rum to augment their daily dose. Richardson may have snickered or been repulsed, but there was little he could do. His collection nevertheless grew to such proportions that luminaries like Charles Darwin visited with the exclusive purpose of examining it.*

Richardson continued to enjoy honours and awards throughout his tenure at Haslar and, in 1846, he was knighted for his achievements. He wasn't entirely finished with the Arctic, however. The Admiralty's interest in arctic exploration had waned after several expensive and inconclusive voyages, but in 1845 they had commissioned the aging

---

* Richardson's thoughts on Charles Darwin's theory of evolution through the process of natural selection are unclear. Richardson corresponded with Darwin throughout his career, sharing information on matters of Arctic biology. Darwin on at least one occasion visited Richardson to study his collections while preparing his book *The Voyage of the Beagle*. Although Richardson himself never mentioned evolution in any of his own writings, he also never publicly opposed it. It appears that he reconciled the concept of evolution with his staunch Presbyterian beliefs.

John Franklin to lead two huge, well-furnished, and rein-
forced ships to make one final push to discover the elusive
Northwest Passage. There had been no word of them for two
years and a grand-scale disaster seemed likely. Richardson,
then sixty years old, approached the Admiralty with a plan for
an overland searching expedition along the same coast he had
explored decades earlier.

Although his age was a major hurdle, he persuaded the
Admiralty to consider his experience and thirty-year friendship with the missing captain. On March 25, 1848, he once
again boarded a ship for North America, where he was to link
up with an energetic and resourceful Scottish fur trader
named John Rae. The two met in Montreal and retraced
Richardson's familiar route north and west, and then followed
the Mackenzie River north. The trees diminished in size until
they were little more than withered bushes and lines of crumbling rock pushed through the skin of the earth like ribs. They
travelled east, leaving cairns and food caches along the stony
shore to help stranded mariners who might stumble upon
them. Richardson devoted himself to frequent prayers and letters home to his family. Despite his age and "weather which
would stop an Indian," he kept up with the younger men until
they abandoned the coast for the winter. Richardson, the
indomitable Rae, and their entourage spent the winter of
1848–49 at Fort Confidence on western Great Bear Lake
under a dome of stars in the brittle cold. It was an introspec-
tive time for Richardson, which he spent reading books
selected by his wife, studying scripture, and pronouncing ser-
mons to the assembled inhabitants of the rudimentary fort.
"The snow geese are still passing in flocks," he wrote one day
before permanent darkness had settled upon the land, "and
we kill some daily, taking also fish by nets and lines set under
the ice of the lake. Our meals make a break in the monotony
of our lives."

Time dragged on and Richardson thought of his family.
The monotony and primitive conditions soon overshadowed

Richardson studied common northern mammals.

the initial excitement of re-visiting the scenes of his youthful adventures. "Three and twenty years have passed since papa spent one of his birth-days on this lake," he wrote to his daughter on his sixty-second birthday, "and many changes of kingdom and family have occurred in that interval of time. It is a long period to look forward to, my dear little child, and to you, I fancy, it looks like a life-time, but I look back on twenty-five years as a dream of the night....I almost fancy at times that I have never been anything but an inhabitant of these wilds." The exertions of his summer journey, and a frightening episode of chest pain, persuaded Richardson that exploration was a young person's job and he made plans to leave the great open land and return to England in the spring. He would leave John Rae, much younger and more robust, in charge of the expedition. It seems that Richardson's final Arctic journey, whether he was conscious of it or not, was as much to experience for one final time the grandeur and desolation of the North American North as it was to help locate his old comrade.

Never again did he venture to the northlands. But he did continue his work in natural history, corresponding with scientific peers in Britain and abroad, focusing in his later years almost exclusively on ichthyology. During his career he described, according to C. Stuart Houston, the editor of Richardson's annotated journal from his first arctic expedition, "forty-three still-accepted genera of fish and well over two hundred new species of fish." In 1857, he contributed three articles to the eighth edition of the *Encyclopaedia Britannica*—a 128-page definitive article on ichthyology, and shorter articles entitled "The Life of Sir John Franklin" and "The Polar Regions."

When he retired from the navy in 1855, however, he found it more difficult to keep abreast of the latest developments in natural history, and his access to the latest books and specimens was curtailed by his new residence in

Lancrigg in the Lake District. "I thought at one time of preparing sets of the lichens for distribution," he wrote to one correspondent, "but I find the time has gone past with me. Want of books of reference and other causes have induced me to give up entirely the study of Natural History and to employ my leisure hours otherwise." He

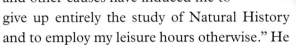

RICHARDSON'S GROUND SQUIRREL

had a strong interest in philology and took an avid interest in the new dictionary of the English language then being created. The *Oxford English Dictionary* was being developed and edited by James Henry Murray at a great scriptorium in Oxford. Richardson employed himself reading the oldest editions of many early English books, sending in annotated notes on each word and the context of its use. He took a special interest in cataloguing the Scottish words used by Robert Burns, along with their definitions in English. With his children either successfully married or established in promising careers, he spent his time reading, visiting friends and family, and running a busy charity practice in the local community.

Richardson's Ground Squirrel is one of many species named after Richardson. His description of its habits and behaviours were so precise that naturalists have added little in over 150 years.

He died on Monday, June 5, 1865, at the age of seventy-eight, much to the sorrow of the many people who knew him. He had a large circle of friends, colleagues, and admirers that included some of the greatest scientific luminaries of the time, as well as unknown tradesmen. Many detailed obituaries appeared in papers and periodicals throughout Britain, and all lamented his passing, heaping effusive praise on him. One friend wrote, "I should think it hardly possible to find a more perfect man, in body, soul, and spirit—strong, deep, and true." Richardson would likely have been humbled by the respect of his scientific peers, touched by the emotion of his comrades and family, but ultimately embarrassed at the florid, ornate, and windy accounts of his life and achievements. His old companion George Back, the last surviving member of his first arctic expedition, perhaps best summed up Richardson's character when he wrote simply that "he was ever a pleasant companion, and, better than all, a moral, good man."

In the field of natural history, Richardson's achievements speak for themselves. In 1930, at the joint convention of the Canadian and British Medical Associations in Winnipeg, Dr. David Stewart gave a speech on Richardson's scientific contributions. "Plants of Northern Canada," he said, "named by and for Richardson would make a garden of respectable size, and animals named by and for him a considerable zoo."

PART FOUR

The Last Field Naturalists

LINNAEUS'S FIRST LIST OF ANIMALS, created in 1758, catalogued and named 4,162 species. It was a considerable number, and naturalists expected that it would be only a matter of decades before every species in the world—all of "creation"—was slotted into the list and defined forever. But by the early nineteenth century, the number of known animal species had more than doubled. By the end of the nineteenth century, after the great natural history craze and the era of the professional collectors, over 400,000 species were known to science. The total number of species in the world seemed to increase in proportion to the number of specimen collectors in the field. Today the figure is well over one million, with new insects alone being discovered at the rate of about six thousand annually (and thousands of other species becoming extinct each year from pollution, deforestation, and other forms of habitat loss).

Between Linnaeus's time and 1862—the year that respected British zoologist Richard Owen tallied the results—species of birds had increased in number from 444 to over 8,000. Naturalists began to suspect that nature would never be defined in the form of a complete list. Not only did the astronomical increase in the number of known species raise disturbing questions, such as how Noah's Ark could possibly have accommodated a breeding pair of this vast and bewildering host of organisms, but too many species had been collected for any single individual to even hope to have an adequate knowledge of them all.

As late as the 1830s, natural history remained a broad pursuit, a blend of collecting, theorizing, and speculating. One of the main reasons for the huge popular interest in natural history in the mid-nineteenth century, apart from the influence of natural theology, was that it was a generalist's pursuit, driven by the desire to know all of nature. Anyone could become involved and believe that they were contributing to scientific knowledge. Not only did the collectors and laboratory naturalists eventually separate and specialize, but by the 1850s, closet naturalists themselves had to further specialize in order to make sense of the multitude of species. The term "naturalist" increasingly became outdated as people preferred more specific titles related to their field of study—botanist, zoologist, ichthyologist, or ornithologist, for example.

Branches of biology such as botany, zoology, or ichthyology, also became more rigorous, focusing on the minutiae of internal biological processes rather than on classification. Having an encyclopedic knowledge of the differences between various species of fish, as John Richardson did in the 1840s, was no longer enough to secure respect from a scientific establishment that was increasingly concerned with detailed explanations of internal organism functioning. As with any new subject of study, theories and principles came after the facts had been gathered—and the professional collectors had done, and were doing, their fact-gathering with diligence and precision.

By the second half of the nineteenth century, natural history was petering out as a scientific tradition. Its great contribution to scientific knowledge had been made and there were few remote regions of the world left to explore. Natural history as a hobby and as a literary genre remained popular, but the role of the old-style naturalists, even the closet naturalists, within the scientific community began to steadily decrease.

In a sense, collectors like Henry Walter Bates were so successful that they contributed to the decline of their own profession by scooping up the remainder of easily identifiable and locatable species. During his decade along the far reaches of the Amazon River, Bates introduced over eight thousand new species to science. He set out for Brazil in 1848, at the height of the interest in natural history, but when his book was published fifteen years later, in 1863, the fascination with natural history and the respect for naturalists as professionals was beginning a slow but terminal decline. Bates tried to make the transition from a naturalist collector into the rank of scientists, but was not entirely successful, in part because of his social background and in part because, ironically, his success as a field naturalist probably tainted his reputation as a scientist.

On the other hand, John Wesley Powell began his career when interest in natural history was already dwindling. The American West had already been largely explored and scoured by earlier naturalists, apart from one lone region—the canyons of the Colorado River. Consequently, he turned his attention to the unique geology of that region and produced a classic tale of adventure replete with a naturalist's wonder at the glory and magnificence of nature. To Powell, however, writing more than a decade after Darwin's evolutionary theory transformed scientific thought, the glory of nature was not evidence of divine creation, but of the power of natural forces—erosion by water, wind, and time. Despite his early career as a naturalist/traveller in one of the few remaining unexplored regions in North America, Powell made the leap to become a respected scientist because of his innovative theories and ideas. He began his career as a field naturalist, but ended it as a powerful institutional scientist. The era of the great scientific travellers and collectors ended in his lifetime.

CHAPTER EIGHT

Henry Walter Bates

*There is something in a tropical forest akin
to the ocean in its effect on the mind. Man feels so completely his
insignificance there and the vastness of nature.*
—HENRY WALTER BATES,
The Naturalist on the River Amazons

Henry Walter Bates
(1825–1892) spent over
ten years in the Amazon
basin and collected and
catalogued nearly fifteen
thousand species of plants
and animals new to science.

fter a turbulent and harrowing Atlantic crossing in a small, cramped vessel in 1848, twenty-three-year-old Henry Walter Bates and his travelling companion, twenty-five-year-old Alfred Russel Wallace, beheld the barren dunes of the Brazilian shore stretching back to a thick mass of mist-enshrouded forest that clothed "the whole surface of the country for two thousand miles from this point to the foot of the Andes." Under an overcast sky, the ship sailed up the Pará River, so immensely broad that the opposite shore could not be seen through the fog. Eagerly scanning the land, the two young men spied "many native canoes, which seemed like toys beneath the lofty walls of the dark forest." The ship docked at the port of Pará (now called Belém) on May 26 and, soon after introducing themselves to several British merchants and establishing a base for their expeditions, they set off into the virgin forest. Although Bates could never have known it, he would spend the next eleven years tramping through the morass of the Brazilian rain forest along the length of the turbid Amazon River. "All the sights and sounds," he remembered, "showed us we had come to a land where perpetual summer, warmth, verdure, and general nature invited the inhabitants to a life of pleasure rather than one of anxiety and toil."

By the time he returned to England in 1859, Bates had made an unparalleled contribution to the study of natural history by discovering and cataloguing a vast harvest of ants, wasps, beetles, moths, and butterflies, in addition to an aviary of birds and a menagerie of larger animals. Of the 14,712 species he collected, approximately 8,000 were new to science. His detailed collections and insightful observations, particularly his theory of mimicry among butterflies (where certain butterflies look like different species in order to avoid their predators), were later used by Charles Darwin to strengthen his arguments for evolution through natural selection. A short, bespectacled man who suffered in England from chronic dyspepsia and frequently recurring bronchitis, Bates was one of the most widely respected entomologists of his day and known to most of the scientific explorers, although he always remained on the fringe of Victorian institutional scientific society.

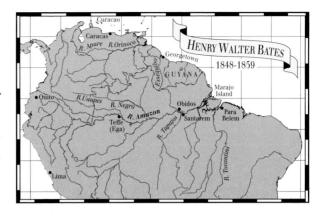

Henry Walter Bates's sojourn along the Amazon, 1848–1859.

It was a simple book published in 1847 that led Bates and his friend Wallace to cast their eyes toward distant Brazil. *A Voyage up the River Amazon*, written by an American naturalist from New York named William H. Edwards, described the Amazon basin as a naturalist's utopia. After several months along the Amazon in 1846, Edwards had sketched out the details of his colourful journey. "At this period," Edwards wrote of one of his destinations, "too vast numbers of trees add their tribute of beauty, and the flower-domed forest from its many-coloured altars ever sends heavenward worshipful incense. Nor is this wild luxuriance unseen or unenlivened. Monkeys are frolicking through festooned bowers, or chasing in revelry over the wood arches. Squirrels scamper in ecstasy from limb to limb, unable to contain themselves for joyousness. Coatis are gamboling among the fallen leaves, or vying with monkeys in nimble climbing, pacas and agoutis chase wildly about.... The exquisite, tiny deer, scarcely larger than a lamb, sniffs exultantly the air, and bounds fearlessly, knowing that he has no enemy here." Edwards also wrote of birds "of gaudiest plumage"; of butterflies "the bigness of a hand, and of the richest metallic blue"; of "myriads of gaily coated insects"; and of "armies of ants in their busy toil." All this seemed fantastic to two adventure-seeking companions trapped in the stultifying labours of the lower rungs of Victorian society. Fascinated by Edwards's account of the wonders of the Amazon, and having little other material to tether their dreamy thoughts to the earth, the two vowed to set sail for Brazil.

Neither Bates nor Wallace was destined for a career in the natural sciences. They were not from aristocratic stock with contacts in the academic world, they had not had the means to pursue formal education beyond the age of fourteen, and neither had ever travelled much outside of England. Bates was born into a financially precarious family of hosiery manufacturers on February 8, 1825, in Leicester. His parents were pious and scrupulously ethical Unitarians who raised their children with great emphasis on reading and personal learning. They sent Bates to boarding school until he was fourteen, when he was apprenticed for seven years to a wholesale merchant. Despite poverty wages and crushing thirteen-hour workdays, Bates continued to pursue his increasing interest in natural history by taking courses at the local Mechanics Institute (organizations that offered educational courses to the lower classes) and availing himself of the library. Initially, he focused his energy on drawing and Greek and Latin composition. During the summers he would go on field trips to the nearby country to collect insects and plants.

By the time he was nineteen, Bates was a recognized amateur naturalist who regularly contributed articles to *The Zoologist* detailing his observations of local beetles and butterflies. He had a remarkable collection of local beetles that he showed to his acquaintance Alfred Russel Wallace in 1844. Wallace was amazed at "the great number of beetles, their many strange forms and other beautiful markings or colouring, and was even more surprised when I found out that almost all I saw had been collected round Leicester." Wallace was a gangly, awkward, and bespectacled young schoolteacher who shared Bates's avid interest in natural history, as well as the younger man's frustrations with a narrow, confining life that seemed to stretch on ahead without end. Like Bates, Wallace had completed most of his education after the age of fourteen at the Mechanics Institute, and was inspired by Darwin's *Voyage of the Beagle*. They were both eagerly searching for a means to follow their scientific interests rather than remaining in dull careers only occasionally animated by a little amateur pursuit of natural history.

In preparation for their monumental undertaking they had visited several leading scientific authorities such as Edward Doubleday, curator in charge of lepidoptera at the British Museum. Doubleday advised them that they could fund their travels and studies by selling duplicate collections of the species they procured. Both Bates and Wallace knew exactly how to prepare specimens that met scientific requirements. They also visited the famous botanist Sir William Hooker at the botanical gardens at Kew. With commissions from Hooker to collect plants, and from Doubleday to collect insects, they were well on their way. One of the most important things they did was secure an agent, who agreed to find buyers for their specimens. Because of the widespread interest in natural history in Victorian England, private collections of rare species, particularly from such romantic and obscure lands as Brazil, were very valuable. There was a growing market for the specimens Bates and Wallace planned to collect, and though the income might prove meagre, it would be enough to support them in Amazonia.

In the 1840s, the town of Pará, near the mouth of the Amazon River, was a pleasant provincial backwater nestled against a thriving jungle that crept up against the fringe of the settlement. The city was founded in 1615 as Belém (as it is known today) and was once a thriving Portuguese trading centre. After Brazilian independence from Portugal in 1822, however, it had diminished in importance, and did not regain its former prosperity until the rubber boom in the late nineteenth century. "The white buildings [were] roofed with red tiles, the numerous towers and cupolas of churches and convents, the crowns of palm trees reared above the buildings, all sharply defined against the clear blue sky. . . ." The town was a curious melange of ostentation and decay. Crumbling mansions of the grandest pretensions sprouted weeds from their cracked sagging walls, while the large public squares were clogged "and impassable on account of the swampy places which occupied parts of their areas." The houses were mostly dilapidated, the walls had partially collapsed and "hogs, goats, and ill-fed poultry wandered in and out through the gaps."

The citizens were "idle, jovial and luxurious," and "amidst all, and compensating every defect, rose the overpowering beauty of the vegetation. The massive dark crowns of shady mangos were seen everywhere amongst the dwellings, amidst fragrant blossoming orange, lemon, and many other tropical fruit trees; some in flower, others in fruit, at varying stages of ripeness." It was a welcoming and comfortable community. With a small congregation of European traders and businessmen, it was a perfect place for Bates and Wallace to ease into their new life. They settled into a comfortable house on the outskirts of town—easily affordable despite their scanty funds—and slipped into the habits that would keep them based there for the next year and a half. The small European community in the town, mostly trading agents, proved to be a disappointment. They were, recalled Bates, "so particular with their dress-coats, polished boots, hats, etc., as to be quite a nuisance." He and Wallace dressed more sensibly according to local style, wearing a loose garments and straw hats.

Freed from the regimen of long hours, poor pay, and low

social standing, the two men found the life of a professional naturalist in Brazil a pleasant surprise. Short, stooped, serious, myopic, and in delicate health, Bates seemed ill-suited to life as a roaming specimen collector. But the fresh air, physical exertion, and genuine

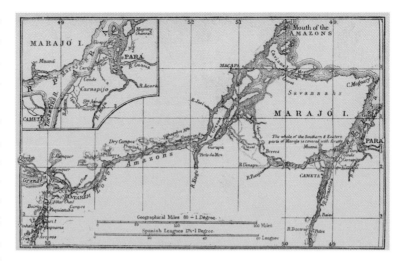

pleasure of his new circumstances acted as a palliative to his former ailments. In addition to a spacious home, Bates and Wallace had several acres of garden containing wild fruits, coffee, and other exotic plants. "All nature was fresh," Bates wrote, "[with] new leaf and flower-buds expanding rapidly. Some mornings a single tree would appear in flower against what was the preceding evening a uniform green mass of forest—a dome of blossom suddenly created as if by magic." The pair ate their meals on the large veranda of their house, and since few people spoke English, they quickly began learning Portuguese.

Bates and Wallace first arrived at the town of Pará and used it as a base for several years. In the 1840s, the hinterland of the Amazon basin beyond the major river systems was unexplored.

Each day they rose at dawn, sipped freshly roasted and brewed coffee, and then "sallied forth after birds." They wandered the luxuriant growth of the nearby forest searching for and shooting unknown or exotic avian specimens—multi-hued toucans, speedy hummingbirds, and other dull-looking species with eerie and haunting calls. After a mid-morning breakfast they abandoned birds, and insects became their prey for several hours, until the midday heat sapped their energy.

They didn't have to stray far to find new things to collect. Within a few hours walk from the outskirts of Pará, Bates collected over 700 different species of butterflies (in comparison, the British Isles have 66 species and all of Europe has only 321 species). He described "velvety-black, green, and rose-coloured" Trojans; "splendid metallic blue" Morphos flapping their "huge wings like a bird"; and the camouflaged Hummingbird Hawk-moth that avoided predators by mimicking the appearance of a hummingbird. The region held, Bates wrote, "an infinite number of curious and rare species...most diversified in habits, mode of flight, colours, and markings: some yellow, others bright red, green, purple, and blue, and many bordered or spangled with metallic lines and spots of a silvery or golden lustre. Some have wings transparent as glass; one of these clear wings is especially beautiful, namely, the Hetaira Esmerelda; which is of a violet and rose hue; this is the only part visible when the insect is flying low over dead leaves in the gloomy shades where it alone is found, and it then looks like a wandering petal of a flower."

In addition to the butterflies and birds, Bates was fascinated by the daily weather patterns, so different from anything he had ever before experienced. Each afternoon a great deluge of warm rain washed the humidity from the sky while "a mighty wind is heard through the forest." After the daily storm "bluish-black motionless clouds" remained in the sky until night. Although there were distinct dry and wet seasons, Bates noted that the difference between them was minimal and that the temperature never varied more than a few degrees throughout the entire year. "It is never spring, summer or autumn," he recalled, "but each day is a combination of all three."

After an early dinner when the storm had cleared, he and Wallace spent the evening preparing their specimens—mounting insects, skinning birds, and consolidating their notes. Occasionally they rested on the porch, lingering in the peaceful solitude of the evening, or wandered back to Pará "to see Brazilian life or enjoy the pleasure of European and American society." It was an easy and productive life and before half a year had passed, they had amassed quite a large collection. Seldom did a day pass without several new discoveries, a feat never duplicated before or since.

Despite the abundance of creatures, Bates wrote that "the number and beauty of the birds and insects did not at first equal our expectations." Most likely this was because those expectations had been built on Edwards's overblown account. Similarly, Bates and Wallace "were disappointed also in not meeting with any of the larger animals of the forest. There was no tumultuous movement, or sound of life. We did not see or hear monkeys, and no tapir or jaguar crossed our path. Birds, also, appeared exceedingly scarce." It was months before Bates realized that animals were not in fact scarce at all, but were wary of humans and, with plenty of room to roam, could stay out of their way. Most jungle creatures led their lives high above ground in the dense latticework of the forest canopy—an arboreal world teeming with life—not in the shadowy underworld where he and Wallace strolled.

Bates was particularly intrigued by the Sauba, the leaf-cutting ants.

Bates found one group of creatures abundant on the forest floor to be most peculiar and fascinating—the wide variety of ants. At the dinner table, he wrote, "pieces of meat, etc., are seen moving, as if by magic." Sometimes the industrious workers could be seen "running away with our specimens as we are setting them." He encountered vast numbers of different ants—from tiny ones as small as the tip of a fingernail to large fat ones with painful stingers. His favourite, however, was the leaf-cutting Sauba that sometimes despoiled whole coffee or orange plantations, their preferred crops. "Their processions," Bates wrote, "look like a multitude of animated leaves on the march." He and Wallace followed one column back to a massive mound of dirt, the portal to the ants' "vast subterranean galleries." Bates spent weeks studying these ants, noting their behaviour and method of feasting. Although the "habit of the Sauba ant of clipping and carrying away immense quantities of leaves has long been recorded in books on natural history," Bates took his investigations much further. He dug deep into the great mounds to determine where the galleries and corridors of the vast network intersected before they descended into the earth.

"In some districts [the Sauba] is so abundant that agriculture is impossible," he recorded, "and everywhere complaints are heard of the terrible pest. . . . It is a great scourge to the Brazilians." On one occasion Bates himself was wakened by a shuffling sound and went to the storeroom of his house to frighten off what he believed were rats. He was astonished to see a vast line of ants "staggering along, completely hidden under their load," which consisted of grain and dissected woven baskets. He and a servant spent hours stamping and squashing them to no avail. The next night he "was obliged to lay trains of gun powder along their line, and blow them up." After several explosions, the ants reluctantly retreated "and we were free from their visits."

After a considerable amount of time observing several colonies, Bates was able to provide answers to what had previously been unknown—to what purpose did the ants use the infinite number of cut leaves? He proposed that the Sauba used the leaves to thatch the roofs of their subterranean dwellings, "thereby protecting from the deluging rains the young broods in the nests beneath." He described how the workers drag their "burthens" back to the colony and "another relay of labourers place the leaves in position, covering them with a layer of earthy granules, which are brought one by one from the soil beneath."* Bates also described the

---

* The actual use of the leaves proved to be more interesting than Bates suspected. Scientists have since concluded that the leaves are used as a fertilized base to grow a fungus that is consumed by the ants. The Sauba were, in fact, engaged in a sophisticated and organized agrarian enterprise that involved the entire community.

social customs of the ants, the various types of workers and their specific roles in the colony, the mating ritual of the queens, and the stages of growth from grubs to workers or winged perfect-sex males and females. He wasn't the first to write about the Sauba, but his observations were detailed and reliable.

Later on his journeys, Bates encountered many other varieties of ants that inspired him further. He had particular fascination for the martial army ants, the Ecitons, that foraged with carnivorous intent throughout the forest. Eventually, he categorized ten distinct species of the foraging army ants—and eight of them proved to be new to science. "Many confused statements have been published in books of travel, and copied in Natural History works, regarding these ants," he wrote, "which are often confused with the Sauba." The Sauba, however, is a vegetable eater, while the Ecitons are carnivorous and "excite terror wherever they go." The first time he came across the Ecitons they were marching in two long, broad columns in opposite directions; one train was empty-handed, while "the other [was] laden with the mangled remains of insects, chiefly larvae and pupae of other ants." They were returning from raiding another ant colony. Bates followed the ant-road to the scene of the battle and observed the Ecitons hovering about the orifices of the ant-mines, dragging the living prey from the tunnels and ripping them apart before carrying them away. "All the work," he noted, "seemed thus to be performed by intelligent co-operation amongst the host of eager little creatures." Bates spent many weeks studying them, using the disquieting metaphor of human warfare to describe their depredations and motives. "The errand of the vast ant-armies," he noted, "is plunder," and their spoils were the mutilated remains of the vanquished.

While they were based in Pará, Bates and Wallace also spent several months roaming along the coast and followed several rivers deeper into the hinterland. One particular journey brought them up the mighty Tocantins River, which runs south from the Amazon. Apart from finding dozens of new species of butterflies and beetles, and collecting numerous specimens of eagles, herons, egrets, hawks, and yellow-billed toucans, Bates was most astonished by a discovery in a small remote village. The village was surrounded by magnificent primeval forest that smothered it against the river. In the corner of a room in the rudimentary home of his amiable host was, against all expectations, a small bookshelf. "I was rather surprised," Bates wrote with great understatement, "to see a number of well-thumbed Latin classics, Virgil, Terence, Cicero's Epistles, and Livy.... It was an unexpected sight, a classical library in a mud-plastered and palm-thatched hut on the banks of the Tocantins."

Bates was also able to "verify a fact relating to the habits of a large hairy spider of the genus Mygale"—as large as an outstretched hand—while canoeing up a subsidiary stream to the Tocantins. The spider's swollen body was covered in coarse gray and red hairs and its shiny black eyes glinted from the shadows. Rumours had this bird-eating monster "sallying forth at night, mounting trees, and sucking the eggs and young of humming-birds." On this day, however, Bates observed the spider hovering above its silky web, in which two small finches, a male and a female, were trapped. He drove the spider away and drew near to the tiny birds. One was dead, while the other, still struggling, was "smeared with the filthy liquor or saliva exuded by the monster." It soon died from the secretions as well. Nevertheless, Bates had settled a long-disputed rumour concerning the bird-eating spider, of which he was able to eventually collect several distinct species. The story of this spider had long been recounted, Bates noted, but by an unreliable source. Although the spiders proved to be quite common, and he encountered several different species in the course of his wanderings, this first encounter was an unpleasant experience. "The hairs with which they are clothed come off when touched," he recounted, "and cause a peculiar and almost maddening irritation. The first specimen that I killed and prepared was handled incautiously, and I suffered terribly for three days afterwards." He was shocked when he saw several children leading one about their house "as they would a dog," by a string secured around the spider's hairy abdomen.

TURTLE FISHING AND ADVENTURE WITH ALLIGATOR.

When they returned to Pará, Bates and Wallace had amassed such a quantity of specimens that they immediately sent a huge shipment to London. They then decided to separate in order to pursue their individual interests. Apart from a brief meeting in 1850, the two naturalists never encountered each other for the remainder of their time in Brazil. Wallace followed the Amazon upstream and then branched off north on the Negro River, entering the region that Humboldt had explored almost fifty years before. Bates, on the other hand, remained almost exclusively on the Amazon and its south-leading tributaries.

After parting ways with Wallace, Bates ascended the mysterious and daunting Amazon River far into the interior near Ega (now called Teffé), where he spent a year before briefly returning to Pará, impoverished and sick with yellow fever. He intended to return to England, but the unexpected arrival of significant funds from the sale of his previous specimens altered his plans, and he quickly set out for Santarem, midway along the Amazon. Broad and deep, draining the water of a third of the continent, the Amazon was the main artery

Bates always lived with the people of the Amazon and recorded local customs and beliefs. Life in Amazonia could be very dangerous without proper knowledge— poisonous snakes and insects were common, and one had to be wary of predators such as alligators.

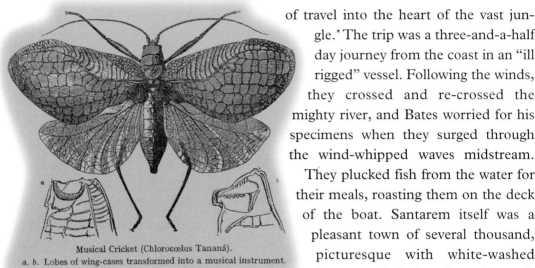

Musical Cricket (Chlorocœlus Tananá).
a. b. Lobes of wing-cases transformed into a musical instrument.

Bates found and collected a single specimen of a rare type of large cricket that continuously chirped. It was the Musical Cricket (*Chlorocoelus tananá*).

of travel into the heart of the vast jungle.* The trip was a three-and-a-half day journey from the coast in an "ill rigged" vessel. Following the winds, they crossed and re-crossed the mighty river, and Bates worried for his specimens when they surged through the wind-whipped waves midstream. They plucked fish from the water for their meals, roasting them on the deck of the boat. Santarem itself was a pleasant town of several thousand, picturesque with white-washed houses, red-tiled roofs, and beautiful gardens. Situated at the mouth of the Tapajós River on the south shore of the Amazon, it was well suited for extended forays into the jungle.

Bates did not undertake strenuous overland journeys into the wildest hinterland, but preferred to remain close to waterways. Although he eventually followed the Amazon nearly two thousand miles into the interior, his habit was to settle into a region for several years at a time. "I wished to explore districts at my ease," he wrote. Establishing a base enabled him to store and preserve the vast quantities of specimens he

---

* Originating in the eastern slopes of the Andes Mountains in Peru, the Amazon is the world's second longest river, approximately 3,900 mi (6,280 km) long. It rolls east through northern Brazil with a maze of twisting sediment-filled channels before fanning out into the Atlantic Ocean near Belém. It drains more land and carries more water than any other river in the world: the Amazon drainage basin consists of more than a third of the entire continent of South America. It is not a steep or quick flowing river. Most of the vast drainage basin is a sprawling lowland jungle—the largest rainforest in the world. Rainfall is heavy, the temperature always hot, and the humidity consistently high. Extensive deforestation in the late twentieth century has resulted in the extinction or threatened extinction of numerous rare species of plants and has contributed to the increase in carbon dioxide in the atmosphere and, perhaps, to global warming.

collected. Although he made many side trips, sometimes for months at a time, he did very little in the way of geographical exploration—scientific collecting was his sole and driving interest, and an economic necessity.

By November 1851 Bates had settled into Santarem and he found that it more than satisfied his requirements. The climate was the best anywhere he had travelled (not too hot in the dry season and not too wet in the rainy season), the people were friendly, and palatable food, including imported luxuries such as tea, was in good supply. He rented a comfortable tile-roofed house on the outskirts of town soon after arriving and hired a family to help him with his collecting and to maintain his home while he was wandering the jungle. His forays from Santarem during the three and a half years that he was based there brought him farther into the remote jungle than he had ever before gone. On one prolonged excursion up the Tapajós River, he spent several months in the interior, where he saw butterflies "of almost endless diversity." Over a period of a month he collected over three hundred species within a half-hour walk of the village in which he was staying. He also found and collected a single specimen of a rare type of large cricket that continuously chirped with notes "the loudest and most extraordinary I ever heard produced by an orthopterous insect."

Bates was inspired and amazed by the variety and luxuriance of the vegetation. Often, a thick haze hung about the damp foliage. Massive wing-based trees shot hundreds of feet into the shadows before spreading their branches wide, blocking all sun and providing a home for thousands of other parasitic vines and creepers. Spongy mosses and slight flowering shrubs sprouted from the detritus at the crooks of ancient branches. He frequently saw "the woody fruits [the

HOWLER.

The incessant droning of the howler monkey was like a mournful dirge to Bates.

BIRD-KILLING SPIDER (MYGALE AVICULARIA) ATTACKING FINCHES.

When Bates first saw the bird-killing spider (*Mygale avicularia*) hovering over two stunned finches, he was offended and shooed the beast away.

Brazil nuts] large and round as cannon balls, dotted over the branches." Thousands of creatures, from sloths and monkeys to innumerable varieties of insects and birds rarely ventured down from their arboreal perches, and the noise from above was varied and frequent. Far below, the shadowy floor where Bates walked was strewn with mouldering branches, cracked green-tinged stumps, and a soft layer of decaying vegetable remains. Snakes coiled from low-lying branches, tiny mammals scurried through the brush, and amphibians peered forth from their swampy pools. Through it all wove a labyrinth of murky waterways, the canoe paths of the natives, spreading out through the low-lying morass. The water was sluggish and turgid, seldom a ripple breaking the surface, and it undulated slowly with the tide, though the coast was hundreds of miles distant. He paddled his canoe, frequently alone, ever deeper into the vast forest, scooping insects from the air with his net and scanning the latticework of vines and branches for new species of beetles. "Art," he proclaimed in awe, "could not have assorted together beautiful vegetable forms so harmoniously as was done here by Nature."

Sometimes the snakes were so numerous that he trod upon them without knowing it until they hissed and disappeared into the shadows. Amazonian serpents came in a spectrum of colours—some were pale green, some variegated and iridescent; others were brown and mottled, or banded black and vermilion. Bates collected species that were long and thin and quick and ones that were rotund and sleepy. He found them lurking in the stagnant pools, slithering through the grasses, and hanging from the trees like dangling vines. "It was rather alarming, in retrospect," he observed, "in entomologising about the trunks of trees, to suddenly encounter, on turning round, as sometimes happened, a pair of glittering eyes and a forked tongue within a few inches of one's head." On one occasion a huge anaconda slid from the river at night, burst asunder the poultry cage in the rear of his canoe and gulped down two chickens before slinking back into the water.

Ever curious, Bates always dissected the bellies of the serpents he captured to determine what they had recently eaten. He was sometimes surprised to discover vast quantities of ants, some still alive, and, in one instance, a whole iguana so large that he couldn't imagine the snake opening its mouth wide enough to devour it. When he killed them and prepared them for shipment, however, he was saddened at how the colour drained from their bodies as life faded. "The state of specimens preserved in spirits," he lamented, "can give no idea of the brilliant colours which adorn them in life."

In 1855, after three and a half years in the vicinity of Santarem, Bates felt he had learned what he could and decided to head deeper into the heart of the continent. He left for Ega in a large canoe through "the yellow turbid current of the Upper Amazons or Solimoens." The Upper Amazon drained a very different terrain than the lower portion of the river nearer the coast. The coastal trade winds or sea breezes never reached more than a thousand miles inland. Santarem itself received only a dwindling wisp of freshness, while the atmosphere farther inland was "stagnant and sultry." The terrain was no longer hilly, but consisted of a sprawling plain, a thousand miles long and several hundred miles wide "covered with one uniform, lofty, impervious, and humid forest." Bates later remarked that "one lives here as in a permanent vapour bath."

The river west of Santarem had an "evil reputation for storms and mosquitoes," and this trip was no exception. Along the river he encountered, in addition to mosquitoes, the dreaded *pium*, a minute fly that swarmed in clouds all

along the upper Amazon—but only during the day, "reliev-
ing," Bates noted wryly, "the mosquito at sunrise with the
greatest punctuality." It was a vicious pest that he had far too
much time to study. They would "alight imperceptibly" on
exposed flesh and "fall at once to work; stretching forward
their long front legs, which are in constant motion…then
applying their short, broad snouts to the skin." They soon
became bloated with blood and slowly lifted off "sometimes
so stupefied with their potations that they can scarcely fly."
The greatest annoyance was that they left puckered, crusty,
and irritable red lesions all over the body. Bates, however,
eventually became immune to their depredations. "All
exposed parts of my body, by that time, being so closely covered with black punctures that the little bloodsuckers could
not very easily find an unoccupied place to operate upon."
One traveller he was with "was laid up for three weeks from
the attacks of the Píum; his legs being swelled to an enormous size, and the punctures aggravated into spreading
sores."

Bates, of course, dissected many specimens while he
slowly voyaged upstream. The vivisection may have been
cathartic; for there was certainly no way of fending off their
assault and no pleasure could be derived from swatting them
because they were too small. "The mouth consists of a pair of
thick fleshy lips," he wrote unsympathetically, "and two tri-
angular horny lancets, answering to the upper lip and tongue
of other insects. This is applied closely to the skin, a puncture
is made with the lancets, and the blood then sucked through
between these into the oesophagus, the circular spot which
results coinciding with the shape of the lips." At least, he
claimed, "no pain is felt whilst they are at work."

By the time he reached Ega, Bates had been in Brazil for
over seven years. He had sent numerous specimen collections
back to London and had received payment enough to keep
him in relative luxury. Ega was a small village four hundred
miles from the coast, situated several miles along the Teffé

River on a clean, dark placid lake enshrouded by looming forest. "It was unspeakably refreshing," he wrote, "to find one's-self again in a dark-water river, smooth as a lake, and free from Píum and Motuca." Bates settled into a spacious palm-thatched, whitewashed cottage secure with his "chests, filled store-boxes and trays for specimens...my little stock of useful books, guns, and game bags, boards and materials for skinning and preserving animals, botanical press and papers, drying cages for insects and birds, and so forth." His life in Ega began as he hoped it would, with the collection of hundreds of new species within a few hours' walk of the town. He wrote that of all the amazing productions of the natural world, the Upper Amazon surpassed every other region—the insects and animals were stranger and more diverse, the vegetation was more luxuriant and overgrown, and the feeling was more alien and somehow eerie and desolate.

The wild and peculiar fruits near Ega, a practical embodiment of the profuse and vibrant natural world, were a pleasant surprise. He feasted upon dozens of these strange plants that grew in healthy clumps, dangling from vines, trees, and shrubs along his path. One of his favourites, found only on the upper Amazon, was the *jabutí-púhe*, a scaled, apple-sized fruit with a thin rind enclosing a "quantity of custardy pulp of a very rich flavour." Another of his specialties was the *pamá*, similar to a cherry, but oblong in shape. It grew from one of the tallest trees in the forest and was obtained by the natives with great difficulty. It had a fatty, bitter pulp that was very nourishing.

The nourishment of his mind in this remote village, however, was not so easily accomplished. The townsfolk were very curious to know for what purpose he wandered through the jungle collecting insects and birds, and he "had no difficulty making them understand that each European capital had a public museum, in which were sought to be stored specimens of all natural productions in the mineral, animal, and vegetable kingdoms." But they had no interest in his studies and only when he explained that he was being paid did they nod in approval. Despite their welcoming and friendly demeanour, Bates found himself lonely in Ega, particularly after several years, for there was no one who shared his interest in science and literature. He eagerly awaited the bimonthly mail ship that brought him reading material—scientific journals and letters from London. Occasionally the ship was delayed or brought nothing for him, and it lowered his buoyant spirit.

During his tenure at Ega, Bates made many extensive excursions hundreds of miles into the jungle, as far upstream on the Amazon as São Paulo near the Peruvian border. On one ill-fated excursion he and a group of fellow travellers were caught unawares by a jungle storm while hunting for turtle eggs on a tributary to the Teffé River. Awakening around midnight to a thunderous deluge of warm rain, Bates at first tried to remain under a sprawling tree. But the downpour became so great that they all rushed to the canoes for shelter. "So there we lay," he remembered, "huddled together in the best way we could arrange ourselves, exhausted with fatigue and irritated beyond all conception by clouds of mosquitoes. I slept on a bench with a sail over me, my wet clothes clinging to my body, and to increase my discomfort, close beside me lay an Indian girl...who had a skin disfigured with black diseased patches, and whose thick clothing, not having been washed during the whole time we had been out (eighteen days), gave forth a most vile effluvium."

The collecting, however, was magnificent. Seldom did a day pass that he did not add a new species of butterfly, wasp, caterpillar, or beetle to his collection. Nearly half of his total haul during his eleven years in Brazil was made here, including, by his own account, "upwards of 7000 species of insects," about 550 species of butterflies alone, including the "crimson and vermilion" *Catagramma Peristera*, which he found clustered about the trunk of an ancient tree. Within a ten-minute walk of his house, he catalogued "eighteen species of true papilio (the swallow-tail genus).... No description can convey an adequate notion of the beauty and diversity in form and colour of this class of insects in the neighborhood of Ega." Sometimes the forest was spacious and open, allowing for easy rambling, while at other times it was "rank wilderness, into which it was impossible to penetrate many yards, on account of uprooted trees, entangled webs of monstrous woody climbers, thickets of spiny bamboos, swamps, or obstacles of one kind or other."

In addition to his study and collection of insects, he devoted considerable attention to aquatic turtles, manatees, dolphins, electric eels, caimans, and other semi-aquatic creatures found in profusion along the winding waterways of the great jungle. "The discovery of new species, however," he noted, "forms but a small item in the interest belonging to the study of the living creation. The structure, habits, instincts, and geographical distribution of some of the oldest-known forms supply inexhaustible materials for reflection." Bates reflected on monkeys, which he found to be "the most interesting, next to man, of all the animals." His studies and observations consumed hours upon hours of his time, and he classified six different species and wrote detailed accounts of their behaviour and characteristics, including the tailless scarlet-faced monkey, the white Uakarí, the Parauacu, the owl-faced night ape, and the barrigudo monkey.

Birds were also plentiful here, and he again noted dozens of new species. "There are scores, probably hundreds, of birds, all moving about with the greatest activity—woodpeckers and *Dendrocolaptidae* (from species no larger than a sparrow to others the size of a crow) running up the tree trunks; tanagers, ant-thrushes, humming-birds, fly-catchers, and barbets, flitting about the leaves and lower branches." He had the distinct "pleasure of seeing for the first time, the rare and curious Umbrella Bird." It was a creature similar to a crow, apart from the tuft of shaggy hairs on its head. The hairs had long bone quills "which, when raised, spread themselves out in the form of a fringed sun-shade over the head."

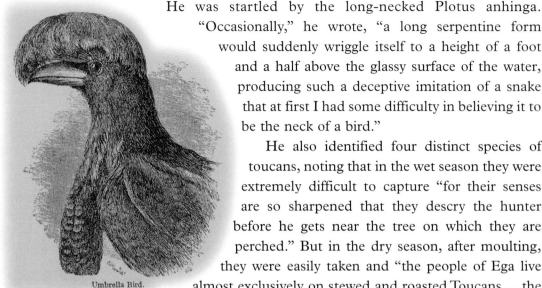

Umbrella Bird.

The "rare and curious" Umbrella Bird (*Cephalopterus ornatus*) was one of the strangest birds Bates studied in Amazonia.

He was startled by the long-necked Plotus anhinga. "Occasionally," he wrote, "a long serpentine form would suddenly wriggle itself to a height of a foot and a half above the glassy surface of the water, producing such a deceptive imitation of a snake that at first I had some difficulty in believing it to be the neck of a bird."

He also identified four distinct species of toucans, noting that in the wet season they were extremely difficult to capture "for their senses are so sharpened that they descry the hunter before he gets near the tree on which they are perched." But in the dry season, after moulting, they were easily taken and "the people of Ega live almost exclusively on stewed and roasted Toucans...the birds being then very fat, and the meat exceedingly sweet and tender." While strolling one day through "a dark glen," he came upon a curl-crested toucan, the most colourful variety, and shot it from a high branch. When he grabbed it from the ground, it let out a startling squawk and "in an instant, as if by magic, the shady nook seemed alive with these birds." They descended from the canopy hopping from limb to limb "some of them swinging on the loops and cables of woody lianas, and all croaking and fluttering their wings like so many furies." They surrounded him, lowering their massive beaks and flapping around menacingly. It was very spooky, and he began reloading his gun "for obtaining more specimens and punishing the viragos for their boldness." The wounded one died, however, and no sooner had their comrade been silenced than the great horde of toucans retreated into the upper foliage and became silent.

The aspect of the Upper Amazon that Bates found most intriguing was the multitude of sounds that the jungle brought forth—distant roars, thundering cracks, terrified screeches, piercing cries, and sudden crashes as if a monstrous tree had shuddered and collapsed to the earth, shattering on impact. Occasionally there were frightful yodels from "some defenseless fruit-eating animal, which is pounced upon by a tiger-cat or stealthy boa-constrictor." Most disturbing to him was the dreadful moaning of the howler monkeys (of which he eventually identified several new species previously unknown to science, notable mostly for the different shading of their fur). "Morning and evening," he remembered, "the howler monkeys make a most fearful and harrowing noise, under which it is difficult to keep up one's buoyancy of spirit. The feeling of inhospitable wildness which the forest is calculated to inspire, is increased tenfold under this fearful uproar."

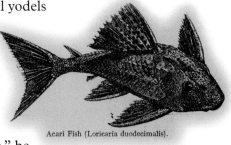

Acari Fish (Loricaria duodecimalis).

Although insects were Bates's specialty, he also collected several species of fish, including the Acari Fish (*Loricaria duodecimalis*).

The eerie sounds, distant squawks, odd scratching, and other unpleasant and unidentifiable noises, coming always from just beyond the limits of where he could see, were a frequent topic of conversation. The natives attributed these sounds to the Curupíra, the wild man or spirit of the jungle. The influence of the mysterious Curupíra was strong among the forest dwellers. Depending on the region, he was sometimes a shaggy-haired, orangutan-like beast that lurked in the upper foliage, or a cloven-hoofed, red-faced being that would skulk on the fringes of town looking for things to steal. "Myths," Bates pronounced with Victorian sensibility, "are the rude theories which mankind, in the infancy of knowledge, invent to explain natural phenomena." But Bates admitted that many of the sounds were "impossible to account for."

One of Bates's adventures on the Upper Amazon would have greatly amused another South American naturalist, Charles Waterton. While staying with a family of German immigrant farmers in a small village along the shore of a tributary to the Amazon, Bates was set upon one night and bled by a bat. He was awakened at midnight by shuffling sounds on the ceiling, and lit his lamp illuminating "vast hosts of bats sweeping about the room." The air, he wrote in astonishment,

ADVENTURE WITH CURL-CRESTED TOUCANS.

Bates and the villagers around Ega feasted for months each year on roasted and stewed toucans. On one occasion when he shot one in an upper branch, the entire flock descended upon him, squawking and flapping menacingly. While Bates reloaded his gun, the wounded bird died and the others vanished into the canopy.

was "blackened with the impish multitudes that were whirling round and round." He swatted at them with a stick for several minutes until they dispersed, scurrying into crevices and skulking behind rafters, and once again went to sleep. The next night, however, several crept into his hammock. "I seized them," he wrote, "as they were crawling over me, and dashed them against the wall." The next morning he observed with resignation a wound on his hip. "This was rather unpleasant," he noted.

The next day he and some helpers rousted the fiends from the house, shooting a great many of them "as they hung from the rafters." The only consolation Bates could take from his unexpected bloodletting was that he identified four distinct species for his collection. He was never attacked by bats again and, in conclusion, noted that "the fact of their sucking the blood of persons sleeping, from wounds which they make in the toes, is now well established; but it is only a few persons who are subject to this blood-letting."*

The hard living in the vicinity of Ega began to take its toll. In the border town of São Paulo, Bates was laid low by a serious attack of the "ague" (probably malaria) that left him "with shattered health and dampened enthusiasm." Poor diet, frequent exposure to the sun, and "the foul and humid

---

* The vampire bat, although he admitted that it was mostly harmless, repulsed him like no other creature he met during his eleven-year tenure in "the naturalist's paradise." No other animal, he noted, "can be more hideous than the countenance of this creature when viewed from the front; the large leathery ears standing out from the sides and top of the head, the erect spear-shaped appendage on the tip of the nose, the grin and the glistening black eye, all combining to make up a figure that reminds one of some mocking imp of fable. No wonder that imaginative people have inferred diabolical instincts on the part of so ugly an animal."

state of the village" produced a gradual deterioration of his health throughout 1858. By early 1859, he was unable to cope with it any longer, and spent much of his time recuperating from illness. He reluctantly left Ega on February 3, boarding a ship with all his collections and possessions and floating downstream to Pará, arriving on March 17. He had been away from Pará for over seven and a half years, and the town had changed considerably in that time. Prosperity and immigration had swelled the population. The dilapidated buildings had been repaired, the swampy squares had been drained, and the crumbling fences had been mended. It was now energetic and thriving with commerce.

Bates, however, also observed the downside of the prosperity. "The noble forest trees had been cut down," he wrote, "and their naked half-burnt stems remained in the midst of ashes, muddy puddles, and heaps of broken branches." The foliage had been cleared back from the town, farms stood in place of trees, and roads were being carved through the forest—the cry of wild beasts no longer resonated from the woods and the calls of birds no longer enlivened the mornings. And a most disturbing practical consideration was the cost of living, which had soared beyond what he could comfortably afford. Bates stayed with old friends while he regained his strength, and began to dream of home and "the rich pleasures of intellectual society." He arranged for his vast collection of specimens to be shipped on three separate ships to avoid the chance of loss en route, and purchased a ticket for himself on an American trader sailing for London on June 2.

The anticipation of returning was not entirely pleasant. "During that last night on the Pará river, a crowd of unusual thoughts occupied my mind. Recollections of English climate, scenery, and modes of life came to me with a vividness I had never before experienced, during the eleven years of my absence. Pictures of startling clearness rose up of the gloomy winters, the long grey twilights, murky atmosphere, elongated shadows, chilly springs, and sloppy summers; of factory chimneys and crowds of grimy operatives, rung to work in early morning by factory bells; of union workhouses, confined rooms, artificial cares, and slavish conventionalities. To live again amongst these dull scenes I was quitting a country of perpetual summer, where my life had been spent...in gypsy fashion, on the endless streams or in the boundless forests."

Despite his misgivings, Bates flourished after returning to London. Although he remained "much depressed in health and spirits" for a long time, particularly since he was compelled by financial necessity to return to Leicester and join his brothers and father in the hosiery business, he began a slow integration into the scientific community. He spent considerable time in London arranging the sale of his final specimens, which yielded him a tidy profit. Bates read with eager interest Charles Darwin's *Origin of Species*, published in 1859, and immediately became a convert—Darwin's brilliant generalizations meshed perfectly with his own observations along the Amazon and he wrote Darwin to tell him so. They became lifelong correspondents and, while Bates supplied Darwin with observable facts on specific species, Darwin publicly supported Bates's presentations and encouraged him to publish a book of his travels.

In the first few years after his return, Bates wrote two theoretical papers, one each for the Entomological Society and the Linnean Society. The first dealt with the relationships of species and their geographical distribution within the framework of evolutionary theory; the second was a detailed theory on how mimicry amongst certain insect species was a clear example of the working of natural selection.

He wrote of the "resemblances in external appearance, shapes, and colours" of butterflies of different species. In the shady forests along the lower Amazon he had noted different species flying amongst the larger group. Although he was unable to distinguish between them "on the wing," he was astonished when his quarry proved to be other than he expected. "These analogies to me appear amongst the most beautiful phenomena in nature," he claimed. His theory has become known as "Batesian mimicry"—protective resemblance, whereby a species appears and behaves like another species to avoid its predators, and therefore has a greater likelihood of surviving and reproducing. "This principle can be no other than natural selection, the selecting agents being insectivorous animals, which gradually destroy those sorts or varieties that are not sufficiently like [the mimicked species] to deceive them.... I believe the case offers a most beautiful proof of the truth of the theory of natural selection." Darwin heartily agreed.

The Victorian scientific establishment, however, was not so open to new theories. With the publication of his papers Bates immediately joined a select, but heretical, circle of the most prominent naturalists, such as Charles Darwin, Joseph Hooker, Thomas Huxley, and his old companion, Alfred Wallace. Far from securing his career in natural history, Bates's ideas served to blacklist him from ever achieving a public appointment. The establishment—the universities and the British Museum—closed ranks. They were almost exclusively anti-Darwinians and were certainly not eager to admit to their ranks a man of Bates's indifferent birth, self-acquired education, and radical ideas. He sought in vain for employment, but was consistently rebuffed, passed over in favour of men with the proper connections and upbringing. It was very disheartening to Bates, a man who had little interest in the life of a provincial craftsman, but whose health had never rebounded sufficiently to enable him to return to the life of a wandering specimen collector.

He slogged away on his book, *The Naturalist on the River Amazons*. When it was published in 1863, it received universally positive reviews and became one of the most popular travel accounts of its time, praised by Darwin as "second only to Humboldt." Still he could not establish a footing in London scientific society. In 1863, Bates married a local

THE ⊚ ⊚ ⊚
NATURALIST
ON THE RIVER
AMAZONS *by*
HENRY WALTER
BATES ⊚ ⊚

LONDON: PUBLISHED
by J·M·DENT·&·SONS·L͟TᴰP
AND IN NEW YORK
BY E·P·DUTTON&CO

Title page from Bates's
immensely popular book,
*The Naturalist on the River
Amazons*, which was still in
print as late as the 1990s.

Leicester girl, twenty-two-year-old Sarah Ann Mason, a butcher's daughter. "Mrs. B. is a plain domesticated woman so there you have it all," Bates wrote blandly to Darwin, although they obviously married out of mutual affection. An intensely private man, Bates seldom wrote anything about his family or personal life. With one daughter already born and another child on the way, Bates contracted out his services for cataloguing specimens for private collectors, marking geography examinations, and ghost writing. While Darwin was independently wealthy and pursued his theories in spite of academic blacklisting, Bates needed the means to support his family.

Continually passed over for institutional natural history appointments, in 1864 he accepted the position of assistant secretary of the Royal Geographical Society, where he edited the society's *Transactions*, helped to organize several scientific expeditions, and advised inexperienced explorers. In this capacity, his years as a traveller were of great benefit, but his training and experience as a natural historian went mostly unused for the twenty-seven years he held the position. Although he became quite well-off, with a comfortable home in London and a summer place in Folkstone, and was the undisputed expert on the taxonomy of butterflies and other insects, Bates never again had the time to turn his mind to original research or evolutionary theory. But according to the many biographical sketches of his life that appeared over the last century, Bates, far from being embittered, was an amiable and social man known for his interesting ideas and stimulating conversation. He and Charles Darwin shared ideas and information freely until Darwin's death in 1882, a year after Bates had reluctantly been accepted as a Fellow of the Royal Society. Bates died of bronchial disease ten years later in 1892 at the age of sixty-seven, leaving his wife and five well-established adult children.

Despite his early promise as a theorist, Bates's achievements as a natural historian ended within a few years of his return to England. His respected and valued role at the Royal Geographical Society seems anticlimactic compared with his unparalleled scientific accomplishments in the Amazon valley. Perhaps he veered from theoretical natural history out of financial necessity, or from frustration at being passed over for appointments in favour of less talented candidates. Perhaps it was only the Amazon that awakened his senses, stimulating his mind with the wild glory and infinite variety of nature's productions, and the return to England dulled his enthusiasm and inspiration. Perhaps as he grew older, his interest and inclinations shifted toward his wife and children, or to assisting other, younger, adventurers plan their journeys.

Deep in the jungle, near the end of his tenure along the Amazon, in 1859, Bates was forced to acknowledge something that he must have wrestled with for a long time. "I was obliged, at last," he wrote, "to come to the conclusion that the contemplation of Nature alone is not sufficient to fill the human heart and mind." For him, at least, this proved true.

During Bates's lifetime, the respect for natural historians as a profession went into precipitous decline. By the 1880s it was no longer possible to make a living as an itinerant specimen collector. Not only because so many specimens had been collected by the 1870s that they were becoming a burden rather than a novelty, but also because there was a shortage of unplundered wilderness. Even South America experienced a massive economic and population expansion during the rubber boom of the 1890s. In the American Southeast, much of the land where Bartram had roamed a century earlier was now crossed by roads or was under cultivation. The population of coastal Alaska had expanded and the unregulated hunting had almost driven several species of aquatic animals to extinction. Oregon Territory had been flooded by a wave of migrants from the eastern United States along the Oregon Trail. The scientifically unexplored regions of the globe were diminishing as human population increased and settlement expanded. There were few unexplored regions remaining, and those that did still exist were not large enough to base a career exclusively upon exploring and collecting. This was the era in which John Wesley Powell began his career as a field naturalist.

CHAPTER NINE

John Wesley Powell

More than once I have been warned by the Indians not to enter this canyon.
They considered it disobedience to the gods and contempt for their authority,
and believed that it would surely bring upon me their wrath.
—JOHN WESLEY POWELL,
Exploration of the Colorado River of the West and its Tributaries

On his death in 1902 at the age of sixty-eight, Major John Wesley Powell had his brain cut from his skull and submerged in a jar of preserving fluid. He had bequeathed the organ to a colleague to settle a bet regarding brain size, which was believed to be related to intelligence. The bet was probably made in good nature, or perhaps to further the study of the human body in a small way, but Powell was an ambitious and competitive man and he wanted to win.

In some respects, Powell, at one time perhaps the most influential institutional scientist in the United States, was an eccentric man. Brain size was only the latest in a series of controversial or seemingly outlandish theories he developed as a career naturalist in a era when the final patches of unexplored American wilderness were shrinking under the onslaught of settlers and mineral prospectors. Much of his posthumous fame was earned not in the accumulation of chance-encountered curiosities during a haphazard wander through previously unexplored regions, like the earlier travelling naturalists, but in the systematic and thorough exploration and documentation of a narrow band of rugged terrain, one of the last large tracts of unknown land south of Canada and north of Mexico—the canyons and basins of the Colorado River. His adventures in the awe-inspiring canyons

Major John Wesley Powell (1834–1902) explored one of the last remaining uncharted regions on the continent north of Mexico and south of Alaska—the canyons of the Colorado River.

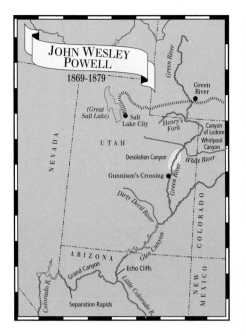

John Wesley Powell's journeys down the canyons of the Colorado, 1869–1879.

and gorges of the Colorado—seen and studied for months from the canyon floor instead of from peering over the edge—led him to pioneering theories on geological formation and erosion. Although his early interest and studies were in the natural history of mollusks, shells, and fossils, his greatest scientific contribution was in explaining the geology and ethnology of this specific region and, later, his theories on resource management in the arid regions of the West.

In 1868, Powell, a small, bearded, one-armed ex-major in the Union Artillery corps, stood on the crest of Long's Peak and gazed down upon the serpentine thread of blue and brown winding its way southwest. He was formulating a bold plan to navigate the entire length of the dreaded and treacherous rapids of the Colorado, from the Green River south to the Virgin River (near present-day Lake Mead). Although parts of the river had already been navigated, never had a single person undertaken the entire arduous journey, and certainly no trained scientist had accurately and reliably recorded and measured what was to be seen and encountered along its shores. Powell already had a general understanding of the mountains surrounding the Green River west of Denver, and an appreciation for the magnitude of his plan. This was his second summer in the West on a natural history expedition. In both 1867 and 1868 he and his wife, Emma, an amateur ornithologist, and a team that included a botanist, a zoologist, a herpetologist, and a mineralogist left Illinois, where he was professor of natural history at Normal University, rode the rails west to Denver, and then headed off into the mountains.

During two years of fieldwork on the frontier, they had collected and tried to classify thousands of insects, nearly nine hundred birds, and hundreds of plants, in addition to reptiles, mammals, fossils, and selections of minerals. But although these collections were valuable to the university, and personally new to Powell and his group, they were not new to science—by this time the majority of easily identifiable species had already been collected and classified (and the specimens brought back by Powell were mostly common plants and grasses, and mammals such as jackrabbits, deer, prairie dogs, badgers, etc.). Unlike the 1830s, when John Kirk Townsend made his cross-country trek collecting new species of birds and mammals, making a significant contribution to natural history or science in Powell's day would require something more specific. Although he was certainly interested in observing the species in the region, the era of the great collectors in North America had already drawn to a close. For an ambitious man like Powell, a mediocre contribution probably seemed like a waste of his time.

THE START FROM GREEN RIVER STATION.

At Green River Station, Powell launched four boats, beginning a journey of danger, hardship and great revelation.

With the approach of winter in 1868, most of the expedition members boarded a train at Green River Crossing and returned east, but Powell and Emma pushed two hundred miles west of the Great Divide to a camp along the White River. Here they spent many dark winter evenings visiting a nearby camp of Ute Indians, learning their language, myths, and customs, and recording a vocabulary of their language. This, at least, hadn't been done before and Powell took great interest in it, an interest that would continue over the next three decades of his life. He was laying the foundations for the study of ethnology. But his immediate interest was in geology, still a primitive, but more conventional, field of study.

This winter expedition gave him the idea that although the vast network of deep-cut canyons and gorges following the White and Green Rivers into the Grand Canyon were virtually inaccessible by land, the region might be surveyed by boat, providing it was stout enough to withstand the incessant pounding and potential swamping by the monstrous rapids. The region of the upper Colorado remained blank on government maps, and Powell planned to extend his explorations through this uninhabited and largely unknown area. The only white settlements belonged to a few Mormon communities. According to rudimentary Mormon sketch maps, there was no white settlement or military outpost for nearly fifteen hundred miles. No one knew what species lived within the confines of the canyons, or what new mineral deposits lay hidden and inaccessible in the forbidding cliffs.

What might lie before them on such a journey, if the rumours could be believed, were worthy of the trials of Hercules—roaring waterfalls, canyons so deep that the sun could not ever reach the bottom, turbulent white-frothed rapids, caverns where the water plunged into sinkholes and disappeared from the face of the earth for miles at a time, leaving nothing but barren dusty rock outcroppings on the surface and a distant rumbling from the bowels below. Swirling whirlpools might suck unsuspecting explorers to their doom, but valuable mineral deposits—gold, silver, diamonds, or coal—might be strewn about the floor of the most inaccessible gorge. Curiosity as to what lay in the West was so strong in the newly unified United States that newspapers frequently reported on the outrageous stories of western travellers. One tall tale proclaimed that "oil [was] floating on a number of small streams entering the main river.... Occasionally a spot could be seen on the land, composed of a sticky, tarry substance, where we found that a number of birds and squirrels had perished in endeavoring to extricate themselves." There were many such bogus claims and it was difficult to separate fact from the fiction. One of Powell's early biographers, W. E. Stegner, wrote in 1954 that "Powell's importance is that seventy-five years ago he pierced through those misconceptions to the realities. His career was an indomitable effort to substitute knowledge for the misconceptions and to get it acted upon."

When Powell set out on his first expedition down the Colorado in 1869, it was the continuation of his budding career as a natural historian, a career that began in his youth but was stalled by the Civil War. Powell was the third child and first son of Welsh immigrants who had settled in the hinterland of New York State and then continued migrating west. His father was a circuit-riding Methodist minister who strongly encouraged his son to follow the preaching life. But the younger Powell had his own ideas and, at an early age, took an avid interest in the natural world. He frequently went on field trips where he taught himself the rudiments of geology, botany, archaeology, and other aspects of natural history. When he began to assemble a primitive museum of fossils, plants, and insects at about age fourteen, his father actively discouraged his interest, eventually threatening to pay for his education only if he studied theology—something the headstrong and curious youth refused to do (Powell remained an atheist even on his deathbed). Consequently, his formal education was sporadic, although it was sufficient to obtain a teaching certificate. To survive, he taught school and worked as a farm labourer. Throughout the 1850s, he amassed a large private collection of plants, snakes, mollusks, minerals, and fossils, and he was part of an ambitious project initiated by the Illinois State History Society to discover and enumerate every plant, animal, and mineral in the state. On his explorations along and around the Illinois and Des Moines Rivers, he began noticing geological features such as gravel deposits left from glacial drift, soil layering, and unusual rock formations—aspects of the natural world not greatly understood or studied in the field at that time.

When the Civil War began in 1861, he put his scientific aspirations on hold and enlisted in the 20th Illinois Volunteers as a private, but soon rose to the rank of captain and later major (a title that so suited him it stuck for the rest of his life). During a lull in fighting he travelled to Detroit and married Emma Dean, a cousin he had known for many years, and returned with her to his post. During the battle of Shiloh, his right arm was blasted by a Confederate minnie ball and had to be amputated at the elbow. This didn't slow him down, however. After a few months of convalescence during which he was nursed by Emma, he returned to active service on the special condition that she be permitted to accompany him to each new post. Although he led his troops throughout the war, he was not injured again and was honourably discharged in 1865.

Powell returned to Bloomington, Illinois, and because of his teaching experience and his work with the Illinois State History Society, was offered a position as professor of geology at Normal University. He found geology alone to be too confining and later expanded his duties to include all aspects of natural history, including botany, comparative anatomy and physiology, zoology, mineralogy, and the study of prehistoric man. Geology meant field work, and so it was that in the summers of 1867 and 1868 he led two small scientific expeditions to the Rocky Mountains west of Denver, where he concocted his scheme to navigate the Colorado. "I have explored the canyon of the Green where it cuts through the foot of the Uintah Mountains," he wrote to the president of Normal University in January 1869, "and find that boats can be taken down. So that the prospect of making a passage of the 'Grand Canyon' of the Colorado is brighter. The canyon of the Green was said to be impassable."

Instead of a trek that would have a broad focus, on which as much could be missed as discovered, Powell vowed to study the geology, flora, and fauna of the region comprehensively and exhaustively. He begged for funds from various governments and universities, obtained free passage on the Union Pacific Railway, and borrowed scientific instruments from the Smithsonian Institution. He proved to be an effective fundraiser, rallying the support of both private and government institutions. By seeking government funding for legitimate research expeditions, he was at the forefront of a new tradition for scientific research that would grow exponentially in the century following his death.

In Chicago, Powell had four boats designed to his specifications—three large, stalwart oak boats and a lighter one of pine to lead the way. He recruited nine other adventurous and curious men to voyage with him, some of whom had been with him on previous explorations, but none who had any particular scientific training or interest. One young sergeant named George Bradley, who was serving out his term at Green River, exclaimed that he would "explore the river Styx" if Powell would take him along and relieve him from tedious army life. By May 24, 1869, the men had loaded the boats with two thousand pounds of bacon, beans, sugar, flour, coffee, and tea. It was enough provisions for ten months, "for we expect," wrote Powell, "when winter comes on and the river is filled with ice, to lie over at some point until spring arrives."

They also brought along axes, hammers, saws, augers, nails, screws, and other tools, as well as two sextants, four chronometers, a number of barometers, thermometers, compasses, and other instruments for taking scientific measurements. Powell planned to take frequent latitude and longitude measurements and barometric readings, collect samples of minerals and strata, and, every fifty miles or so, to take astronomic readings to create a map after the survey was completed. He also made provisions for detailed compass readings at every bend in the river, with observers in each boat estimating the distance between points, three daily measurements of altitude at the waters edge, and calculations of the height of the canyons. Any new plants and animals would also be collected.

After two weeks of training, they pushed the four heavily laden boats into the rushing waters of the Green River in the Wyoming Territory, leaped in, and began a three-month-long string of frightening and unexpected hardships and adventures. For the first three days it was a pleasant float. At the end of each day they camped on a comfortable-looking patch of level ground beneath twelve-thousand foot cliffs, among cottonwood trees and tall grasses. On his evening strolls Powell was struck by the stark beauty of the terrain they traversed. "Barren desolation is stretched before me; and yet there is a beauty in the scene. The fantastic carving, imitating architectural forms, and suggesting rude but weird statuary, with the bright and varied colors of the rocks, conspire to make a scene such as the dweller in verdure-clad hills can scarcely appreciate....Dark shadows are settling in the valleys and gulches, and the heights are made higher and the depths deeper by the glamour and witchery of light and shade. Away to the south, the Uinta Mountains stretch in a long line; high peaks thrust into the sky, and snow fields glittering like lakes of molten silver; and pine forests in somber green; and rosy clouds playing around the borders of huge, black masses; and heights and clouds, and mountains and snow fields, and forests and rocklands, are blended into one grand view."

The floating remained easy as the four boats drifted down the canyon. Startled deer bounded into the brush and wild geese took wing from the willows. Soon they entered a deep canyon through which the river slowly meandered. "It is the grandest scenery I have ever found in the mountains," wrote ex-lieutenant Bradley, "and I am delighted with it. The river winds like a serpent...but instead of rapids it is deep and calm as a lake." Soon they entered Flaming Gorge, a "flaring, brilliant red gorge...composed of bright vermilion rocks... [that] come down with a gentle curve to the water's edge on the nearer slope of the mountain." Powell knew, from his previous explorations, that they would be entering the Uinta Mountains and that their pleasant jaunt would not last. After resting at Henry's Fork for a few days, taking measurements and collecting specimens, they pushed off into the river, prepared for rougher days.

The four boats surged clumsily through the rolling waves, spinning around rocks, and blindly plunging around corners.

They passed through rapids made dangerous by high rocks lying in the channel. Powell quickly noticed that riding the rapids of a river would be very different from the waves on a lake or ocean. "The water of an ocean wave merely rises and falls; the form only passes on, and form chases form unceasingly," he wrote. "A body floating on such waves merely rises and sinks—does not progress unless impelled by wind or some other power. But here, the water of the wave passes on, while the form remains. The waters plunge down ten or twenty feet, to the foot of a fall; spring up again in a great wave; then down and up, in a series of billows, that gradually disappear in the more quiet waters below; but these waves are always there, and you can stand above and count them."

In the next few days the waves grew much larger and began to wash over the gunwales of the loaded boats, and they had to bale furiously to keep their supplies dry. Their lack of experience was obvious. Oars akimbo and boats spinning wildly, they plunged ever forward. The first of June was a glorious day, where the river rolled "down the canyon at a wonderful rate, and with no rocks in the way, we make almost railroad speed.... The boats go leaping and bounding over these like things in life." During a one-hour period, they were whisked more than twelve miles along the river without accident.

They entered Swallow Canyon on June 4, where huge numbers of swallows built their "adobe houses" along the river's cliffs. "The waters are deep and quiet," Powell wrote, "but the swallows are swift and noisy enough, sweeping by in their curved paths through the air, or chattering from the rocks. The young birds stretch their little heads on naked necks through the doorways of their mud houses, clamoring for food. They are a very noisy people." The next day he was wakened by a "chorus of birds. It seems as if all the feathered songsters of the region have come to the old tree. Several species of warblers, woodpeckers, and flickers above, meadowlarks in the grass, and wild geese in the river." Beautiful flowers covered the dusty earth like a canopy, "crimson velvet

FIRE IN CAMP.

One ill-fated evening the campfire spread to the surrounding grasses and Powell's men fled to the boats to escape burning. Unfortunately they left behind valuable provisions and supplies that were sorely missed in the days to come.

flowers, set in groups on the stems of pear-shaped cactus plants; patches of painted cups are seen here and there, with yellow blossoms protruding through scarlet bracts; little blue-eyed flowers are peeping through the grass, and the air is filled with fragrance from the white blossoms of a Spiraea." The canyon existed in timeless tranquility, separate from the goings-on of the busy world above.*

By mid-June they were entering the gateway to the Canyon of Lodore. The canyon, wrote Powell, "opened like a beautiful portal to a region of glory," but by evening, when "the vermilion gleams and rosy hues, the green and gray tints are changing to somber brown above, and black shadows below. Now, 'tis a black portal to a region of gloom." Two weeks after setting out, they experienced their worst rapids yet in the doom and gloom of the Lodore. So great were the rapids that several times the boats were spun broadside into the surging waves and swamped in the rushing milk-like foam. They clung dearly to the submerged hulks of the boats and were dragged through swollen spumes of churned water, twisting around bends and disappearing downstream. One time a boat, perhaps too swamped to be controlled, failed to heed the major's signal and surged forward through a foaming chute without pulling up at the shore with the others. The beleaguered boat, with three men yelling and furiously rowing, rolled on over the dangerous rapids toward a cluster of massive rocks strewn across the river. They survived the first

---

* In the east, John A. Risdon, a swindler and convicted horse thief, claimed that the entire expedition had been drowned. He presented himself as the sole survivor and petitioned the government for additional funding to search the wreckage. But Powell's wife, Emma, knew too many details of the expedition and exposed him as a fraud.

fall, a standard run of ten or twelve feet, but lost control when the winding chasm dropped another forty or fifty feet "in a channel filled with dangerous rocks that break the waves into whirlpools and beat them into foam." The boat spun broadside in a swirling eddy, struck a boulder, and broke into pieces. The oars were sucked away and the men clung to the wreckage as it was whisked downstream.

When a small island appeared midstream, the three men managed to crawl up onto it where they lay exhausted for several hours until the others arrived. Only with great difficulty, in the heavy current, were they rescued and brought ashore. "We were as glad to shake hands with them," wrote Powell, "as though they had been on a voyage around the world, and wrecked on a distant coast." Almost everything on board had been destroyed and carried away by the mighty river, including rations, supplies, and scientific instruments, guns, ammunition, pistols, knives, cooking utensils, and the barometers, bedding, and clothes for the three men. "All's well that ends well," wrote Bradley optimistically, "but the end is not yet."

The next day, they could see the wreckage downstream and it didn't look so bad in the cheery morning sun. Two men immediately volunteered to take the smallest boat out and survey the debris. As they were retrieving what appeared to be the barometers and thermometers, the men on shore let out an exuberant shout—and the major was proud that they were as pleased as he that the barometers were salvaged. When the boat reached shore, however, it turned out that the keen eyes of the men were fixed not on the barometers, but on a three-gallon keg of whisky, which had somehow survived the mishap. "Now I am glad they did," Powell wrote, "for they think it will do them good, as they are drenched every day by the melting snow, which runs down from the summits of the Rocky Mountains."

It took a gruelling four-day portage to get the other boats safely past the foaming cataract, hauling the sacks of flour and bales of bacon over slime-slicked stones and through a marshy quagmire. The men cursed the injustice of it all—apparently floating, however dangerous, was preferable to slogging. "The Major as usual has chosen the worst camping-ground possible," wrote a disgruntled adventurer after a day working like a galley slave. "If I had a dog that would lie where my bed is tonight I would kill him burn his collar and swear I never owned him.... Have been wet all day.... The clothes in my valise are all wet and I have nothing dry to put on."

Powell called for a rest after the portage to recuperate, dry out clothes, and, perhaps, have a sip or two of whisky. It was a pleasant respite, and he took advantage of it to work on his map and scientific recordings and observations. The Canyon of Lodore, however, stretched on for another few days of boiling and unknown rapids. More portages and rapids followed, and when two men climbed a peak along the canyon edge they found it to be twenty-seven hundred feet above the turbulent river below. "On the east side of the river," Powell wrote, "a vast amphitheater has been cut, with massive buttresses and deep, dark alcoves in which grow beautiful mosses and delicate ferns, while springs burst from the farther recesses and wind in silver threads over floors of sand rock."

They hauled the boats and equipment over three more portages the same day, with the river plunging a hundred feet down during one half-mile stretch. They aptly named the treacherous circuit Hell's Half Mile. Oddly, though, it was not the rapids that led to the greatest disaster on this stretch of the journey, but a wind-whipped wildfire that sprang into the brush while the men were cooking dinner. The flames took hold among the dead willows and sagebrush and spread madly in the gusting wind. The men dodged through the flames to the boats, leaped in, and ran a dangerous rapid in the poor light of dusk to escape the fire. Several had their hair and clothing burned off, and the cook, who had stumbled while clambering into the boat, dropped all the cooking and eating utensils into the river. The mess kit for ten men was reduced to one pan for making bread, a kettle, a frying pan, three spoons, three tin plates, and five bailing cups. The bailing cups now had to be shared for morning coffee. If they were roughing it before, things had just become a lot more uncomfortable. Most of the remaining clothing and blankets showed signs of rot from the constant wetness. It took several more days of frightening rapids before they emerged victorious from the confines of the Lodore.

Powell, alone in his optimism and excitement, admitted that although the Canyon of Lodore "has been a chapter of disasters and toils . . . it was not devoid of scenic interest, even beyond the power of pen to tell. . . . Its walls and cliffs, its peaks and crags, its amphitheaters and alcoves, tell a story of beauty and grandeur that I hear yet—and shall hear." The canyon led through mysterious and eerie geological formations that were thousands of years old and became the kernel of Powell's pioneering theories on canyon formation and erosion years later. He was particularly interested in the different types of gorges and chasms they floated through and the mineral composition of the cliffs.

The next segment of their geological float was easy and relaxing. From the mouth of the Yampa River at Echo Park (named by the men after they heard their voices constantly returned to them from the rock walls of the canyon "with startling clearness, but in a soft, mellow tone, that transforms them into magical music"), they coasted down a series of fast-flowing, but even, descents to the mouth of the Uinta River. They drifted through Split Mountain Canyon and Whirlpool Canyon, but these were as playthings compared with what they had already passed through.

At the Uinta River, Powell and several others hiked into the reservation of the Uinta Indians, twenty-five to thirty miles inland, to send off mail. One of the men refused to return to the boats, choosing to brave the desert rather than the river, leaving only nine in the three remaining boats. For days they lingered at the confluence of the Uinta and the

Green, feasting on ripe currants and resting for the ordeal ahead. They had voyaged for five weeks and three hundred miles. They next planned to head down to the mouth of the Grand River, another two hundred miles farther on. Although Powell had acquired additional flour at the Uinta Agency, provisions were running dangerously low. The bacon had gone rancid, the beans sour, and the flour was damp and had to be sifted to remove mouldy lumps. When they spied a small untended Indian garden just south of the Uinta River they pulled ashore. Eagerly, they dug up the diminutive, ill-formed tubers, threw them into a great pot and boiled up a satisfying stew. All but one of the men devoured the pulpy mass with relish—and were soon suffering from "severe vomiting." Powell recorded that "we tumbled around under the trees, groaning with pain." Emetics rid them of the pain, but it took several days of rest to fully regain their strength. Soon after they got underway, blasts of scorching air buffeted them from above, funnelled down from the plateau—they were now floating in the midst of a barren desert, with no known route to safety but downstream.

On July 8, they passed the Canyon of Desolation. "The walls are almost without vegetation," Powell wrote, "a few dwarf bushes are seen here and there clinging to the rocks, and cedars grow from the crevices . . . ugly clumps, like war clubs with spines." Despite the otherworldly landscape—miles upon miles of cracked pebbly earth dotted with stunted bushes and spiny cacti, with lumpy knobs of rock hummocking the earth as far as the eye could see—the boating was not difficult. Boiled beaver and a few fish augmented their meagre and insufficient diet. Although the incessant rapids failed to let up, they covered a great distance due to the speed of the river between the narrow confines of the gorge. By July 13, they passed Gunnison's Crossing in Utah, where "the course of the river is tortuous, and it nearly doubles upon itself many times."

When he climbed to the lip of the ledge in the Land of the

Standing Rocks on July 17, Powell was in awe of the "naked, solid rock—a beautiful red sandstone, forming a smooth, undulating pavement." It was a landscape of eerie hoodoos, jagged, dusty rock outcroppings, prickly pear cactuses, sagebrush, and rattlesnakes, dusted with a dry hot wind. "Wherever we look there is but a wilderness of rocks—deep gorges where the rivers are lost below cliffs and towers and pinnacles, and ten thousand strangely carved forms in every direction." Powell, however, was the only one interested in the magnificent wonder of the scenery. The others were preoccupied with food and rest. When he suggested that this spot would be ideal to observe a solar eclipse predicted for August 7, the men let it be known he would be observing it without them if he stayed.

Bowing to their demands, Powell led the convoy of boats farther into the unknown. The provisions slowly degenerated so as to be almost unpalatable, and only shooting a goat or deer or catching the occasional fish staved off malnutrition. By the end of July they had reached the junction of the San Juan River. Since they had passed the confluence of the Grand and the Green, they had laboured over eighteen portages and run forty-five treacherous rapids. After months of staring at layers of rock in the cliffs, Powell began to compose his theories on the process of canyon formation and pressed for additional time to study the land, in spite of the diminishing coffee and flour rations. One of the men wrote in his diary, however, that although he "ought to get the latitude and longitude of every mouth of a river not known before and we are willing to face starvation if necessary to do it but further than that he should not ask us to wait, and he must go on soon or the consequences will be different from what he anticipates." Although Powell's journal indicates a strong concern for the welfare of the men,

HORSESHOE CANYON.

Horseshoe Canyon was one of a seemingly endless series of canyons that hemmed the explorers in and kept them floating inexorably downstream.

THE GRAND CANYON.

The Grand Canyon was a wild and terrifying abyss. "Wherever we look," Powell wrote, "there is but a wilderness of rocks—deep gorges where the rivers are lost below cliffs and towers and pinnacles, and ten thousand strangely carved forms in every direction."

he apparently didn't show too much fear or concern, and they began to believe he was callous and unconcerned with their survival.

Soon the food was almost too sour to eat, and one of the men noted in his journal that "the men are uneasy and discontented and anxious to move on. If Major does not do something I fear the consequences, but he is contented, it seems to think that biscuit made of sour and musty flour and a few dried apples is ample to sustain a laboring man. If he can only study geology he will be happy without food or shelter but the rest of us are not afflicted with it to an alarming extent."

By mid-August they were roaring through the Grand Canyon, a magnificent and terrifying abyss. The rapids grew worse and the river faster still, as the men grew weaker on their meagre diet—which now consisted only of sour unleavened bread. Some nights they had to sleep in crevasses or on narrow ledges perched along the cliffs when there was no room to make camp. The unceasing roar of the river and the frightful nights allowed no respite. Powell was alone in his appreciation of the landscape, continuously collecting geological specimens and storing them in the boats. The others saw only the increasing of the canyon depth, the quickening of the river, the greater size of the rapids, and the diminishing provisions. By now most of their clothes had rotted away completely and their hair had grown long—they looked like a band of forlorn vagabonds.

On August 25, they started on the last sack of flour and calculated that there was only enough food to last a week. Two days later the chasm narrowed like the maw of a giant beast, foam-flecked water flew about the canyon, and the endless roar of the water was like a menacing growl. It was the most forbidding chute yet—a foaming angry torrent that stretched around the bend into the gloom. "The water dashes against the left bank and then is thrown furiously back against the right," wrote one of the men. "The spectacle is appalling to us." Rather than risk the terrible cataract, on August 28

AN INDIAN VILLAGE.

three of the men decided to abandon the expedition and risk an overland dash to safety. Although Powell assured them that according to his calculations, the Virgin River and a Mormon settlement was only forty-five miles ahead, they either disbelieved him or were too frightened to risk the final obstacle. They were adamant. After accepting a share of the scanty provisions and a rifle and ammunition for their overland trek, they scaled the rock face and stood watching as the remaining six men prepared to shoot Separation Rapids.

Powell was able to obtain some basic provisions from the Uinta Indians near the junction of the Uinta and Green Rivers.

Before launching themselves into the swirling maelstrom, Powell's group reluctantly abandoned one of the boats, the majority of his fossils, and geological and plant specimens. The water was rough, and partway through the perilous gorge they pulled into an eddy to bail the boats that were already "half full in a perfect hell of foam." The ragged water pulled continuously at the tethered boats, pounding them together and circling them around, grinding them against the slick rock face. The rope holding one of the boats in the eddy was strained to its limit and finally snapped when one of the men was onboard bailing. The river grabbed hold of the boat,

THE HEART OF MARBLE CANYON.

After months of running rapids studying the walls from the canyon floor, Powell was led toward pioneering theories on geological formation and erosion.

suddenly released from bondage, twirled it around madly, and shot it downstream. It was over in a second. The boat bobbed lightly over the crest of the most forbidding and foreboding chasm on the three-month journey and pulled safely into an eddy below. In a state of euphoric disbelief, Powell leaped into the other boat and taxied it also to safety.

In a few days they had escaped the canyons. The hills mellowed and the cliffs shrank away in the distance. Near the mouth of the Virgin River, they pulled to shore when they saw a Mormon family fishing and were regaled with a feast of roasted sweet squash, melons, and fresh fish. "Now the danger is over," exclaimed Powell, "now the toil has ceased; now the gloom has disappeared; now the firmament is bounded only by the horizon; and what a vast expanse of constellations can be seen!" The last great unexplored region of the United States had been conquered. But Powell was still thinking of the men under his command whom he had left behind. "The river rolls by us in silent majesty," Powell wrote, "the quiet of the camp is sweet; our joy is almost ecstasy. We sit till long after midnight talking of the Grand Canyon, talking of home, but talking chiefly of the three men who left us. Are they wandering in those depths unable to find a way out? Are they searching over the desert lands above for water? Or are they nearing the settlements?"*

By the time he returned east Major John Wesley Powell

*The three hapless wanderers were shot and killed by Shivwit Indians who mistook them for another group of whites who had murdered a woman. Ironically, Separation Rapids was the last daunting obstacle of the three-month ordeal.

was a famous man, in demand on the lecture circuit. Powell loved to lecture and, while he planned a follow-up expedition to continue his scientific study of the canyon region, he toured the cities discussing his adventures and propounding his evolving theories on hydrology and erosion, the age of the canyons, and the influence of water on the formation of unique topographical features. Scientifically, he hadn't yet accomplished anything significant, but in the coming years he would build on his fame and influence. After catapulting himself to prominence with a daring adventure, Powell spent the next decade pursuing his scientific objectives.

His second expedition in 1871 was a well-funded, government-sponsored campaign of study—a longer, more systematic scouring of the entire region, involving accurate mapping and a careful survey of all lateral canyons and plateaus. Supply wagons trundled across the desert and awaited the boats at designated points along the route, and food and scientific instruments were never in short supply. Powell took frequent leaves of absence to visit Emma, who was going through a difficult pregnancy in Salt Lake City. She gave birth to their only child, Mary Dean, on September 8, 1871.

Powell's second expedition, eventually referred to as the "United States Geographical and Geological Survey of the Rocky Mountain Region, J.W. Powell in Charge," was an ongoing survey that continued seasonally for almost nine years. Powell spent much of his time visiting the Ute, Paiutes, and Shoshone Indians, recording their customs, mythology, arts, vocabulary, religious ceremonies, social institutions, and ways of life. Several decades later, Powell helped legitimize and pioneer the first university courses in modern ethnology and anthropology. He had secured the support of the Smithsonian—later becoming the director of the Bureau of American Ethnology—and worked toward the amalgamation of various government surveys under the U.S.

Geological Survey, of which he became the director in 1879.[*]

In 1875, after his second trip down the Colorado, Powell wrote his most popular book, *The Exploration of the Colorado River of the West*, describing in eloquent prose the combined story of his two Colorado River expeditions. It was story a of grand adventure and heroism in the tradition of travelling naturalists of the past century. The science was restricted to the end (and was presented in a more detailed companion book, *Geology of the Uinta Mountains*, published one year later). Stephen J. Pyne, writing on the history of the Grand Canyon in 1998, commented that "in truth Powell's was a final gesture on the Humboldtean adventurer, and his account belongs with Samuel Baker's ascent up the Nile, Henry Bates's travels up the Amazon, and David Livingston's passage along the Zambezi."

After his adventures in the West, Powell proved to be a master fundraiser for his scientific objectives. As the director of the Geological Survey, he was likely the nation's most influential scientist, despite his lack of formal education, and he used his position to continue the study of mineralogy, paleontology, and stratigraphy, as well as of the new disciplines of geochemistry and geophysics. For all his contributions, nepotism was rife under his leadership. He put many of his relatives and close associates into choice positions of authority and, in one instance, sold his influence to promote the approval of the Great Southern Railroad in return for pressure for continued survey work in the West. Robert Elman, writing in *First in the Field, America's Pioneering Naturalists* in 1977, observed that as a person,

---

[*] In the 1870s there were three other great surveys of the American West being conducted under the auspices of various government departments— Clarence King led the United States Geological Survey of the Fortieth Parallel; Lieutenant George Montague Wheeler led the Geographical Surveys West of the 100th Meridian; and Ferdinand Hayden led the United States Geological and Geographical Survey of the Territories.

Powell had his flaws. "He was often inconsiderate of subordinates," Elman wrote, "occasionally imperious, somewhat disdainful of rivals. He could be intentionally forgetful—devious, in fact—in sending collections of plants, fossils, minerals, archaeological artifacts, and so on, not always to the institutions to which they had been promised but to those most likely to support future projects. He made impulsive decisions. He indulged in bureaucratic and Congressional politicking..."

Many of Powell's theories were radical and revolutionary, particularly his conviction that mountains and uplands were created slowly, over eons, and given their form by the work of water—uplift, erosion, and sedimentation. Formations, except volcanoes and sudden earthquakes, he believed, were created at an imperceptible rate by natural processes that are still working and can be measured. The idea wasn't new, but it gained a new life after Powell's tireless promotion, and it challenged the dominant view that great topographic formations were the result of sudden cataclysmic upheavals.

"The lifting of the rocks was so slow that the rains removed the sandstone almost as fast as they came up," Powell wrote. "The mountains were not thrust up as peaks, but a great block was slowly lifted, and from this the mountains were carved by the clouds.... We speak of mountains forming clouds about their tops; the clouds have formed the mountains. Lift a district of granite, or marble, into their region, and they gather about it, and hurl their storms against it, beating the rocks into sands, and they carry them out into the sea, carving out canyons, gulches, and valleys, and leaving plateaus and mountains embossed on the surface." The creation of the canyons was the result of the enormous energy of running water, like a giant saw cutting ever deeper into the earth as the surface rose. One of Powell's associates, Clarence Dutton, further developed the concept into the law of the persistence of rivers. It was not until the early twentieth century that these theories were expanded upon and accepted.

OUR MESSENGER.

During the course of his subsequent scientific studies of the Colorado region in the 1870s, Powell spent much of his time visiting the Ute, Paiute and Shoshone Indians, recording their customs, mythology, arts, vocabulary, religious ceremonies, social institutions and way of life. Several decades later, Powell helped legitimize and pioneer the first university courses in modern ethnology and anthropology.

Powell also used his influence to promote his concern for public administration of natural resources. In 1878 he wrote his greatest contribution to the understanding of how differences in the natural world affect human settlement— *Report on the Lands of the Arid Regions of the United States.* It was a revolutionary book in which he suggested that the lack of accessible water in many areas of the West warranted different land management policies than in the East. The limited water sources of the arid West should be universally accessible, he argued, and should not fall into the hands of a few connected individuals or businesses. It was an unprecedented argument—for government interference in the use of private land—that seemed to run counter to the prevailing notions of individual enterprise and personal freedom. He pointed out that in a region where land could only be productively settled with extensive irrigation, whoever controlled the water effectively dominated large, and otherwise dry, tracts of land. Most of the arid lands in the West were essentially valueless without access to water. He disputed the prevailing theory that "water follows the plow," and one of his great objectives was to create a comprehensive listing of all the choice sites for water reservoirs, dams, canals, and other water distribution and storage systems that he believed should be controlled by the government.

In essence, he demanded an end to unregulated and unclassified land use, and successfully lobbied for vast tracts of public land to be set aside to conserve water, minerals, timber, pasturage, and other limited natural resources. In 1889, as part of the Senate's select committee on irrigation, he spoke at North Dakota's constitutional convention about the need for public control of limited water resources. "There's almost enough rainfall for your purposes, but one year with another you need a little more than you get.... There are waters rolling by you which are quite ample...and you must save these waters.... Don't let these streams get out of the possession of the people.... Fix it in your constitution that no corporation—no body of men—no capital can get possession of the right of your waters. Hold the waters in the hands of the people."

Throughout his tenure at the Geological Survey, Powell attempted to mold public policy to address the arid reality of lands in the West. Yet, despite his position of authority, he was not entirely successful. He was forced to resign from his post as head of the Geological Survey in 1894, partly due to his controversial land classification policy. Most of his suggestions were ignored for decades or only partially implemented. And although he was later praised as being one of the founders of a federal land policy and of the conservation movement, he is also criticized because of the environmental damage that resulted from rampant dam construction and land drainage, where short-term benefits resulted in long-term deterioration. Powell continued to write on geological subjects for a number of years after his resignation. He passed away at the age of sixty-eight on September 17, 1902, at a cottage in Maine, after having suffered a stroke the previous autumn. His wife, Emma, and daughter, Mary Dean, survived him.

Powell's final conquest came a decade after he died. Dr. Edward Spitzka examined and carefully weighed his brain, compared it with the brain of one of his colleagues, W. J. McGee, and proclaimed Powell the victor. "Major Powell was endowed with a superior brain," he announced with an assurance that might produce a chuckle from scientists today. Whether or not he had a superior brain, Powell certainly had a driving ambition and curiosity for natural history that led him to great hardships and adventure in one of the remotest regions yet remaining in the United States, in an era when such places were quickly diminishing. But he was much more than an adventurer and collector. He developed pioneering theories on erosion and canyon formation, founded the study of ethnology as a respected scientific endeavour, and, perhaps most significantly, he established that organized systematic research in the natural sciences was a legitimate responsibility of government. As one of the last great scientific travellers, he bridged the gap between the old-style naturalists and the modern professional scientists.

Whatever his brain size, there are probably few who would disagree that he used it well.

Epilogue

The publication of Darwin's *Origin of Species* in 1859 was the final nail in the coffin of the natural history craze of the nineteenth century. If species were constantly changing and evolving through a natural process, then the great hierarchical schemata of living creatures many had been labouring on for years was an artificial and unattainable goal. If studying the natural world was no longer a way to understand "creation"—the immutable and static world of God—then natural theology could no longer be the motivating force behind scientific inquiry. Darwin's theories completely wiped out the underlying premise of nearly a century of work that was centred on collecting and defining the world's species. "The reason why species gathering slowed down after the 1860s," writes Lynn Barber, "was not because the work had reached completion, but simply because Darwin's theories provided a new line of inquiry for naturalists to embark on, so that fewer and fewer of them were prepared to devote their lives to classification."

Interest in the natural world, however, did not end overnight. Darwin's theory only slowly filtered down from scientific circles into public discourse, and it was not universally accepted. It had a corrosive rather than an explosive impact on natural theology. Barber has noted that popular natural history books in the decade following publication of *The Origin of Species* hardly mention evolution through natural selection, apart from the occasional joking reference to the relationship between humans and monkeys. But it marked the beginning of the end of the natural history craze.

Darwin's theories liberated scientists from their obsession with the classification of species that had limited and stultified biological inquiry for nearly a century and, ironically, brought to a close the simmering quarrel between the field collectors and the closet classifiers. By suggesting that all living creatures were in the process of evolving to better suit their environment, closet naturalists could no longer name, describe, and preserve a species specimen and believe that the work was complete. And if nature and natural processes were far more complex than what could be revealed by studying an individual specimen, more field work would be required to observe and study the process by which species evolved.

But field work could no longer be the preserve of amateurs. It became the domain of a new breed of professional scientists who set out to view species within the greater framework of an entire ecosystem. It was impossible for amateurs to keep up with all the developments and new theories. "In the past," according to Barber, "an amateur had been able to make himself an expert in, say, coleoptery without ever necessarily doing anything more than collecting a very large number of dead beetles. But now the coleopterist was expected to know, not only what his beetles looked like, but where they lived, how they behaved, what they ate, how they digested, how they bred, and how they related to all the other species which shared their habitat, which meant studying them in the field and under a microscope perhaps for years." Post-Darwin naturalists could no longer be curious amateurs with a theological purpose to justify their travels and adventures.

In Darwin's new world, humans were no longer privileged beings near the apex of a great hierarchy of life with only God above them, but were one species among many co-inhabiting the planet. The early interest in natural history generated a growing awareness of the need to protect nature and, in the twentieth century, led to the realization that some of the species that had been so arduously collected and studied were now disappearing because of pollution and the destruction of habitat.

The term "ecology" first appeared in the 1870s to describe the study of species in relation to their environment—the interrelationships of an entire ecosystem—rather than the casual observation of a particular species and its behaviours. Darwin himself in *The Origin of Species* hinted at this when he suggested that we can conclude through observation that cats eat mice, mice eat bees, and bees pollinate flowers, and therefore "it is quite credible that the presence of a feline animal in large numbers in a district might determine through the intervention first of mice and then of bees, the frequency of certain flowers in that district!" A seemingly simple concept today, at the time it was a radical breakthrough that refocused the direction of scientific thinking. With the development of binoculars and sophisticated photography by the 1890s, information from the field became verifiable evidence, and turned field biology into a respectable scientific endeavour. The whimsical descriptions of William Bartram, Charles Waterton, or even Henry Bates no longer had any scientific value.

With the advent of the theory of natural selection, the purpose of the old-style naturalists, discovering and naming new species, was eviscerated. Like an oxbow lake, it was slowly severed from the stream of scientific inquiry, finally existing only in its own curious and stagnant backwater. Natural history as a line of scientific reasoning had reached its natural conclusion, and the golden age of the travelling naturalists drew to a close.

Selected Bibliography

Adams, Alexander B. *Eternal Quest: The Story of the Great Naturalists*. New York: G.P. Putnam's Sons, 1969.

Aldington, Richard. *The Strange Life of Charles Waterton, 1782–1865*. London: Evans Brothers Ltd., 1949.

Barber, Lynn. *The Heyday of Natural History, 1820–1870*. London: Jonathan Cape, 1980.

Bartram, William. *The Travels of William Bartram: Naturalist's Edition*. Edited by Francis Harper. New Haven: Yale University Press, 1958.

Bartram, William, and John Bartram. *John and William Bartram's America: Selections from the Writings of the Philadelphia Naturalists*. Edited by Helen Cruickshank. New York: The Devin-Adair Company, 1957.

Bates, Henry Walter. *The Naturalist on the River Amazons*. Foreword by Robert L. Usinger. 1864. Reprint, Berkeley: University of California Press, 1962.

Botting, Douglas. *Humboldt and the Cosmos*. London: George Rainbird Limited, 1973.

Cutright, Paul Russel. *The Great Naturalists Explore South America*. New York: The Macmillan Co., 1940.

Coats, Alice M. *The Plant Hunters*. New York: McGraw-Hill, 1969.

Douglas, David. *Journal Kept by David Douglas During his Travels in North America*. London: William Wesley & Son, 1914.

Elman, Robert. *First in the Field: America's Pioneering Naturalists*. New York: Mason/Charter, 1977.

Ewers, John Canfield. *Views of a Vanishing Frontier*. Omaha: Joslyn Art Museum, 1984.

Franklin, John. *Narrative of a Journey to the Shores of the Polar Sea, in the Years 1819, 1820, 1821, 1822*. New introduction by James P. Delgado. Vancouver: Douglas and McIntyre, 2000.

———. *Narrative of a Second Expedition to the Shores of the Polar Sea, in the Years 1825, 1826, and 1827: Including an Account of the Progress of a Detachment to the Eastward by John Richardson*. Edmonton: Hurtig Publishers, 1971.

Goodman, Edward, J. *Explorers of South America*. New York: The Macmillan Company, 1972.

Harvey, George. *Douglas of the Fir*. Cambridge, MA: Harvard University Press, 1947.

Humboldt, Alexander von. *Personal Narrative of Travels to the Equinoctial Regions of the New Continent, During the Years 1799–1804*. Translated and edited by Thomasina Ross. London: G. Bell, 1852.

Merrill, Lynn L. *The Romance of Victorian Natural History.* New York: Oxford University Press, 1989.

McIlraith, John. *The Life of Sir John Richardson.* London: Longmans, Green, 1868.

Powell, John Wesley. *Exploration of the Colorado River of the West and Its Tributaries.* 1875. Reprint, New York: Dover Publications, 1961.

Richardson, John. *Arctic Ordeal: The Journal of John Richardson, Surgeon-Naturalist with Franklin 1820–1822.* Edited by C. Stuart Houston. Montreal: McGill-Queens's University Press, 1985.

Stegner, Wallace E. *Beyond the Hundredth Meridian: John Wesley Powell and the Second Opening of the West.* Boston: Houghton Mifflin Co., 1954.

Townsend, John Kirk. "Narrative of a Journey Across the Rocky Mountains to the Columbia River." In Thwaites, Reuben B., ed. *Early Western Travels, 1748–1846.* Cleveland, Ohio: The Arthur H. Clark Co., 1905.

Waterton, Charles. *Wanderings in South America.* London: Unit Library, Ltd., 1903.

Wied-Neuwied, Maximilian Alexander Philipp. *People of the First Man: Life Among the Plains Indians in Their Final Days of Glory: The Firsthand Account of Prince Maximilian's Expedition Up the Missouri River, 1833–1834.* Edited by Davis Thomas and Karin Ronnefeldt. New York: Dutton, 1976.

Whittle, Tyler. *The Plant Hunters: 3,450 Years of Searching for Green Treasure.* London: Heinemann, 1970.

Worster, Donald. *A River Running West: The Life of John Wesley Powell.* New York: Oxford University Press, 2001.

Acknowledgments

Turning a manuscript into a book is a much more involved task than I had imagined. It requires creativity, skill, experience, and a great deal of time. I would like to thank all the excellent people who helped to create this beautiful book, including Anne Denoon, Andrea Knight, John Lightfoot, Peter Maher, Jean Peters, Alison Reid, Susan Renouf, Louise Ward, and especially my editor, Michael Mouland. I would also like to thank my agent, Frances Hanna, for her constant perseverance on my behalf. The Alberta Foundation for the Arts awarded me a writing grant in the early stages of this project, which allowed me to focus on it as the months rolled by. Most important, I would to express my gratitude and thanks to my wife, Nicky Brink, the first reader of everything I write and my partner in all things.

Index